D1860288

Gandhi's Legacy and A New Human Civilization

Gandhi's Legacy and A New Human Civilization

Edited by

B. MOHANAN

GYAN PUBLISHING HOUSE
NEW DELHI-110002

GANDHI'S LEGACY AND
A NEW HUMAN CIVILIZATION
[*Politics, History, Culture, Philosophy, Economics*]

ISBN: 81-212-0645-6

© B. MOHANAN

All rights are reserved. No part of this book may be reproduced in any manner without written permission.

Published in 1999 in India by
Gyan Publishing House
5, Ansari Road
New Delhi 110 002

Laser Typeset at 'Darpan Graphics', New Delhi.
Printed at Chawla Offset Printers, New Delhi.

Contents

PART - III

List of Contributors

Prof. (Dr.) N. Radhakrishnan	:	Director, Gandhi Smriti and Darshan Samiti, New Delhi.
Prof. (Dr.) M.G.S. Narayanan	:	Former Member Secretary, Indian Council of Historical Research (ICHR), New Delhi.
Prof. (Dr.) K.P. Karunakaran	:	Former Professor of Political Science, Delhi University, Delhi.
Shri. M.R. Rajagopalan	:	Secretary, Gandhigram Trust, Gandhigram, Tamil Nadu.
Dr. A.K. Tharien	:	Christian Fellowship Hospital, Oddanchatram, Dindigul, Tamil Nadu.
Dr. T. Rajendran	:	Sr. Lecturer, Department of Sociology, Gandhigram University, Gandhigram, Tamil Nadu.
Prof. (Dr.) Devavrat N. Pathak	:	Peace Research Centre, Gujarat Vidyapith, Ahmedabad.
Prof. (Dr.) S. Uma Devi	:	Prof. & Head, Department of Economics, University of Kerala, Thiruvananthapuram.
Dr. K. Sreenivasan	:	Prof. (Rtd.) Dept. of English, University College, Thiruvananthapuram.
Shri S. Muraleedharan	:	Sr. Lecturer, Dept. of Economics, Victoria College, Palakkad, Kerala.
Shri S. Arunkumar	:	Lecturer in Economics, Sri Sankara Sanskrit University, Kalady, Kerala.
Dr. P. N. Sankaran	:	Reader, Department of Eco-nomics, University College,

		Thiruvananthapuram.
Prof. Ramashray Roy	:	NISWASS, Bhuvaneshwar, Orissa.
Prof. (Dr.) T. Kalyani	:	Department of Political Science, Madurai Kamaraj University.
Prof. (Dr.) Gnanapragasam	:	Head, Department of Political Science, Institute of Distance Education, Madurai Kamaraj University.
Dr. Midatala Rani	:	Sr. Lecturer, Dept. of Studies in Political Science, University of Mysore, Manasagangotri, Mysore.
Prof. (Dr.) N. Durairaj	:	Head, Department of Rural Development, School of Eco-nomics, Kamaraj University, Madurai.
Dr. Kala Rani Rengasamy	:	Lecturer, Dept. of Rural Develop-ment, School of Economics, Kamaraj University, Madurai.
Dr. Padma Ramakrishnan	:	Reader, Dept. of Political Science, University College, Thiruvananthapuram.
Dr. P. Gopinathan Pillai	:	Director, CACEE, University of Kerala, Thiruvananthapuram.
Dr. P. Chinnathurai	:	Research Scholar, Department of Political Science, Kamaraj University, Madurai.
Dr. K.C. Sreekumar	:	Reader & Head, Dept. of Political Science, Mahatma Gandhi College, Thiruvananthapuram.
Dr. V.K. Muthu	:	Sr. Lecturer, Faculty of Rural Health and Sanitation, Gandhi-gram University, Gandhigram, Tamil Nadu.
Shri N. Arumugam	:	Deputy Librarian, Dr.G.Rama-chandran

		Library, Gandhigram University, Gandhigram, Tamil Nadu.
Shri P. Gopinathan Nair	:	Former President, Sarva Seva Sangam, Wardha. President, Kerala Gandhi Smarak Nidhi.
Prof. (Dr.) K. Raman Pillai	:	Chairman, Institute for the Study of Developing Areas, Thiruvananthapuram & Chairman, Indian Institute of Public Administration, Kerala Regional Branch, IMG Complex, Barton Hill, Thiruvananthapuram.
Dr. A.S. Narayana Pillai	:	Former Professor of Philosophy, University College, Thiruvananthapuram.
Shri T.N. Jayachandran	:	I.A.S. (Retd.), Formerly Commissioner & Secretary, Department of Higher Education, Government of Kerala and Director, Institute of Management in Government (IMG), Thiru-vananthapuram, Vice-Chancellor, University of Kerala and University of Calicut.

Introduction

Modern western civilization took off with the promise of creating a new human civilization. When capitalism was found incapable of ushering in a new world, communism took up the task of creating the same. In spite of all its achievements in its dual forms of capitalism and communism, modern western civilization seems to have entered into a perennial crisis of its own making. The failure of western developmentalisms as exemplified by the collapse of the erstwhile communist regimes in the former Soviet Union and Eastern Europe, has clearly brought out the fact that the basic premises of modern civilization have become redundant. The intellectual vacuum following the setback suffered by leftist ideologies, in general, and Marxism in particular, as well as the absence of creative thinking, have led to the return of several national governments to the capitalistic development techniques which have historically been proved irrelevant.

Humanity has been tremendously benefited by the spectacular achievements of modern science and technology. However, an examination of the hitherto revealed facts regarding the dreadful and negative impacts of the technological advancement which have rendered most of these achievements irrelevant, more so, when viewed in the light of the ultimate destiny of humanity. The degeneration of socioeconomic and political life of modern man, on the one hand and the impending ecological tragedy on the other, has underlined the fact that modern man is incapable of resolving the multidimensional crises confronting humanity. Any attempt to resolve these problems within the framework of the existing thought patterns and value systems with the help of the means which created these problems will end up in failure. In this situation, only an ideology—which can provide a humanitarian approach and a world vision as an alternative to the vision of modern western civilization and society, in order to assimilate and translate these ideas into its day to day existence—can be a prelude to a better life for mankind.

The Gandhian ideology, evolved in the light of the experience of the post-industrial world development would perhaps provide a basis for a novel beginning of an enduring path. Gandhian vision of a new human civilization assumes special significance in the context of the historically proved irrelevance of modern western civilization. A development, which does not contribute to the development of the human self will be self-defeating. Unlike other modern thinkers, Gandhi approached political and economic problems from a highly ethical and humanistic point of view. According to him, the acute economic disparity between the rich and the poor was the creation of the foreign rule and the exploitation that accompanied it. It was also the product of the "capitalist industrial civilization of the west as embodied in the big machine".

Gandhi's religion was neither conventional nor traditional. He raised his voice of protest against religious obscurantism and dogmatism. However, he regarded politics and religion as inseparable. He waged a constant struggle against the divisive forces of communalism. He stressed on the equality of all religions and thereby laid the foundation for a secular India. His world view was *SHi generis.*

What was Gandhi's concept of Social change ? Did Gandhi develop an economic philosophy, relevant to the developing nations ? What according to Gandhi should be the interface between religion and politics ? How did Gandhi view the achievements of science and technology ? What are the salient features of Gandhi's world view ? These and related issues were discussed in detail in the two-day national seminar on 'Rediscovering Gandhi', which I organised in Thiruvananthapuram (Kerala) under the auspices of the Institute for the Study of Developing Areas, and at the Department of Political Science and Development Administration, Gandhigram University, Gandhigram, Tamil Nadu.

These two seminars were spread over four sessions besides the inaugural session and the valedictory session. The four major sessions were on :

(1) 'Gandhi and Modern Civilization'

(2) 'Contemporary Relevance of Gandhi's Economic Philosophy'

(3) 'Gandhi and Social Revolution' and

(4) 'Gandhi and Secularism'.

The participants of the seminar were drawn from Gandhian thinkers, practitioners of Gandhism, academicians and social workers.

The topics discussed under each of the thrust areas were as under :

Gandhi and Modern Civilization

Modern civilization : Gandhian critique; Gandhi's view on modern science and technology; Gandhian alternative: Gandhian vision of a new human civilization; Rama Rajya; Gandhian concept of appropriate technology: A critique; Gandhian concept of a new world order.

Relevance of Gandhi's Economic Philosophy

Gandhian critique: Modern man's economic pursuit; Gandhian view on economic development; Relevance of Gandhian theory of bread-labour-trusteeship; Economy of permanence: Gandhian alternative; Relevance of Gandhian view on man-nature relationship; Environment.

Gandhi and Social Revolution

Gandhian Analysis of Indian Society; Gandhian concept of Social change; The relevance of Gandhian strategy for social change: A critique; Gandhian concept of self-government: End and means; Truth and nonviolence; Satyagraha, Gramswaraj and Sarvodaya; Educational philosophy of Gandhi.

Gandhi and Secularism

Gandhian view on the role of religion in social life; Material and spiritual Gandhian approach: Religion and Politics: Gandhian view; Gandhi and the Hindu-Muslim question; Gandhi as a living model of secularism : A critique.

Apart from the papers presented at the two seminars, mentioned above, the present volume carries a few articles originally appeared in various issues of the *ISDA Journal.*

This volume is a tribute to the Mahatma in the 50th year of his martyrdom.

B. Mohanan

Part I

1

Gandhi and the Challenges of the 21st Century

N. Radhakrishnan

The challenges from the growing consumerism and materialistic culture which recognizes no values other than the worth of money is the biggest menace faced by humanity today. The fast dwindling natural resources, the suffocating environmental degradation and repudiation of moral values are the three major aspects that deserve our attention as we get ready to enter the next century. Gandhi seems to have anticipated this frightening scenario as early as the first quarter of this century.

Humanity started moving in a different direction with the industrial revolution and Gandhi warned humanity against the enveloping materialistic civilization. He described it as monstrous and soulless. No one cared then. During the last 50 years that separate us from Gandhi, humanity has witnessed breathtaking achievements in science and technology and even the texture and rhythm of our life seem to have been altered. All of a sudden—thanks to science and technology—this vast universe and our world have been shrunk both in size and distance and the talk of the hour is global village, globalization and global citizenship. Gandhi who believed in the dictum that an ounce of practice is worth tons of theory, offered an alternative world vision : A life in harmony with nature, a life of simplicity, a life which recognises the pain in others, and a society which ensures minimum for everybody to live like decent human beings. A world vision which extols the virtue of "Vasudhaiva Kutumbakam?" (The world is one family).

This world vision of Gandhi was described to be utopian by the champions of unlimited growth. Can we afford to have unlimited growth in a finite world? This is one of the major challenges faced by humanity in the next millennium. If man is the measure of everything, an answer to this challenging question is to be found by man alone and not by some other creature from outer space. Knowing this truth, Gandhi insisted on individual change. He also offered an alternative lifestyle, alternative world vision and a viable set of strategies and methods for social transformation, peace and stability.

When Gandhi came back from South Africa in July 1914 and started mobilising the dumb millions who either did not know how to articulate their grievances or were afraid of doing so for a variety of reasons, people could not believe that this great man of destiny, who devised new methods to mobilize millions—to whom even the basic right of self-expression, leave alone basic human rights, was denied—could succeed in doing that. The first major initiative Gandhi took was the Champaran Satyagraha. It marked the birth of Satyagraha in India. It may be remembered that it was not with any political ambition that Gandhi started the movement in Champaran. It was to invite the attention of the authorities to the existing poor living conditions, which denied indigo workers the basic minimum living facilities and freedom to live like human beings. Gandhi was invited to visit the place and make a study of what was happening. On his arrival, Gandhi was prevented and barred entry there. Undeterred, he continued his mission and made a report which altered the situation, almost overnight. The awakened people convincingly demonstrated that they could never be subjugated by a tyrannical set of rules and formulations whosoever be the perpetrators of this crime—be it the biggest Empire in those days, over which the Sun never set.

Let us remember again the significance of what Gandhi was able to achieve in South Africa where incidentally he began his innings in April 1893. Gandhi had not gone to South Africa to start an agitation as we know. The young Gandhi had felt that he could not be successful in India as a lawyer under the Raj and it would be humiliating all the way to pursue an honest profession in India. It was at that time the offer came to him to work in South Africa.

Let us not look at Gandhi as a god. The biggest mistake, many of the Gandhian scholars and admirers of Gandhi and many others in this country have done during the last many years, is to look at Gandhi as a god and think that all that he did or said and formulated was beyond questioning and that he is infallible. Let us not miss the obvious when we try to look at the graph of the amazing growth of his own mind and his perception of life around him. From an ordinary school child who did not display any special trait or talent, he matured into a sensitive, truthful votary of human dignity, freedom and justice. We know all these things and the initial difficulties that he had in the school. What is to be remembered is how Gandhi grew from each of the trials. How many of our young men and women in schools, colleges or universities even put or raise a question to a teacher during a discussion ? Often they do not dare. Rather they are more worried as to how this question will offend the teacher or whether he will like it or not. Further, we are afraid of our children, both at home and in schools or colleges. In a sense, we should be ashamed of having nurtured our students in such a way that they are even afraid of raising legitimate and sensible questions. Considerations of internal marks, job assessment, recommendations and many similar things inhibit our children. If this is the situation in the university classes, what would be the situation in lower classes?

When the teacher himself wants a student to copy from another student surreptitiously, the correct spelling of a word he had misspelt, how many young students would have the courage to ignore the goading of the teacher? Young Mohan Das had this amazing power. If a boy at the age of 9 or 10, could resist this temptation, that proved the basic mettle, the stuff which he was made of. But then, that stuff was not an intellectual stuff. As a child he was very timid, very ordinary but God-fearing and obedient. He also did all the pranks most children are capable of doing, which you and I would have done. But, at least I would have no courage to say that I stole a little thing from my father's pocket or my uncle's pocket. You and I do not have the courage to admit, "when I was in UK or USA as a student, I was tempted to go to a brothel", if ever such a situation arose. Gandhi had the courage to admit the temptations he had at various stages. He confessed in his autobiography about the 'double shame' he was subjected to, following his father's death. While he had the courage to admit various lapses about which he atoned, there was something emerging which was noble and which sustained him and shaped his character as he grew up.

Now let us look at the other formative influences on the young Gandhi. As already stated, he went to South Africa not to lead any movement and certainly not to become an agitator. Somebody had offered him the job of an assistant lawyer of an Indian firm. On arrival what did he see there? Many poor labourers, recruited by the British colonial masters from Gujarat, Madras Province, Bihar and some other parts of India, were found living a life which was subhuman in all respects. Imagine a situation when a child is unable to identify openly his parents, a situation when a young mother is prevented from recognising her child in the open for fear of inviting punishment. Imagine the tragedy of a man who is unable to identify his wife in the open. They were all unable to raise voice against the inhuman laws. What else was this but denial of human rights? The western world which was taking pride in the fact that the people there were champions of human rights, protesting against human rights violation in South Africa did not see what was happening there.

It may not be an exaggeration to say that human rights movement assumed an organisational frame with Gandhi only. In known history very few before Gandhi had brought together such a large number of people who fearlessly launched the biggest sustained onslaught against the forces of oppression. In this process Gandhi emerged as a revolutionary par excellence by organising people to think of their rights and identify those who deny them their rights. It becomes evident, when we look at the graph of the development of Gandhi's strategies, the methods that he devised and the manner in which he was looking at human problems to put them together and to find out which were the applicable ones and which were the fetters to be just discarded or broken. He did it by looking at the basic human elements and looking at the whole thing. When he came back to India after the heroic work of 21 years in South Africa, he had almost become the Mahatma and was no longer the young man who left the Indian shores in April 1893 to plead a case in South Africa.

In fact, the first major work that he started in Champaran, created the flame of national resurgence and awakening which brought people of several categories together. The Champaran Satyagraha opened a new phase in human rights protection. We know the non-violent movement for freedom under Mahatma Gandhi assumed the shape of the biggest mass movement for social justice. Now let me invite your attention to two or three aspects for discussion.

Gandhi is respected as the Father of this Nation. Very few know what it is ? We remember him on two occasions every year Gandhi Jayanti and Martye Day. There are universities in his name which have nothing to do with Gandhi except their names. We have departments of Gandhian Studies and chairs of Gandhian Studies have also been instituted in several universities. There are a number of Gandhian organisations directly funded by the Government or those which are getting substantial funds from the Government. There are also countless bogus organisations which receive fabulous funds from abroad to propagate Gandhian ideals. There are so many professors and scholars (and I am not excluded) who go regularly to many universities to lecture on Gandhi. On an average, 50-60 books are written on Gandhi, in India, in English every year and further about 130 books are written in different Indian languages. Gandhi Memorial Lectures are also organised in at least 60 centres throughout India every year. A number of Ph.Ds are being awarded by various Indian universities on topics related to Gandhi. Besides, 340 M.Phil scholars, full-time as well as part-time, are working on Gandhi. There are six universities where M.A. in Gandhian Studies and M.Sc. in Peace Making are being offered with a total enrolment of 300 every year. Again, we hear exhortations from everybody everyday right from 6 in the morning on the All India Radio, in support of Gandhian programme. So, there is no dearth of initiatives. The Government has done well in a way, in publishing the monumental 100 volumes of the *Collected Works of Gandhi*, which is a big tribute, any nation can pay to its founding father. Recently they have instituted an International Gandhi Peace Award which is similar to the Nobel Prize. Then, there are several voluntary organisations doing fairly good work. Gandhi Peace Foundation is the nerve centre of a lot of activities which this premier organisation has been able to organise in different parts of India. Gandhi Smarak Nidhi has generated nationwide interest in Gandhi and has done meaningful constructive work. But the big question is, what is their impact today in a materialist and consumerist culture? Where are the Gandhians of the day?

However, the answer could be that there is no point in blaming anybody. As a nation we have failed to carry forward the flame of liberty, the flame of introspection, the initiative for social awareness, the cause for ensuring social justice, with dignity which Gandhi gave us. In fact, the Gandhian passion for social transformation in a way ended with Gandhi himself. The post-Gandhian leaders, with their own priorities, fell short of the expectations. They could not be called un-Gandhian but the Gandhian vision of Swadeshi, the Gandhian vision of developing self-sufficient villages and the Gandhian striving for each of the five lakh Indian villages being given basic necessities could not be translated into reality. Social justice to those people to whom equal right even to walk along the common roads was denied, could not be taken beyond a level by a leadership which was probably obsessed with the idea of development in science and technology. Those people who were prevented even from drawing water from the common well and from worshipping in the common temple, were all given the tools of protest by Gandhi. What happened after Gandhi, is known to all of us.

We should make honest attempts to understand why we have failed and where we have failed? The Government is our government, elected and run by the people. Those who are part of the bureaucracy are also our own brothers and sisters. We may have political differences. We may have differences with 'X' as the Prime Minister or 'Y' as the Prime Minister, but what is to be realised is that it is our own national Government. Our Government during the last 50 years could not be described to have failed us as a nation. The improvements that we have registered in several aspects of life are tremendous, of which any of us should be proud. But then, the most serious thought that comes to us despite all these things, is that nearly 40% Indian population lives under subsistence level. You know what living under subsistence level means. These people do not have sufficient clothes to wear, they do not have enough—in many instances even a single square—meal a day, they do not have a roof over them, they do not have minimum medical facilities, even after 50 years of freedom. Is it not a matter of shame? How did it happen? All of us continue to shed crocodile tears about the dehumanization, about the grinding poverty and still the people have to live in the slums in this country. How lucky are you and I, sitting in this hall? How privileged we are. Go to a slum and see how even some pigs and dogs have a better and more decent living than those 'human beings'. We throw some food to the animals we domesticate and there are people who spend substantially on their pet animals. Is this the way we perpetuate the Gandhian legacy of sharing and justice? What was the Gandhian method to remove poverty from this country?

The real challenge of the 21st century is how we tackle poverty, hunger and malnutrition and ensure redistribution of wealth, to which all should have equal accessibility. I was just reading a small unpublished piece, a letter which my father had received from Gandhi. He wrote: "Freedom will mean hollow if people who are committed to my ideals don't dedicate to remove the poverty of this country". Obviously, he was very clear about it and we call Gandhi utopian and old fashioned. In London, when he was a student he could see the vulgar face of industrialisation. How industrialisation changed the texture and contour of our century and brought about the present day consumerism and materialism, about which all of us are worried. We are living in a society which no longer respects or recognizes anyone on the basis of his scholarship or any other achievement. The criteria today is the bank balance or your purchasing power, whether you have Contessa Car or whether you have a Maruti Car or whether you have a Ciello Car or whether you are staying in a multi-storeyed building or whether you possess this and that? Gone are the days when the worth of an individual was decided and when he was respected on the basis of the essential qualities of a human being. I respectfully remember even the teachers who taught me in my primary school. I get up as a mark of respect whenever I see them. How many of our students, whom we love and to whose well-being most of us are committed show even one-tenth of that awareness and respect?

What I want to tell you is that our perception has changed. Our concept of values is now assessed in terms of money. Even the concept of value has changed. Why do we go after Japan, Germany and United States? The role of Japan and Germany during the World War II is well known. Still, Japan and Germany are eligible to become permanent members in the Security Council. But, according to the American perception, India, the largest democracy in the world with all its credentials, with all its support to noble causes everywhere, is not fit for the same. We respect Japan because of the power of its wealth. We go after Germany because of what Germany can offer us. Everybody tries to make a beeline to the United States because it has emerged as the biggest economy with enormous clout. So money has become the only criteria in the world now and not scholarship, not intellectual achievements, not one's capabilities, not our concern for ethics, not our concern for human fellow beings and rarely anyone's artistic abilities. Who respects an artist nowadays if he is poor?

It was against this frightening scenario of the extending consumeristic mesmerism and the tightening grip of materialism that we have to look at what Gandhi can offer? Instead of quoting Gandhi let us ask whether we can imbibe some lessons and practice them in our own day-to-day life. Many of the formulations of Gandhi, could probably be outdated but the basic formulations and the kind of life that he lived and the message that he left for us, gives us a concrete framework for a dependable and exciting future. In *Hind Swaraj* which he wrote in 1909, he described the western civilization as 'Satanic' and 'soulless'. Even his friends had advised him to withdraw this book as they feared that the views expressed in the book would give a negative image of Gandhi. After three decades, when Gandhi reissued the book and published it, he said in the press statement that 'even today after 20 years of his writing it, originally in 1908-09, he stood by every sentence of what he wrote. Nothing had changed to compel him to have a second look of his views.' When Gandhi pointed out that 'there would come a time when, if we are not taking care of Nature, if we are consuming more than what we need, we would run short of what the Nature provides us. In a world of finite resources, infinite consumption would lead to catastrophe.'

A World Watch Report which is available to us says that by the year 2020, over 100 cities in the world will have no water to drink. Gandhi never used such expressions as 'Green House Effect', but he understood what would be the effect if we don't take care of Nature.

He was not a conventional philosopher. He lived a certain kind of life and he left it to others to interpret and follow or understand whatever it was or if it suited them, to follow. He said that the living conditions in the world would become very suffocated very soon unless timely corrective measures were taken up. So, we had to plant a lot of trees and we should not take more than what we needed from Nature. We should not eat more than what our body need. He feared that there would come a time when there would be acute shortage of resources in this world. So we had to simplify our lifestyle. Have we done that? Let us go to any house or come to my house. Though I try to resist all the temptations of the market, I am also a worldly man and I have my wife and children. We have also made our house a sort of mini showroom. Every drawing-room in a middleclass or upper middleclass or a rich person's house is a showroom now. There is probably no escape. There was a time when television was a luxury but can we say that now?

So, let us assess Gandhi within the parameters and the requirements of his time and the realities as they existed then and find out those which have permanent value, which are those which need to be left behind and which need to be sustained? Can any of us quarrel with somebody when he insists on the need to make truth the basis of our life? It does not become irrelevant just because Gandhi said so? Do we want a life to be built around 'a farce' and self-abuse or falsehood? Self-abuse leads to hypocrisy. Hypocrisy leads one to a double life and a double life leads to all kinds of dangers which we see and how many of us including those of us who are here today can declare in tune with Gandhi that 'My life is my message'. Supposing today somebody asks us for a message. What we might do is that we will dictate and type out and give a wonderful message clothed in moving language and sentiments of the highest order. Messages, it appears, are meant for others and not for one's own self. Gandhi could say, "My life is my message". How many of us can tell our children to live as we live. I am not able to say so to my children though by training and conviction I try to live a very simple life. I confess with all honesty that it is impossible for me to say to my children that my life is my message. You look at the lifestyle of any of the national leaders. A nation's life is influenced and shaped by national leaders, by and large. Let us close our eyes for a moment and ask: Do we have one national leader today who could be emulated in any way? Do we have anyone who could be described to be a role model? Everything has become politics of survival, and politics of manoeuvring and politics of manipulation and in a large number of cases even between husband and wife, the relationship is by and large manipulative now. Between the teachers and the taught also there is total lack of communication.

Can we say that the Gandhian insistence on simple life, truth, purity between ends and means, core values that sustain humanity should be followed? Gandhi was not taken seriously by us, let us be very honest; Gandhi was not taken seriously in many parts of the world. He was just dismissed. Some of the scholars from here and there get passionate to understand anything. Gandhi was able to persuade the British to leave India in good faith. He influnced the British phsyche and the British leadership considerably and they realized that it was time that the British left India. The Gandhian insistence on hate and evil and not the evildoer under any compulsion, under any temptation, under whatever circumstances, won both Gandhi and India many friends. He asked to hate the English system which was perpetrating colonialism and suppression but not the Englishmen. Gandhi's belief that nobody does any evil on his own volition, that everybody is a spark of the divine and nobody is capable of doing anything that would hurt anybody, went well with a conisderable segment of international community. How many of us are able to do this? So, we have to look at the Gandhian message that emanates from him. It distinguishes Gandhi from all other philosophers and teachers we have. What is known today as Gandhian philosophy flows out of Gandhi's acitivies and the life that he lived. We remember him for what he did and not for what he said. This is the major aspect that distinguished Gandhi from other conventional philosophers.

I strongly aruge that we need to adopt a new method to understand Gandhi and to discover Gandhi. Gandhi cannot be discovered through thoughts or through a conventional debate. Gandhi cannot be discovered through an academic approach either.

2

Gandhi's Legacy and A New Human Civilization

M.G.S. Narayanan

Gandhi discovered a new method and strategy for resisting organized evil in the form of the State.

From the earliest phase of known history, man had to carry on a struggle against the forces of nature and against other men also. Here, we discuss the second aspect, though the first also comes into the picture in some ways, as the two cannot be separated easily.

Evil and Resistance to Evil

The State, with its laws and law-enforcing agencies, was formed to see that justice was rendered to all men alike. However, these very instruments intended to promote justice and ensure peace, were often abused by those who wielded authority. As many thinkers including Karl Marx have pointed out, all history was largely the history of class struggles, sometimes open, sometimes concealed. The weaker sections within society or the weaker States within the community of States, continued to be victimised by the mighty ones. Oppression took the form of physical harm or mental torture or social injustice. Brute force was augmented by intellectual skills and moral pressures. Even philosophy and religion were brought into legitimised tyranny. The examples are so numerous and so well-known that it is not necessary to cite them here.

Resistance to injustice was also continuously growing in history. It often took the form of prayers, protests, propaganda, revolts, wars and revolutions. However, the results were not satisfactory or durable.

When a specific instance of cruelty or partiality was remedied by the show of strength, that very movement of conflict, expressed in the form of revolt, war or revolution, generated hatred and produced revenge. New engines of tyranny were created. History was repeated with increasing violence. It was a vicious circle without an escape route. Revolutions are notorious for their habit of swallowing their own children and inviting counter-revolutions that occupy the stage sooner or later.

Gandhi's new technique of satyagraha is variously described as the application of the principle of non-violence, the invocation of soul-force, and the appeal to the higher court of public opinion. Respect and love for the enemy, absolute honesty and openness in behaviour, maximum readiness to sacrifice and compromise on all issues and the adoption of purificatory vows of silence and starvation—all these are integral parts of the technique of satyagraha.

Religious Antecedents of Satyagraha

On a close scrutiny of the practice of satyagraha adopted by Gandhi and his arguments and explanations, it is clear that the method is not entirely original or unprecedented, but familiar in the history of great religious teachers. It is based on a simple and well-known principle, that of invoking the God inside man, even the threatening hostile adversary, and making him act sincerely and openly in the best interests of both sides. The foundations of satyagraha go deep into the philosophy of the great religions of the world. How to grapple with and overcome evil within oneself and within society was the central problem of religion throughout history.

All prophets and avatars were concerned with practical steps to improve secular life even though they are, often wrongly depicted to my mind, as other-worldly in outlook and impractical in their approach to life. This is why the ordinary man or woman, harassed by the most ordinary troubles arising out of ignorance, poverty and tyranny and burdened with sorrow and failures, but endowed with common sense, was irresistibly and instinctively drawn towards religion.

What is acceptable to the great majority of mankind through centuries must be good for mankind, as long as our goal is the greatest happiness of the greatest number. While the thinking minority of scholars and philosophers were habitually skeptical about it, the ordinary folk who were closer to nature and somehow preserved the faculty of intuition, always opted for religion. If we try to see through the ornate jungle of words and rituals and focus on the essence enshrined in the core of the great religions, we observe a common factor--faith in God. Though the concept of God cannot be defined easily in words, it refers to the intuitive comprehension of the fact that-the creative force of will behind manifest nature, is the embodiment of supreme power, wisdom and justice. Faith in God is advocated as the foundation of good life. What the mind apprehends naturally, man tries to coach in rational terms in philosophy and theology.

In other words, God, the idea of supreme power, perfect justice and infinite wisdom, is the most obvious fact in the world, though it is not audible, smellable, visible, tastable or tangible. The normal human mind can perceive it automatically. The natural leaders of mankind have always taken it for granted and recognized its existence in the heart of every human being. Religious leaders have often tried successfully to bring it out into action. The function of religion in history has been to propagate this idea and activise this principle for solving the problems of life.

There are several concrete instances in the life stories of prophets and religious teachers telling us how they successfully encountered bad characters and converted them. These people recognized the divinity in them, drew it out and helped them to recognise this divinity in turn, so that they were transformed into men and women of God, and led a good life. This pattern is endorsed by the stories of Gautama Buddha and the robber Angulimala, Ananda and the courtesan Vasava Datta, Jesus Christ and the courtesan Mary of Magdeline, Mohammed (PBH) and the Arab swordsman and numerous other episodes in the lives of religious teachers. Many popular stories about miracles can be traced back to the operation of this principle. There are instances of a crude form of Satyagraha called Pattini which the rural folk practised in medieval Kerala. May be in other parts of the country also, the people adopted such methods, when they had no other means for obtaining justice.

Birth of the Scientific Formula

Gandhi's satyagraha also fits into this pattern and emerges from the religious tradition, but he has modified and adapted it for application in modern society. A distinctive feature of the modern age is the dominance of the scientific and rational spirit which attempts to organise things in a systematic way, making it possible for any person of intelligence to understand and verify. Everything is analysed and published so that the element of mystification is removed. What was the prerogative of a small number of saints and scholars at one time comes within the grasp of ordinary men and women who show the necessary patience and persistence.

Being thoroughly modern in his outlook, Gandhi did something more in the field of Satyagraha in conformity with the spirit of the age. He separated it from the Hindu-Jain religious complex and started using it in the context of secular public life in the period of the national movement in India. He mastered the technique of using the newspapers through statements, interviews and public speeches. He made the maximum use of the improved facilities of transport and communication during the British regime. Perhaps for the first time in the history of the world, this method was employed on a large-scale on several occasions in civil noncooperation, not only by Gandhi himself but by hundreds of Satyagrahis in towns and villages under his guidance. As a result of this, a vast empire was overthrown and an enslaved nation gained its independence.

Gandhi had started experimenting with it in South Africa, slowly groping his way towards perfection through trial and error and by the time he took up the leadership of the national movement in India, he had attained such mastery in the field that he almost became a wizard performing on the world stage.

He could not have achieved this if he had not gone through the first hand experience of modernity in the world capital of the modern age. When, in London during the early years of the present century, he participated in a dizzy dance of wealth and fashion, trying to adjust to it but failed. He took lessons in western music and dance but, did not continue that line. A teetotaller and pure vegetarian, he felt like fish out of water in a city of drunkards and meat-eaters. Being in a small minority, at loggerheads with the majority trends, he seems to have been forced to cultivate the society of similar souls. He read the Bible, and read much of Tolstoy, Ruskin, Thoreau and others who were the Western critics of modernity at that time. To be able to choose these masters of protest as his gurus, he must have had to wade through much that was currently being produced in the English language.

It is amazing that this conservative, awkward, Gujarati Bania boy was able to acquire mastery over the English language, cultivating a sharp and precise style of expression. Moreover, he also realized the tremendous power of the press, and picked up the art of using it with great effect for intervening in public life. The journalistic training that he gave himself in South Africa was employed with great advantage, when he reached India. People often forget that Gandhi, the man of action was also the most prolific and most graceful writer in the English language in India.

His isolation and bitter experiences in England and in South Africa gradually equipped him to stand up and stand alone against the entire world of profit and consumption oriented Western industrial culture. He was able to see clearly the contrast between the frustrating egoism of the money-loving, power-hunting neurotic society of the imperial capital and the happy innocence of many of his own countrymen, steeped in material poverty but rich in spiritual joy. The latter were bound together with family affection and traditional simple faith. His chief concern in later life was to find a way to recover freedom for the Indian people without losing this quality of life. It was a post-modernist attitude, born out of criticism of modernity and deriving inspiration from the ancient Eastern (Hindu) and Western (Christian) philosophy and ways of life. The search was intensified by his personal suffering and produced the method of Satyagraha.

Failure of other Forms : War and Revolution

This is a powerful weapon in the hands of the weak and unarmed persons or groups of persons against any form of evil. We have to reckon the fact that it does not always guarantee success in the worldly sense, but its chances of success are certainly greater than that of any other method, rebellion or war or revolution. The latter have proved again and again their inability to arrest the downward trend, to put an end to the chain reactions of insult and revenge. Even if the resister is destroyed in the process of satyagraha, he scores a moral victory over his adversary who can never go back to the old forms of cruelty in future. A small personal sacrifice will save posterity and eventually the entire human race.

When you scan the history of resistance movements before and after Gandhi, you become convinced that the Gandhian remedy is the only choice for a suffering humanity. The progress of science and technology, propelled by greed and ambition, has brought the world to a point where we find ourselves on the brink of disaster. Compulsions in modern society drive us to destroy natural environment, damage bio-diversity and most probably commit collective suicide through nuclear and chemical warfare. This historical emergency has made the adoption of moral resistance, powerfully advocated and poignantly demonstrated by Gandhi, all the more imperative. While it represents the quintessence of all ancient religious wisdom, it is also the most advanced modern scientific formula to check the frightening progress of tragedy on the world stage.

The last hope of mankind before the advent of Gandhi lay in communism. Though it was defeated in the capitalist countries of Europe, semi-feudal Tsarist Russia staged a revolution, and a 'communist' regime survived there for three quarters of a century. Cuba, China and several backward and developing nations of Asia pinned their hopes on communism. The disintegration of the Soviet Union and the liberation of Eastern Europe spelt the doom of the system. China changed her ways and adopted a market economy and Cuba got isolated and frustrated. These events mark not merely the fall of those particular regimes, but the final defeat of an ideology which claimed to offer an alternative to the exploitation, anarchy and wars, generated by the capitalist order. Much expectation was aroused by this movement in several parts of the world including India, but by this time it is clear that communism is as bad as capitalism or even worse. Whatever else it is, it does not produce a clean remedy for the man-made problems caused by man's injustice against man.

It is here in the context of the early demise of communism and the Satanic new forms assumed by capitalism and imperialism that the Gandhian path of satyagraha assumes new significance. Though produced in the Indian soil, its efficacy has been tested in the liberation movement of the blacks in South Africa and America. Environmentalists, feminists and pacifists all over the world are discovering slowly through encounters that a lasting solution is possible only through the real conversion of the enemy through appeals to the heart and to the divine spirit inside man. The human being has to be transformed, through education and demonstration, but the first step is, according to Gandhi, the transformation of the would-be reformer himself through self-discipline and self-sacrifice. This discovery took Gandhi closer to the great religions and its explanation in rational secular terms along with its practice before the entire world, thanks to the new information media, made him a social scientist as well as practical man of action.

Testimony of Social Science

One more important point has to be raised here. Prophetic power lies in the ability to see things which are still in the womb of time, to identify the enemy and prepare to meet him before he actually pounces upon us, to describe the future in clear terms before anyone else. The early critics of industrial revolution were just those lords who were disturbed in their siesta by noise and smoke in their village paradise. Many vigorous intellectuals perceived the advent of utopia, a new millennium of universal happiness, in spite of the increased misery of the lowest classes, which they dismissed as a temporary phase. Many scientists and social philosophers of the new age of enlightenment in Europe felt the euphoria of the conquest of nature. Only a small number of saintly persons like Tolstoy and Ruskin were able to comprehend the inherent evil implications of the machine age. That Gandhi joined this company is remarkable. It speaks for the spiritual strength of the Indian tradition which he had imbibed from the mother's milk and the free air of the village.

Quite recently, after the experience of the second world war and the atomic bomb, social scientists in the West are confirming the insights of the saintly critics of new technology. The historians of science are exposing the roots of scientific activity in the soil of 18th century - 19th century European society. They have been able to show that even scientists like Isac Newton and Charles Darwin were influenced by the concepts of alchemy and racial prejudice. Much of the inspiration and the financial support for laboratory work and fieldwork in the age of enlightenment came from greedy and unscrupulous pioneers in colonial enterprise. Here again the intuition of Gandhi is vindicated by social science. The same process is visible in the anti-communist stance of Gandhi also.

The attitude of Gandhi in relation to modern science and technology, capitalism and communism which are organically related, form the basis of a new non-European variety of neo-modernism. This has to be taken in their totality, separated and abstracted from their Indian background, rephrased in the context of the new explosion of knowledge and the expanding sphere of democracy.

Gandhi's philosophy is capable of providing a theoretical foundation for environmentalism, since his concern for nature, like that of the Jain and Buddhist monks, was built upon the conviction that the vast universe including human beings, animals and plants, formed an organic whole in which all parts are interrelated. Similarly, it can give the *dalits* and tribals a new confidence based on the belief that they were God's own people, possessing an inherent right to survive. It can invest feminism with new meaning and status related to Indian tradition and Gandhian practice.

These are worth a serious trial, especially since all other methods have failed to click. If we succeed in creating a new, morally strong, human being, as envisioned by Gandhi, the new human civilization will take care of itself in due course. If not, men and women, driven compulsively by their own conflicting greed and ambition will succumb to the tyranny of the machine, they constructed and bring about the end of their civilization through collective suicide. It is a moot question, whether such a holocaust will include all life on the face of the planet earth, or just the human race.

References

Gandhi, M.K. — *An Autobiography* or *The Story of My Experiments with Truth,* Navajivan Trust, Ahmedabad, 1927, Reprint 1996 *India of My Dreams,* Compiled by *R. K. Prabhu, Navajivan Trust, Ahmedabad,* 1947, Reprint 1997.

Joyce, Appleby et al — *Telling the Truth about History.* W.W. Norton & Company, Newyork, London, 1994.

3

Gandhi's Views on the Reconstruction of a New Civilization

K.P. Karunakaran

Very many studies have appeared on Gandhi's rejection of the civilization which existed in his times. These have focused attention on the evils of this civilization which were based on materialism and large-scale production of goods by machines which, by their supply, increased man's appetite for easy life and his desires and wants. Apart from many maxims, Gandhi put forward against this human tendency in his book, *Hind Swaraj*, published in 1908, he stressed on his point of view, in many speeches and writings. Later, Gandhi developed the ideas he expressed and enriched them by new contributions. When we try to assess Gandhi's views on the then existing civilization, we must take a note of these in the context of the impact of his work on his total philosophy. When asked for a message, Gandhi often said that his deeds were his message. In a crowded life, Gandhi behaved dynamically and he occasionally moved from position to position and from one view to another. It is difficult to sum up his views and the meaning of his deeds, which were scattered here and there. But a total look at them is called for, as he was reacting to events and trying to give a lead to many a social reform and political movements, but this was a difficult task. However, there is a uniformity, underlying his thoughts and it is not difficult to connect them and analyse them. This uniformity arose from a moral approach and a desire to lead an active and creative life. Often it was also directed against injustice.

It is wrong to conclude that Gandhi was against all the currents of modern life and that he wanted to turn to the past. No other single leader of his period earned as much popularity as Gandhi had and no other leader had received as much respect as Gandhi did from his political opponents. It is also true that after his death, many students and scholars have enriched his ideas by making new contributions. They are mostly western scholars, who have no sentimental approach towards Gandhi. In fact, very often they begin where Gandhi left.

Here, I do not mean to say rigidly that Gandhi was not against modern civilization as such. Often he made an exaggerated attack on it and used expressions and epithets which gave a misleading view about it.

Gandhi's Basic Approach

In public life, Gandhi provided leadership to many social reforms and movements based on fraternity and rationalism and also to various political campaigns connected with the freedom of individuals and the country, as a whole. At first, his basic attitude towards many problems is noted here.

1. Far from being a Hindu fundamentalist, as far as the social organisation was concerned, Gandhi was a religious and social reformer. He fought against such practices as hereditary priesthood, untouchability against the so called low castes and the prohibition of entry to temples to them. He conducted many campaigns, based on social equality and scientific spirit for the cause of these social reforms.

2. The urge for social equality, was the source of inspiration for Gandhi's agitation, for the removal of discrimination, based on racial differences in South Africa. Of course, Gandhi confined himself to the demands of the people of Indian origin in that continent. But its impact was visible on others in Africa later and on the struggle, the American black people launched in their country.

3. Another feature of Gandhi's thought, which had a bearing on his views on civilization, was his opposition to materialism. His rejection of machine-dictated civilization also arose from this. Gandhi was not against machines as such but against the inhuman application of machines and human beings becoming slaves of machines.

4. Another aspect of Gandhi's thought on culture and civilization was his rejection of violent methods by individuals and groups of individuals. This must be

considered separately because it is very important. But the connection between weapons and violence is to be noted here, because of their disastrous nature.

Gandhi : The Prophet of the Atomic Era

Very often, Gandhi's teachings on the rejection of violence and the positive aspects of nonviolent methods for social and political emancipation are primarily remembered as the most important ones. Gandhi was the first major political leader who, by his example, made it clear that nonviolent methods could be used collectively by the masses of people in their struggle for liberation.

Toynbee, the historian of the world, maintained that in the atomic era, as in the pre-atomic age, revolutionary political change could not, and would not be averted. But the use of violence for conducting a revolution would now take a new shape. The political process, associated with violence in the radical, political process of a revolution may, in future lead to disastrous consequences.

Similarly, Mao's view that the revolution could come through the barrel of the gun, can also not be accepted. The customary violence used in a revolution or in an armed conflict between two States might lead to mass suicide in which no party might win and all parties might be destroyed. In the words of Toynbee:

> Gandhi by his revolutionary new political strategy of nonviolent noncooperation made it possible for India and Britain to part from each other in peace and friendship. Martin Luther King consciously applied Gandhian methods in his leadership of the ex-African citizens of the United States in their struggle for human rights, equal to those of the fellow citizens of European origin.

Toynbee also added that, if the human race refrained from mass suicide it might come, into retrospect, to recognise Gandhi as one of its saviours.

This is true of the consequences of a war between nations and of the need for coming to an agreement between them. War is no more 'diplomacy by other means', because no major power will win in a war between big powers. Everyone will end in complete destruction that is why the cold war between the two powers ended. But it has not yet reached in an international order based on mutual faith and cooperation. As Gandhi had not come into grip with the problem of war in the nuclear era, his teachings did develop ideas of mutual goodwill and cooperation. In an open letter to Hitler, written during the World War II, he had elaborated some of these ideas.

One of Gandhi's critics once pointed out the limitations of Gandhi's teaching because he used the idioms and language which appealed mostly to the Indians. In his reply, Gandhi pointed out:

> I am aware of the danger pointed out by my critic, but it seems to be inevitable. I am in the position of a scientist who is in the midst of a very incomplete experiment and who, therefore, is unable to forecast large results and larger corollaries in the language which is capable of being misunderstood. The shortest way, therefore of making it (my message) effectively heard is to let it to speak for itself at least for the time being.

Public Opinion as a Factor

Gandhi always realised that the roles of violence and force were undesirable and that they should be reduced to the minimum in public life. But later, their use became disastrous in the atomic world because of the inventions of atom and nuclear weapons. So now the violence should be averted completely. Gandhi's teachings have become more relevant now than in his times. Gandhi also noted that along with destructive powers, the progress in science and technology has placed at the hands of the people many new inventions, which would help the transmission of information and views between the people. This has helped humanity's progress towards larger and larger groupings.

According to Gandhi, the mobilization of opinion of the people in favour of good causes, was a source of power to those who champion these causes, Now the as a result of many new inventions and the extensive use of radio and television, new dimensions are added to this source of power and its mobilization. Now the boundaries of one State can not stop the transmission of news and views and censorship can not be effectively enforced. That was why the walls of separation, like the Berlin wall, collapsed. Gandhi was not fully aware of the impact of these new inventions, but he realized that the means of communication in his times were effective. It was apparent even in the solo performances, when his fasts were accompanied by extensive propaganda in his favour.

Gandhi once told a representative of the Jews of Germany that with their extensive connections and resources in the world, they could bring pressure on Hitler and eliminate his attacks on them. Perhaps, he was exaggerating it, but in post-Gandhian era, the world public opinion emerged as a great factor. This was true in regard to the United States withdrawal from Vietnam, the American hesitation to the use of force in Iraq and the Soviet Union's withdrawal from Eastern Europe. Of course, there were many other factors which favoured these developments.

When some one pointed out to Gandhi that the non-violence of the cow had no appeal for the tiger, he replied by saying that his main enemies-the Englishmen-were not tigers and that they were human beings. One can even say that the success of Gandhi's non-violent campaigns against the British was partly the result of the response of the British, who had a high level of culture and civilization. Even in regard to the gradual removal of discrimination based on racial differences, the high cultural level of the whites in the United States and Africa was a factor.

There were two aspects to the interrelation between public opinion and non-violent struggles. One was the conversion of the enemy to a noble cause. Another was bringing pressure on him by mobilizing public opinion. Gandhi, himself used both these aspects of public opinion to get support for his struggle. Even a movie made by a Westerner on Gandhi was a vehicle to spread his view in the world. This is true of many scholarly books written on Gandhi and his ideas. Some Westerners, who were their authors, had no sentimental approach towards him and their approach was scientific. The working of some international organisations like the United Nations has also helped the mobilization of world public opinion in favour of good causes in the contemporary world.

These are areas in which Gandhi's ideas have to be enriched. He, himself has noted that the sense of direction of the progress of the world was towards larger and larger grouping. This has not led to the emergence of an effective 'one world organisation' which can enforce its decisions. But, there is no doubt that there is now a trend towards an international order. Gandhi's ideas had anticipated them.

The following were the social reform movements and political campaigns, Gandhi launched in which he made extensive use of public opinion in their favour:

(1) the removal of the discrimination based on racial differences in South Africa;

(2) the Indian nation's liberation from the British rule;

(3) the removal of untouchability and the termination of discrimination against the so called low castes such as the denial to them of the right to enter the temples;

(4) the abolition of the treatment by Hindus towards the Muslims based on intolerance and on the belief that they were *maleech* (impure people).

On the Potential Strength of the Individual

So far, I have discussed Gandhi's views on the reconstruction of social and political life of the people. He thought and wrote at length on the individual's personal life. One can add that this is connected with the social life also, because the society is a collection of individuals. I have noted them earlier. These refer to the control of desires and wants. I may add here some views connected with the exercise of bringing out the potential in man. Gandhi's aim was to create conditions which would help man to maintain good health and develop his psychological and spiritual powers. What he said on these subjects, is not necessarily ignored in the discussions on modern civilization, but these are very often eclipsed and overshadowed by some other features.

Even at the risk of repeating what has been said earlier, Gandhi's emphasis on simple life must again be noted. He emphasized the importance of a balance in psychological activities. Gandhi, for himself, observed a day of silence every week. He was against the individual's going in search of momentary excitements, which according to him, were unwanted pleasures. He continuously emphasized the importance of human beings developing tremendous discipline and powers of concentration. Doing these according to Gandhi could increase their spiritual and physical strength, and also their intellectual powers.

According to Gandhi, a simple life could bring out the best potential in man and there should be no dissipation of his energies for excitement and pleasure. In many of these matters, he was influenced by *Bhagavat Gita*, one of the sacred books of the Hindus. He learned a good deal from Tolstoy and Ruskin also. On another matter like organising resistance to injustice, Thoreau's work had a tremendous impact on him. In regard to the importance of physical work, Gandhi was influenced by many Russian thinkers who glorified bread-labour.

Even in regard to one's diet, Gandhi had strong views. The collection of his writings on this subject are compiled and published under the title, *Diet and Diet Reform*, Gandhi was against human beings yielding to one's palate and eating food, which is harmful to health.

Life and World Affirmation

Gandhi's rejection of materialist philosophy gave some the impression that he thought that the worldly life was a *maya*—an illusion. This is far from the truth.

While explaining his view on a Hindu religious saint (sanyasi) he said; "A sanyasi is one who cares for others. He has renounced all selfishness. A sanyasi, therefore, true to his creed of renunciation, must care for swaraj, (the independence of the country) not for his sake, but for the sake of others. He has no worldly ambition for himself. This does not mean that he may not help others to undertake their place in the world". With this basic approach, Gandhi developed a philosophy of life, which he put into practice.

No other Indian leader of the modern period was as much concerned with real world life as Gandhi was. He was engaged in organising many battles for the causes he wanted to promote. He was also interested in building many world organizations for education and for economic production.

Gandhi realized that there was much to do in this world. He wanted to destroy many things and build many others. As far as he was concerned, he never wanted to escape from life. He was a man, involved in incessant activity. There was nothing passive in him.

The Local and the Universal in Gandhi

The political styles and idioms, Gandhi used made a tremendous appeal to the Indians and particularly to the Hindus of his generation. This was only in regard to the reforms. The content of the message of his deeds and words was universal in character. He made use of the techniques which were very effective at that time in India. Later, when these were to be used to apply to other countries, these were required to be used with new styles and idioms. When Gandhi was invited to other countries to spread his teachings, he used to say, if his work was effective in India of his times, it would be taken up later by others. This is what exactly happened when Martin Luther (Jr.) in the United States and others in Sicily and in Africa carried his ideas forward from where he had left them. Moreover, while doing so they enriched Gandhi's ideas and did not confine themselves to mechanically repeating his words and ideas. The situations in countries other than India in later periods were different from those of India of Gandhi's times. It was, therefore, necessary to apply creatively Gandhi's philosophy in these countries and give it a new shape.

Gandhi saw no contradiction between his role as an Indian social reformer and political leader on one hand and as a teacher of mankind on the other (of course, he did not claim that he was a teacher of mankind). He even thought that the one supplemented the other. Refuting the view of a critic that Buddha and Jesus were not interested in the momentary issues surrounding them in their times, Gandhi said:

> What was the larger symbiosis that Buddha and Christ preached? The Buddha fearlessly carried the war into the enemy's camp and brought down on its knees an arrogant priesthood. Christ drew out the money-changers from the temples of Jerusalem and drew down curses from heaven upon the hypocrites and the pharisees. Both were for intense direct action. Buddha would have died resisting the priesthood if the majesty of his love had not provided equally to the task of bending priesthood. Christ died on the cross with a crown of thorns on his head, defying the might of the empire. And if I raise resistance of a nonviolent character, I sincerely and humbly follow the footsteps of my great masters named by my critics.

Gandhi's Teaching : the Immediate and the Lasting Influence

This is true that there is an interrelation between the immediate impact of Gandhi's teaching and its significance for the future. While trying to apply Gandhi's ideas in future, one must not try to do so mechanically. Some of the essential aspects of Gandhi's ideas will have to be accepted, some will have to be modified and some will have to be dropped altogether. That is why Gandhi, himself said that he did not want to leave behind him a straight jacket as Gandhism. The basic approach towards Gandhi's views in regard to the reorganisation of modern civilization and culture is not that simple, but the total rejection of machinery is unrealistic. So is Gandhi's view that self-control is the best way of birth control.

While Gandhi thought his role as an Indian leader of his time supplemented his role as a teacher of mankind for the future, Jawaharlal Nehru saw an apparent contradiction between the two. He noted, "Always there has been that inner conflict with him (Gandhi) and in our national politics between Gandhi as a nationalist leader and Gandhi as a man with a prophetic message which was not confined to India, but for humanity and the world. It is never easy to reconcile a strict adherence to truth, as one sees it, with exigencies and experience of life, especially the political life. There is an element of truth in what Nehru observed. In Gandhi's own words:

> I shall work single handed in implicit faith that what I failed to make clear to my country men today, shall be clear to them someday by itself or if God wills it through some apt word He may put in my mouth or some apt work He may prompt me to do.

The Traditional and the Modern in Gandhi

Gandhi's use of the idioms and style have occasionally given the impression that Gandhi was a Hindu revivalist. Nathuram Vinayak Godse, who assassinated Gandhi, knew this more than others. He realised that Gandhi was a threat to the narrow social behaviour of the Hindus. Towards the end of Gandhi's life, the Mahatma was undermining the traditional, social behaviour of the Hindus based on their communalism and sectarianism. In a sense, he was the least Hindu of all Hindu leaders of his generation. He wanted the Indian social and political life to be organised on the basis of modern, democratic, social and political life of western Europe.

As far as the encounter between the two civilizations was concerned, Gandhi observed:

> I want the cultures of all lands to blow over my house. But I refuse to live in other people's house as an interloper, a beggar and a slave.

Gandhi also occasionally thought that he had a mission to spread new ideas to the world. Most of the scholars have maintained that Gandhi used the traditional methods to promote the novel ideas. It was from the Christians that Gandhi learned the importance of doing missionary work by those who were religiously inclined.

The Western democratic methods, particularly making mass mobilization by holding meetings and spreading ideas by pamphlets, had a tremendous impact on Gandhi. It was again from the West that Gandhi learned the importance of representative institutions. Many of the techniques Gandhi used for mass mobilization were Western in origin.

Arnold Toynbee, made this observation:

> In the spiritual travail of a Gandhi or a Lenin in our generation, we can watch the impact of Western civilization upon Hinduism and upon Russian orthodox Christendom in the act of transformation from external encounter between Western society and its neighbours into an inner experience of Westernised world. The life and energy with which they inspire their anti-western holy wars is actually drawn—that is the spirit of their vigour—from the western source and that is the crucible of their ardent souls an anti-western movement is transmitted into a new manifestation of the spiritual force against which it is directed. A Gandhi or a Lenin find it impossible to take spiritual action without being moved by the spirit of western civilization. It is as though the western spirit were a kind of psychic electricity which has now electrified the whole mankind with such effect that there could no longer be an extension of human psychic.

What Toynbee refers to here as the source of inspiration and western current of thought is not necessarily western in origin. It was present in different groups of people at different times. But it was in the west that at the first this current of thought moved millions of people on the basis of civilization. It is again in the west that at first, at the beginning of the modern period, a new civilization with all its negative and positive features, became very popular. While criticising its negative features in a letter to a friend, Gandhi wrote in 1909:

> There is no impossible barrier between East and West. There is no such thing as western or European civilization, but there is a modern civilization which is purely material.

Some features of modern civilization which stood for democratization of political life and reorganisation of social structure on the basis of equality, liberty and fraternity have a spiritual dimension also. In modern times there was also an emphasis on those aspects of human activity connected with creative, rationalism and scientific approach. Gandhi accepted all these aspects of modern civilization which came to India from the West.

Summing up of Gandhi's Views

The economic changes that took place in Gandhi's times and later in India and the emergence of new social classes helped the popularization of modern ideas which Gandhi tried to spread in his times.

In regard to the negation of violence and the prospects of conducting social and political movements, Gandhi was ahead of his times. That is why he was referred to as the prophet of the atomic era.

From the negative position of not using violence, Gandhi moved to a positive position of showing regards and regards towards others..... even towards the political opponents who did not easily respond. It was from acting in this position that Gandhi preached affection and regard towards the Muslims towards the end of his life. This was the basis of Gandhi's basic attitude towards civilized life. As some organized sections of Hindu fanatics were not influenced by Gandhi's views, one from among them assassinated him. He became a martyr. What he could not achieve in his life, he achieved by his death. There will again be 'ups' and 'downs' to the pursuance Gandhi's ideas in India. But the sense of direction of the political march and social movements in contemporary India is clear—it is towards modernization. This was taken forward later by those who succeeded Gandhi. But they have not accepted what Gandhi had suggested as corrective to some excesses of modern civilization. Those ideas remain as ideals.

4

Gandhi's Philosophy and a New Human Civilization

M.R. Rajagopalan

We are living in times where the future is rather bleak. The environmental crisis has arrived and except for a few responsible persons, many of us do not seem to notice it. The crisis started with the invention of ploughshare and wheel and man's ability to produce surplus food grains by agricultural practices. But the western thinkers glorifying the individuals rather than the society, telling them about the survival of the fittest encouraged the exploitation of earth's resources. Then came the industrial revolution leading to large-scale destruction of forests and pollution of the soil and atmosphere. The invention of the steam engine and the establishment of coal as an energy source aggravated the situation. In the 20th century, motor cars made their appearance, so did petroleum products as their fuel. Both coal and petroleum have been formed in the earth over billions of years by degradation of plants and marine organisms. We are rapidly exhausting these non-renewable energy sources. Alongwith to the consumption of energy, economic growth and distribution of goods and services increased. All these activities have led to the pollution of atmosphere, ozonal hole, deforestation, soil loss, desertification, water scarcity and its pollution, urban sprawls, toxic wastes, unsustainable energy use, species loss, ecological refuses, etc. This is the development which is ecologically not sustainable. The human being has become, in the words of James McHall "the most dangerous organism that the planet has ever hosted."

India has a tradition rooted in spiritual values. Our Vedas, our Upanishads, *Ramayana* and *Mahabharata* and *Gita* lay stress on higher values—spiritual over temporal values—in life. Only India could produce Ashoka, the emperor who renounced war and violence after a victory.

This is the land of Buddha, Mahavira, Adi Shankaracharya, Ramanuja, Madhwacharya and the likes who were persons of lofty character. They were able to gather around them a large following and extend the sway of their respective systems. Likewise came Gandhi, as a man of peace and sacrifice. Millions of people accepted his teachings which indeed came to constitute a separate religion, namely, Gandhism. If a system owes its growth to the excellence of the philosophical principles on which it is based, Gandhism ought to be at its peak of glory today. But what do we see in reality?

We have aped the western values, its materialism and consumerism, self-interest and the rat race. We are also destroying our environment. Barring a few occasions in the year, it appears that we have forgotten the values preached and practised by Gandhi.

We are going to talk about a new civilization. I suppose that civilization in itself is a tricky word. Human society is supposed to have evolved from a barbaric state to a civilized and advanced one. Then the question arises, "What the pre-civilized society was like"?

Without going deeply into this controversy, we could stick to a few parameters for a civilized society. It is a society where there is a fair amount of production and distribution of essential goods like food, clothing, housing, etc.

The second parameter is one of value—where security of life is assured for citizens—where they enjoy the freedom to choose their way of life and freedom of thought and expression. The third parameter arising out of the first and second is that this kind of civilized society would be tolerant, non-violent and based on mutual trust and respect among persons, following different ideologies and values in life.

Has such a situation ever existed? It is difficult to answer this question in the affirmative. Though in every human society and almost in every age, great persons have preached lofty ideals and values, human beings seem to be surviving only in the midst of quarrels, controversies and violent wars.

Toynbee comparing Gandhi with earlier world leaders, extols his courage and compassion in plunging into the gutter of politics in order to cleanse it and the inner purity which enabled him to emerge unscathed. To quote Toynbee again, "Gandhian prescription alone is the sole and sovereign remedy for the maladies of modern man".

I would like to recall the words of Pandit Nehru on the eve of

Gandhi's assassination.

> The light has gone out of our eyes and there is darkness everywhere.........The light has gone out, I said, and yet I was wrong. For the light that shone in this country was no ordinary light. The light that has illuminated this country for these many years will illumine this country for many more years and a thousand years later that light will still be seen in this country and the world will see it and it will give solace to innumerable hearts. For, that light represented something more than the immediate present. It represented the living truth—the eternal truth reminding us of the right path drawing us from error—taking this ancient country to freedom.

Surely Gandhi's legacy will survive for thousands of .years to come. For his messages of non-violence and truth are moral imperatives, if human society has to survive. Likewise, his khadi and village industries alone could help us cope with the environmental crisis. Only his constructive programme could lead us to a new civilization.

5

Gandhian Ideals for the New Civilization

A.K. Tharien

Introduction

We are at the threshold of a new millennium and are about to step into the new century. We have just celebrated the golden jubilee of our independence. Science and technology have made great strides in recent past. Reproductive science claims that it can now create a baby of one's choice; the complexion, sex, height, brain qualities and so forth by genetic manipulation. A baby can be produced from the tissue of a woman asexually without any contact with a man, by cloning. I was attending a WHO conference in Geneva a few months ago, when the scientists were sharing these startling achievements. Today, ethical, moral and even human values are being threatened.

It is in this context that we are looking at the theme of 'Gandhi's legacy and modern civilization.'

What is Civilization?

Civilization is defined by some as the bringing up from an ignorant social condition to a higher one. It implies an advance, in the state of culture. A community acquires this status depending on climate, soil, water, natural barriers, instinct of self-preservation, effective response to challenges, economic well-being, leisure, knowledge, trade and social and political climate.

What is Culture?

The term culture refers to the social heritage of a group of people, a way of living. It includes daily material needs of a person such as food, clothing, shelter, and non-material aspects such as customs, habits, manners, attitude, ideas, perceptions and values which are transmitted from generation.

History of Mankind

Civilization is estimated to be 7000 years old. The history of mankind has been broadly classified into two periods.

1. Prehistoric-from 1000000 BC to 5000 BC
2. Historic-from 5000 BC to the present day.

   Historic age is again classified into:

   a) Ancient world-5000 BC to 500 AD

   b) Medieval world-500 AD to 1500 AD

   c) Modern world-1500 AD to the present day.

First, let us look into the ancient civilization.

River Valley Civilization

The river valleys were the cradles of civilization and they were:

1. The Nile Valley Civilization (Egyptian) : 5000 BC
2. Mesopotamian Civilization; (around rivers Tigris and Euphrates in Western Asia): 3000 BC
3. Yellow River Valley Civilization (Chinese, considered to be the oldest): 7000 BC
4. Indus Valley Civilization (Indian) : 5000 BC
5. Harrappa Culture in Punjab and Mohan Jo-Daro in Sindh.

Dravidians were the original inhabitants of India. Aryans came from Central Asia around 1500 BC They had no castes in the beginning. Later, castes were formed on the basis of occupations. The four castes were, Brahamins (priests), Kshatriyas (soliders), Vaisyas (traders and farmers) and Shudras (servants).

Sixth century BC had great religious leaders like, Mahavira and Buddha. From the time of Ashoka, Indian culture had permeated into the neighbouring countries.

Origin of Modern Civilization

Columbus discovered America in 1492 and the Spaniards defeated the native Mayans. When Constantinople fell into the hands of Turks, European traders looked for sea routes to trade with rich India. Four centuries ago, in Emperor Jahangir's time, India was described as the richest country, attracting many foreigners. Portugal established a trading settlement on the west coast in 1498.

British Colonization

In 1600 AD the British East India Company established a small trading settlement at Surat.

The British territorial expansion started with the decline of Mughal empire. They acquired land, by skilfully manipulating one local ruler against the other.

By 1857, Queen Victoria became the empress of India with more than 500 Nawabs and Rajas paying obeisance to Her Majesty. British trade flourished, while India's hand-woven cloth making system and other such cottage industries were curtailed. The Indian weavers, who wove the finest fabrics in the world, were brought to Murshidabad and their finger tips were cut off. Raw materials like cotton from India were exported at low cost and manufactured cloth from Manchester and other manufactured goods from other parts of UK were sold in India. Thus, the British established monopoly over the rich Indian market and in turn ruined the Indian artisans. Commercialization of agriculture destroyed the Indian peasantry. British bureaucracy sapped the life vitality and dynamism of the people in India. British youth found easy employment in all key positions in government in India. In short, in two centuries under British rule, they bled the Indian subcontinent white.

French occupation of Indo-China, Dutch occupation of East Indies, enslavement of the vast continent of Africa, slave trade of the Negro population, etc., speak of the same story of exploitation of the blacks by the whites.

Capitalism was born in the womb of imperialism and grew up on the nourishment of external dynamics, arising out of an empire-colony relationship. British rose to power by exploiting their colonies in Asia and Africa. Churchill, while signing the Atlantic Charter, declared that he would not be a party to liquidate the British empire. But Attlee of the labour government that followed, had to grant independence to India and other colonies and the British empire slowly collapsed with it.

Establishment of Modern Civilization

The keynotes to modern civilization are:

(1) Increasing application of science to industry and agriculture

(2) Increasing standard of life

(3) Increasing sense of equality

(4) Uncontrolled consumerism

The USA has epitomized these, in a remarkable way. But today it seems to have lost its dynamism and vigour. Unfortunately they were only concerned with the white man's world. People of Asia and Africa instead of chalking out their own indigenous path of development, tried to imitate the west blindly. Though Gandhi warned against imitating the west, by and large, India unfortunately did not follow his advice. Soviet Union collapsed as they failed in their productivity because of non incentive slave labour.

The Threat to Civilization

After the Second World War, Russia and USA became super powers. They divided the world between themselves into spheres of influences. They switched over from conventional arms to nuclear weapons. The nuclear scientists fear that even if there is no nuclear war the continued tests and nuclear wastes will set a nuclear winter which can destroy plants and life on earth.

Some time ago, at one of the United Nations sessions, I listened to Prof. Lester Brown a noted economist. He said that environmental degradation and ecological deterioration had reached a critical point and if we did not take preventive actions, the result would be irreparable and tragic.

Euro-American Fall of Civilization

Arnold Toynbee, in his study of twenty two civilizations, states that civilizations make progressive forward moves when they are able to respond successfully to the challenges that arise in their forward march. But a particular stage is reached in their onwards march, when they lose its creativity, to meet fresh challenges.

Dr Ram Manohar Lohia has gone deeper and outlined his theory of 'maximum efficiency versus total efficiency'.

Our own Indian civilization moved for maximum efficiency in a particular direction, instead of striving for total efficiency. Modern civilization has lost its creativity. It has stratified.

The maximum efficiency achieved in science and technology could not solve the basic problems of mankind such as poverty, ever-rising, unemployment (in India, the number of unemployed youth was 38.7 lakh in July, 1997), lack of basic health care and the eroding purchasing capacity of the masses.

Permissive western society's fall of moral values has landed mankind to 'AIDS', the new plague. In the final analysis of modern civilization, resulting in the debasement and degradation of the human person, we have lost the joy of life. Virtue seems to be possible, as Roussau said, in simple societies where people lived austere and frugal lives as Gandhi advocated. In the modern sophisticated culture man is corrupt; greater the sophistication, greater the corruption.

Unplanned Industrialization

Ours is a G.N.P. (Gross National Product) oriented civilization. Instead of harnessing the forces of nature and living in harmony with nature, modern civilization started systemic rape of nature. The seas, earth, air and even outer space are polluted. Even mother's breast milk is contaminated, as revealed in a study in Coimbatore.

Globalization and Multinationals

India is being already sucked into the vortex of globalization, losing the core of its cultural identity.

Since 1950, world's economic output has increased 5 to 7 times. It has also increased the human burden on the planet's regeneration systems. It has intensified competition between the rich and the poor for the resource base. For instance, the World Bank sanctions projects which will displace the poor, to generate economic returns for the benefit of the rich. The multinationals cut corners on safety, lessen remunerations and dump untreated toxic discharges into the rivers.

Trade agreements like WTO (World Trade Organization) and NAFTA (North American Free Trade Agreement) are to protect the interests of multinational corporations. Economic planning should be a local, rooting power to the people and communities. Life is for living and not for merely consuming. Material deficiency can be filled up with social, cultural, intellectual and spiritual abundance that place no burden on the planet.

World Trade Organization (WTO)

WTO was established to remove tariffs and other restrictions, for free international trade and for creating new economic opportunity and prosperity. India finds it hard to compete in the world market.

Gandhi's Philosophy

In this century, the world has produced two unique phenomenon, the atom bomb and Mahatma Gandhi. Atom bomb symbolizes achievement of science and technology and material progress. Gandhi represents Spinoza's eternity. He rediscovered a new vision, a new dimension and a new meaning to life which had been forgotten by people for a long time.

Gandhi's entry marked a new era. He was a political genius. He galvanized millions of people into his philosophy. He was influenced by Thoreau, Russel and Tolstoy.

Allen Octaveon Hume founded the Indian National Congress in 1885. It had two groups, one led by Gopal Krishna Gokhale, known as moderates and the other fiery group, led by Bal Gangadhar Tilak known as extremists. Gandhi brought them together in 1921 under the concept of Ahimsa and Satyagraha (non-violence and truth) He applied the Ahimsa of Buddha and the moral and spiritual principles taught by Jesus Christ.

Gandhi emphasized the spiritual value that good ends should have good means also. Mao's idea of achieving good through violence has already proved its futility following the disintegration of the erstwhile Soviet Union. He believed in the total transformation and transmutation of the individual and his society. Both in South Africa and in India, he tried his utmost for emancipation of the oppressed and neglected, whether it be Dalits or women or the poor. He declared: "Unless we eradicate untouchability, we have no moral right to call for independence."

Culture of Peace and Love

Peace is the foundation of the highest spiritual and ethical values. It is the norm of conduct and the basis of democratic and liberal values. Throughout his life, Gandhi tried to identify himself with the most ordinary people. This was his approach towards life—the non-violent approach to life. If we want a society based on non-violence, we have to make radical changes in our lifestyles also.

Religion was the essence of Gandhi's life. Religion touches the deepest elements of the human psyche. The expression of his religious conviction was through love, compassion and non-violence. He preached *Sarva Dharma Same Bhave*—a more positive expression than secularism. Gandhi made the inimitable attempt to establish the inter-communal, inter-religious and international relationship on peace. Gandhi tried to establish love out of its domestic seclusion and introduced it into the world polities.

Gandhi spoke of Rama Rajya (kingdom of God) which was a moral concept, not religious in which there would be no consideration of caste, creed, colour or gender in which everybody would be entitled an equal share.

Truth and Ahimsa

An unqualified insistence on pursuing truth (*satyagraha*) and justice (*nyay*) not by hook or crook but by the method of absolute non-violence (*ahimsa*) is the essence of Gandhi's message both in the moral and political movements.

Gandhi's Economics

Today economics speak of sustainable development and ecological values. Gandhi was not against industry. But as he predicted it could not give people more employment. His constructive programme was to give employment to all whether it be khadi, gobar gas or tree plantation, where all can be engaged in constructive work. Gandhian Economics is an alternative to overcome the exploitation of both capitalism and communism for the exponents of humane social order. In the 1992 Earth Summit in Rio-de-Jenerio the green activists high lighted Gandhi's economy which is an alternative to overcome the failures of both capitalism and communism, having components of a harmonious social order.. The basic factor is not the elimination of competition but complimentary interdependence.

Interdependent World

India is a land of diversities—different religions, races and languages. There is a great variety in the way people live, dress and eat. But there has been a basic unity among the people—peaceful coexistence.

Man being a social animal, has to live in relationships. He has to depend on others. His needs are fulfilled by cooperation and interdependence.

India is the largest democratic country. Our constitution guarantees six fundamental rights to safeguard against abuse of power by the government.

We are living in an interdependent world. Can a nation state exist in seclusion from the community of nations and world authority? Experiences of Stalinist Russia, and Mao's China are before us. USA and European allies found it difficult to face the oil embargo of OPEC.

A New World Order

Nation states of Europe after 300 years of fighting are moving towards a single European community with a common parliament, a common currency and a single army, for survival. The next step may be to strive for a world government, which can mobilize the entire resources of the world and utilize them for removing poverty and restructuring a new world order.

Today, the world is spending about USD 8,000, billion for military expenditure—10 per cent of this is enough to provide basic needs for all, like food, health care, education, and safe water. Cost of constructing a nuclear plant is same as of building a dam. How much of our resources are wasted on defence!

Conclusion

Today, we live in a world of injustice, corruption, exploitation, discrimination based on wealth, and religious fundamentalism. We also have problems.of environment pollution and nuclear threats. We have people in Asia. Africa and Latin America, becoming poorer and the rich becoming richer. How to solve this problem? Experiences of Palestine and LTTE in Sri Lanka have shown that violence and armed conflicts cannot bring lasting solutions. As Gandhi taught, love and compassion, combined with righteous indignation should reign the hearts of the new generations. Mahatma Gandhi has given us the weapon of love, of Satyagraha and of non-violent resistance.

It will epitomise the humanism of Ikkinition of Egypt the millennium of Hebrew prophets, the essence of Upanishads, the wisdom of Lao Tse, the compassion of Buddha, truth of Socrates, brotherhood of Mohammed (PBH), the sacrificial love taught by Jesus Christ and universalism of Lohia. This will usher in an era of new civilization drcamt by Mahatma Gandhi, for peace harmony and prosperity of the human race.

Conclusion

6

Indian Civilization-Versus-Modern Civilization

Sociological and Gandhian Perspectives

T. Rajendran

Concept of Civilization in Sociological Perspective

For enlightened thinkers, the notion of civilization was inextricably connected with the idea of social progress, namely the triumph of rationality over religion, the decline of local customs in particular and the rise of natural science.'

Civilization was originally derived from the verb, civilize, from, civic and 'civilitas', explaining the acquisition of qualities of politeness and amiability on the part of superiors to inferiors. Sociologists use the term in a general way and a vague manner as for instance, mentioning about 'modern civilization' by which is usually meant contemporary urban and industrialized societies. In this regard, there is a relationship between civilization and culture. Civilization tends to be equated with high culture, which refers to the fine arts, classical music, live theatre, and other activities that usually require special preparation to be fully appreciated and this form of culture is patronized by a small group of wealthy and highly educated people in contrast with popular culture which refers to the forms of culture pursued by a larger number of middle and working class people, which include spectators of sports, television movies and rock music (Richard P. Appelbaum and William J. Chambliss, 1995). Sometimes, culture is contrasted with civilization and not identified with the latter, because in this context, civilization is looked in terms of 'a more complex social phenomenon, including the organisation of material and technological qualities as well as the beliefs of art forms, literature and the body of ideas and values of a people; which is more specifically termed as 'culture'. Alfred Weber has analysed civilization as process.

The term civilization is used for referring to a highly complex or advanced culture in contrast with a relatively simple culture and also for a culture that has developed writing, domesticated animals and formed a stable and settled agricultural complex. Further, civilization is defined in terms of the institutionalization of a system of ethical and religious traditions and ideologies that dominate a society or a number of related societies. (Arnold Toynbee). This has an example in western civilization.

Civilization may refer simply to the presence of some established social order as opposed to its absence, as for instance in the pairing of civilization and barbarism, common in early societies. Generally, it is applied to a particular type of society. (Greek civilization or industrial civilization). In this sense, it borders on and merges with the concept of culture. The main difference lies in the tendency of using the term civilization in order to give a greater emphasis to sociopolitical structure and historical process.

According to J.L. Gillin and J.P. Gillin, civilization is a more complex and evolved form of culture, 'A culture becomes civilization only when it possesses a written language, science, philosophy, a specialized division of labour, a complex technology and political system.

Maciver and Page say that civilization includes all those things by means of which some other objective is attained such as a typewriter, press, lathe, motor, etc. It also implies basic technology which refers to the authority of man over natural phenomenon and social technology which deals with man's behaviour. Whereas culture is concerned with knowledge, belief, art, philosophy, religion, literature, music, and all other capabilities obtained by man as a member of society.

Characteristics of Civilization

1. Civilization primarily comprises scientific and technical knowledge and the command which they give over natural resources. (Alfred Weber, 1950).

2. Civilization has a precise standard of measurement on the grounds of efficiency (e.g. a motor car is faster than a bullockcart).

3. Civilization is all the time going forward with a continuous upward trend.
4. It is passed on without effort and connected with external life of man.
5. Civilization is what we have; culture is what we are (Maciver and Page).
6. It is borrowed without change and loss. (e.g. Radio, Television, X-ray)
7. Civilization and culture are interdependent. The anti-facts, the articles of civilization are influenced by mentifacts, the objects of culture.
8. Civilization and culture are interactive. (e.g. The technological development influences culture as the printing press influences the literary art).

Gandhian Concept of Civilization

Gandhian concept of civilization is characterised by moral approach and that mode of conduct which points out the man and his path of duty, duty oriented moral values, moral progress, identification with the exploited and suppressed people, humanitarian service, a quest for truth, simplicity, integration of spiritual and moral elements, predominance of religious ethics, social purification, social justice, voluntary reduction of wants, thereby promoting real happiness and contentment and the capacity for service, nonviolence, Sarvodaya, etc.

Modern civilization is characterised by the features of :

- Greed
- Aggression
- Imperialism
- Colonialism
- War technology
- Star wars
- Inequity
- Exploitation
- Poverty
- Extravagance and luxury

- Unbridled individualism and vulgar materialism
- Alienation
- Total destruction either by design or by accident
- Bodily comforts
- Immorality
- Valueless and commercial education
- Development of unconcerned innate tendency and apathy
- Terrorism
- Keeping peace in place of making peace
- Narrow-mindedness and selfish tendency
- Gradual depletion of non-renewable resources, etc.

Indian Civilization : Gandhian Perspectives

The tendency of the Indian civilization is to elevate moral being and is based on a belief in God. Indian civilization represents, in its essence, the Divine Force.

That is why Gandhi says with daring certainty that : Our civilization with a proper and perfect cultivation of the quality of ahimsa, which is its active form, means that purest love brings the whole world to our feet. Through our civilization we have a message to deliver to the whole world.

Modern Civilization vs Indian Civilization : A Gandhian Perspective

In the words of Gandhi :

Modern civilization is chiefly materialistic as ours is chiefly spiritual. Modern civilization occupies itself in the investigation of the laws of matter and employs human ingenuity in inventing or discovering means of production or weapons of destruction. Ours is chiefly occupied in exploring spiritual laws.

Modern civilization as represented by the west of today, has given matter a place which by right belongs to spirit. It has, therefore, put violence on the throne of triumph and held under bondage truth and innocence.

Modern civilization represents forces of evil and darkness.

Our land has very little to learn from modern civilization which is based on violence of the blackest type, largely negation of the divine in man and which is rushing headlong to its own ruin.

Gandhi calls modern civilization Satanic if it stands for multiplication of wants and machinery devised to supply them, mad desire to destroy distance and time, to increase animal appetites, and go to the ends of the earth in search of their satisfaction.

Conclusion

Indian civilization is in contrast with modern civilization, in the sense that Indian civilization is based on spiritual, moral and ethical values and norms whereas modern civilization diverts man's thoughts from the main purpose of life;

Bodily comfort stands before soul's growth and the man has no time today even to know himself. He prefers newspapers and such other things to be left alone with himself for thought.

Civilization points out to man the path of duty and it consists not in multiplication, but in the deliberate and voluntary restriction of wants.

This alone paves the way for real happiness and contentment and for promoting and strengthening the capacity for service.

References

1. Nicholas Abercrombie, Stephen Hill and Bryans Turner; 1984, *The Penguin Dictionary of Sociology*, p. 38, Penguin Books.
2. G. Duncan Mitchell (ed.); 1968 *A New Dictionary of Sociology,* p. 27-28, Routledge and Kegan Paul, London and Thenley.
3. B. Bhushan, 1989, *Dictionary of Sociology*, p. 27. New Delhi : Anmol Publications Pvt. Ltd.,
4. Michael Mann (ed.), 1983 *Macmillan Student Encyclopaedia of Sociology,* p.44, Macmillan Press, London.
5. T. B. Bottomone, 1962, *Sociology : A Guide to Problems and Literature,* p.121. *Revised Edition,* Third Impression, Blackie & Sons (India) Limited.

6. *Hind Swaraj,* p. 91.
7. *Speeches and Writings of Mahatma Gandhi,* p. 329.
8. *Modern vs. Ancient Civilization,* p. 48.
9. *Speeches and Writings of Mahatma Gandhi,* p. 329.
10. *Young India*, March 9, 1922.
11. *Speeches and Writings of Mahatma Gandhi,* p. 329.
12. *The Indian Review,* (Dec. 1909), p. 134.
13. *Young India, March* 17, 1927.

7

Gandhi's Vision : A Search for Lasting Peace and Security

Devavrat N. Pathak

Recent years have witnessed events that are dramatic and profound in their significance and have far reaching effects. The cold war has ended, bringing down the curtain on the forty year old ideological rivalry and military confrontation. The fall of Berlin wall (1989) symbolized an era of freedom, similar to the French Revolution, two hundred years ago. With the assertion of independence by the East European countries and the constituent states of the Soviet Union, its federal structure collapsed.

Events happened in quick succession. A new era of reconciliation and harmony was inaugurated in South Africa. Free elections took place at various places marking the new age of democracy. Peace process was started in West Asia. All these seemed to mark a new era of peace and cooperation. For the first time after 1945, the UN was free from the East-West confrontation and the fear of veto. The Gulf War of 1991 clearly indicated the commanding position of the USA as the only super power in the world. President Bush termed it as a defining moment of history and called for a New World Order. Fukuyama characterised the New Era, as the 'end of history'. Market economy and freedom of enterprise underlined the triumph of liberalism and a new age of globalization with a promise of freedom, democracy and respect for human rights.

The previous decade of 1980's was aptly termed as a 'lost decade' for the developing world. Military expenditure had gone up reaching the dizzy height of one trillion dollars per year. On the other hand, mountains of debt burdened the developing countries.

Developing countries paid $ 160 billion in debt service charges in 1992, more than two and a half times official aid and $60 billion more than private financial flows. Debt serving has been hampering the ability of the developing countries in meeting their urgent human development needs.

These dreadful trends were reversed on account of Gorbachev's policy of disengagement, relaxation, disarmament, moratorium on nuclear tests and transition to a peaceful economy. Global military spending has been declining since 1987 at the rate of 3.6 per cent a year and has resulted in a cumulative 'peace dividend' of US $ 935 during 1987-94.

In the words of Gustave Speth, Administrator of UNDP :

> It is time to respond to the new compulsions of human security, time to reiterate very clearly that, without the promotion of people-centered development, none of our key objectives can be met, neither peace, nor human rights, nor environmental protection, nor reduced population growth, nor social integration.

Human Security is relevant to people everywhere, in rich nations and the poor nations, as well. Its reach is global now.

As the report comments :

> "Famines, ethnic conflicts, social disintegration, terrorism, pollution and drug trafficking are no longer isolated events, confined within national borders. Their consequences travel all over the globe and concerns for human security are more globalized today than even global trade."

Emphasizing the importance of development and peace, the Secretary General of the U.N. observed :

> "Development is in crisis, in danger of fading from the forefront of the world's agenda and being dramatically undercut by a post-cold war avalanche of new problems and inundating both rich and poor countries".

Five dimensions of development—peace, economy, environment, social justice and democracy—are an integral part of the whole.

- without peace human energies cannot be productively employed.
- without economic growth, there can be no sustained, broad based improvement in material well-being.
- without protection of the environment, the basis of human survival will be eroded.

- without social justice, mounting inequalities will threaten social cohesion.
- without political participation in freedom, development will remain fragile and perpetually at risk.

Development is not only a fundamental human right; it is also the most secure basic peace.

North-South Disparity

Unfortunately, the cause of peace and security as well as development in the long-term interest of mankind are being lost. The collapse of East-West divide has highlighted the North-South disparity, between the developed and underdeveloped, perpetuating the income transfer from the poor to the rich. Economic disparity is greater than ever. The richest 20 per cent of the world (mainly the industrialised countries) receive more than 150 times of the income of the poorest 20 per cent of the world. About 1.3 billion are submerged in absolute poverty; 17 million die from diseases and 800 million do not have enough food. Some 35 million lead the uncertain life of refugees. 850 million subsist in areas of desertification; two-thirds of women are illiterate and 34,000 children die of malnutrition everyday.

Alongwith the South, the North also has its pockets of poverty and deprivation. Over 100 million are beneath poverty line and some 30 million are unemployed. Even Canada, rated highest in Human Development Index, has one million children living in poverty, while two million depend on welfare assistance, 104 miliion rely on food bank and over a quarter million are homeless.

Multidimensional Crisis

The world is suffering from multidimensional crisis. Hunger and unemployment, poverty and illiteracy, paucity of resources and pollution of environment, deforestation and desertification, swelling number of migrants and refugees, ethnic and subnational violence and terrorism, drug trafficking, AIDS, etc.,—all these together constitute a grave danger to the peace and security of the world.

New policies of globalization, reliance on market, retreat of the state from its welfare commitment and resort to privatization do not necessarily work to the benefit of the poor and deprived people of the world, more so in the developing world. Pressures of global integration have led to curtailment of social welfare. Conditions imposed by the World Bank and the IMF compel structural adjustment that work to the detriment of the needy, keeping the policies and goals of private capital at a second fiddle. In short, the development paradigm that depends mainly on economic growth seems to ignore the demands of equity.

In specific terms the global crisis can be spelt out in the following terms:

(a) The state and civil society relations have not worked out in satisfactory terms, for many social needs of people have remained unmet, resulting in denial of human rights, economic security and social welfare.

(b) New agenda under the external pressure of globalization has distorted development process making the state lose its credibility and·capacity to serve its own people, adequately.

(c) Prospects of peace are dim, in spite of reduction in arms, the military predominance remains the top priority for big powers. Developing world is full of internal conflicts and ethnic feuds.

(d) Crisis of resources remains unresolved, exacerbated by a chronic and unequal distribution of wealth. Inequalities within and across nations have not only persisted but are on the increase.

(e) People's aspirations for a new equitable international order have remained unfulfilled.

The inescapable conclusion of all this is that neither the state nor the market can meet the emergent needs of people. With growing literacy and sociopolitical awareness, demands for equality have sharpened. Development paradigm so far tried has ignored the claims of social justice.

The world today presents a paradoxical contrast. There is poverty amidst plenty, overproduction vs undernourishment, affluence and wasteful life in contrast to bare survival, overdevelopment vs. underdevelopment, economic growth vs ecological crisis, consumerism for a few as against denial of basic needs for many, explosion of knowledge as against vast masses of illiterates, globalization vs intense parochialism and ethnicity, science and technology, instead of being utilised in the service of humankind, are used as instruments of domination, exploitation and destruction.

The need of the hour is to adopt a human angle, where man is the centre of our concern, and where development is of the people, for the people and by the people and where a holistic attitude that covers all humans and the whole humanity is kept in view.

Gandhi's Vision Acquires Meaning

It is in the context of this emergent state of the world that Gandhi's vision acquires meaning, significance, urgency and importance. Rooted in fundamentals of ethics and spirituality, Gandhi's transcendental vision embraced the entire human life in all its ramifications.

The present day human problems are essentially global and call for new social and community ethics, comprehensive and all-embracing in its scope and ambit. Gandhi's ethico-spiritual world view provides the direction that the world will have to adopt for its future guidance and development.

While fighting against human oppression, Gandhi believed in the essential unity of mankind. Colonialism was an anathema to him, chiefly because it was a violation of moral order that was essential for human life and society. Colonialism was a denial of human freedom and stunted the growth and development of society. Gandhi may not have talked about the cent and the periphery, but there is no doubt that he had an intuitive perception of the unnatural relationship between the oppressed and the oppressor. He saw violence in all forms of exploitation and struggle to replace it by a non-violent society.

In general, colonialism involved four processes:

(i) Exploitation

(ii) Penetration

(iii) Fragmentation and

(iv) Marginalization.

Exploitation shapes the international division of labour and perpetuates a vertical relation between the centre and the periphery (metropolis and the countryside, the North and the South). In penetration, the centre through local elites, establishes bridgeheads compromising with the autonomy of the periphery. Fragmentation forges links with the centre and divides the people at the periphery. The process of marginalization reduces the people at the periphery to a secondary position without any say in the determination of its policies. All the processes stand for verticality and have to be replaced by a horizontal relationship. For achieving it, exploitation must be replaced by equality and penetration by participation. Needless to say, Gandhi stood for all these four values indicating the direction and the goal of a non-violent and peaceful world.

Apart from ridding the world of these numerous evils, the world needs an inclusive vision that makes life meaningful and peaceful in all the fields of human endeavour–viz, social, economic political, and cultural. We need a philosophy which is value-based, humane, just, participatory and the one that is feasible and practical. Gandhi's vision covers individual and social transformation, replaces violence by non-violence and stands for harmony between man and nature. His thought traverses the span between micro and the macro, the individual and the world community, man and woman, across religions, linguistic and racial barriers, the spiritual and the material, health and hygiene, politics and ethics, ecology and economics, rights and duties and defence and development. His wide ranging philosophy hardly left anything untouched. He saw life as a whole and saw it steadily.

In spite of arms control agreements and reduction of arms, there remain 30,000 nuclear warheads with an overkill capacity. Apart from the hegemony of nuclear powers the world is facing the danger of nuclear terrorism.

In contrast with the conflict-stricken world, Gandhi stands for non-violence, love and fearless human spirit. For Gandhi, dominance and oppression, imperialistic or otherwise, connote exploitation and an eventual violence. Gandhi was the first person to have successfully practised non-violence on a large canvass in the sociopolitical life of man. For him non-violence stood for an alternative vision of the life that promised peace and security for all.

The word, non-violence stands for the dignity and autonomy of the individual. Respect for human rights, irrespective of sex, colour or creed, is an inherent part of it. Nonviolence means a principled life, which in the ultimate analysis, carries the message of self-sacrifice. In a nonviolent world relationship between man and man and between man and nature would be peaceful, accommodative and harmonious.

If civilization means restraint, then Gandhi's man and his society would observe restraint in every walk of life. Self governing individuals would lead to an ideal self-government. Nonviolence avoids verticality of relations and stands for horizontal and equal relationship of 'Oceanic circles'. A nonviolent society is a classless society.

Gandhi also thought of non-violent defence through various peaceful but effective techniques. His Shanti Sena was an answer to militarism and violent wars.

One of his outstanding achievements was in the realm of conflictology. He launched his satyagraha against injustice and carried it to successful ends in a perfectly peaceful manner. As against the zero-sum game of war, satyagraha followed the sum-sum game which produced gains for the parties concerned. In fact, it was an enriching experience that involved learning on both sides and leading to supremely satisfying results with benefits for both the parties. Satyagraha is an innovative technique of conflict resolution with unlimited potentialities for building a peaceful society.

Ecological Humanism

Gandhi saw clearly that all the issues facing mankind were interrelated and mutually interdependent. For him the world was one single framework. R.R. Diwakar aptly termed his thought as one of "ecological humanism". Gandhi's thrust in essence was civilizational. As early as in 1908, writing his famous tract *Hind Swaraj* he had criticised western civilization as burdensome, exploitative and aggressive in nature. He had anticipated the present day environmental crisis and advocated through his constructive programme the main tenets of sustainable development. As he rightly maintained, "There was enough for everybody's needs but not for everybody's greed. The western highly industrialised civilization was too wasteful to be followed by the whole world."

Gandhi's clear distinction between wants and needs went to the root of the environmental crisis and hinted at the carrying capacity of the earth. He viewed that there was only one earth and its resources were limited and not to be wantonly squandered away. Limitation of wants, satisfying the basic needs of all, acceptance of voluntary poverty, emphasis on quality rather than quantity, 'to be' rather than 'to have', strict adherence to values, close relationship between means and ends, respect for human rights, removal of racial and sex differentiation and above all, creation of a non-violent, peaceful society in which disputes could be resolved in a non-violent fashion—all these constituted the ideal society of his dreams. It was a utopia but a relevant, feasible utopia that coincided with the new ideas that were slowly finding their relevance in the contemporary world.

Central to Gandhi's philosophy was man. Self-expression, self-discovery and self-transformation were the main theme of his thought. Autonomy of the individual was precious to him and his entire thought was built on that foundation. He had faith in the common man. He was perhaps in agreement with Lincoln who had said, "God seems to love the common man, otherwise he would not have created so many of them". Empowerment of people was the bedrock of all his movements. People's solidarity and their participation in the decision making were the cardinal principles of his thought.

In place of 'top-down' and 'trickle-down', theory of development, Gandhi's concept of constructive programme worked from 'bottom up' and relied on grassroot support and sustenance. As against elite-based, urban-centered programmes of development, Gandhi stood for people-based, rural-centred approach to development. For Gandhi, people were the mainstay; they were the major vehicle of his action and movements. People's power (*lok shakti*) was the most dynamic element of his thought. Today's grassroot movements derive their inspiration from those traditions that Gandhi lived through his life. Mobilization of people in a disciplined way opened out a creative avenue for our future society.

Gandhi wanted to create a new man and a better and saner civilization. The new men had to live a life under his own strict vigilance, a life that was dedicated to the observance of eleven vows, namely, Satya, Ahimsa, Brahmacharaya, Astheya, Aparigraha, Aswad, Adhaye, Asprushyat, Nivaran, Sharair-Shran Swadeshi and Sarvadharma Samabhav. A lifestyle based upon such high quality virtues was bound to generate waves of change and transformation through its demonstrated example and pave the way for a society of peace and harmony. For Gandhi, Swarajya meant control over one's own self to start with and only thereafter the self-government. In the same fashion individual transformation preceded social transformation. He stood for permanent and total revolution, permanent because it was to continue for ever. It was not once for all transformation. It was a dynamic, ever-moving and ever-evolving system. It was also total since it involved the whole man and the entire human race.

In our age of specialisation, we divide the man into spheres of Homo Economics, Homo Politics, etc. Man's life is compartmentalized and so also his pursuits. Economics is separated from Ecology and Politics from Ethics. Such reductionist approach may be useful for academic analysis but would lead to a disjunctive attitude that has led to an ecological crisis and unscrupulous pursuit of power, detrimental to values and moral sensibility. Gandhi takes a holistic, unified view of life where there is no place for dualism and dichotomous view of life. The distinction and division between the internal and the external, between means and ends, politics and ethics, economics and ecology (both rooted in the term "eco") vanish. Gandhi stands for transparency as the very basis of a democratic and open society. This has to be extended to become the world society. If the present world has turned into a 'global village' then it should be livable, accessible and amenable to the common man. Needless to say, such a development would eventually lead to peace and harmony in the world.

Environmental Disaster

The issue of environmental disaster is perhaps the single most critical problem before the world. The more one thinks about it, the more one feels that it cannot be solved except through an approach that is essentially Gandhian.

In the first place, while it envelops the world, it has to be handled at local level.

Secondly no state is capable of doing so. A global issue has to have global remedies. In short, it needs cooperation of all and that too at several local levels. A constructive and cooperative effort by people emerges as a clear necessity. Local problems are to be locally solved with local initiative of local people. Empowerment of people is the natural outcome. The Chipko movement is an excellent instance highlighting the nature of environmental issues.

Thirdly, environment is not amendable through pursuit of military means. It calls for a peaceful approach and understanding. In fact militarization on vast scale throws a heavy burden on natures' resources. Since weapons are used for destruction, natural resources are wasted in an unproductive way, leading to paucity and pollution of resources. Environment is better protected under conditions of peace.

Fourthly, Gandhi's idea of trusteeship easily and logically can be extended to environment. Environment is a sacred trust which, when properly preserved, can be passed on to the succeeding generations, the present generation being in temporary charge of it.

Fifthly, environment and its proper usage is closely linked with the concept of sustainable development. Sustainability is closely related to equity. Here it is not the numbers which are critical but rather who consumes what and how much. This in turn is, dependent on relations of power—on who decides what is to be done with an area's natural resources. In essence, the issue is political, since politics has been defined as a realm of studies in which decisions are made about who gets what, when and how. Nature's resources are a common heritage of mankind and Gandhi looked to nature with respect and reverence and would make the most economical use of them. He was equally averse to inequity and injustice. The modern concept of sustainable development fits in with the major premises of Gandhian thought.

Closely associated with sustainability is the evil of consumerism, spreading like a wild fire all over the world. Apart from being a burden on earth's resources, the practice is self-defeating and in the long run, unsustainable. Amlan Dutt has rightly observed:

> If the way of life which is now so common in the industrially developed countries is to be made available all over the world, the number of cars in the poorer countries, for instance, will have to be increased, say ten times, with consequences which may be imagined. If, on the other hand, that way of life remains the preserve of one thirds, the world community will suffer a psychological pollution which may be no less killing with demonstration effects of conspicuous consumption carried by electronic media to every nook and corner of the world. The prevailing consumerism culture has intensified psychological distress all around. This is a disease which central planning, spawning a consumerist bureaucracy, has been unable to prevent and the market economy has only aggravated. In fact, it appears to be inseparable from modern industrialism in the form in which it is conquering the world.

Crossroads of History

The world has reached the crossroads of history when the very survival and future of civilization depends upon the ecological balance and the preservation of environment. Man is part of nature and he is to live in harmony with nature. Indeed man's security has to be redefined in terms of the state of the biosphere. With the dwindling resources, the wars of the future are likely to be fought for the resources of the earth. The Gulf War of 1991 is a case in point.

Both peace and security would be safeguarded if Gandhi's prescription is followed. In our age of transition and transformation,

Gandhi's vision inspires and guides us like a beacon of light. In the memorable words of General Omar Bradley:

> Ours is a world of nuclear giants and ethical infants. We know more about war than we know about peace and more about killing than we know about living. We have grasped the mystery of the atom and rejected the Sermon on the Mount.

The world is infested with over-militarization, weapons culture, violence, terrorism, widespread environmental crisis, repression of human rights and denial of basic needs to the majority of people. At stake is the very survival of mankind. Our peace and security can be ensured by adopting a value-based approach rooted in ethics and faith in the unity of mankind. Gandhi's thought and vision emerge as imperative for mankind.

More than 1600 scientists, including 102 Nobel laureates, underscored this point by collectively signing a 'warning to Humanity' in late 1992. It states, "No more than one or a few decades remain before the chance to avert the threats we now confront will be lost and the prospects for humanity immeasurably diminished. A new ethic is required and a new attitude towards discharging our responsibility for caring for ourselves and for the earth. This must motivate a great movement, convincing reluctant leaders, reluctant governments and reluctant people themselves to effect the needed change"

ANNEXURE 1

A COMPARATIVE ANALYSIS OF VIOLENCE VIS A VIS NON-VIOLENCE

Violence/War	*Non-Violence/Peace*
Hard politics-Militarism,	Soft politics-Health,
Real politick	Education-Human Rights
Centralisation of Polity/	Decentralisation of Polity/
Economy	Economy
Urbanization/Megacities	Small towns/Villages
Mass Production	Production by masses
Competition	Cooperation
High Speed	Slow movement
Demands on Nature	Harmony with Nature
Short-term gains	Long-term interests
Zero- sum gains	Sum-sum gains
Atomistic/Reductionism	Holistic/Overall
Discrete/Disjointed/	Interrelated
Nationalist Warfare	Global Welfare
Security of one/National	Security of all/Global
Artificial fertilizers	Organic manure
Consumerism/Lifestyle	Simplicity/Lifestyle
Throw away society	Serving/Conservation
Capital intensive	Labour intensive
Curative (Health)	Preventive (Health)
Elitist/Pro-rich	Peopled oriented/Pro-poor
Want based	Need based
Nuclear power/Arms	Non-nuclear power
Capital intensive energy	Bio-gas
Non-renewable source	Renewable source

ANNEXURE 2

DEVELOPMENT PARADIGM

	Traditional	*Gandhian*
1.	Elitist	People oriented
2.	Urban based	Rural based
3.	Wants	Needs
4.	Nation-unit	People centered
5.	Affluence	Simplicity
6.	Dependence	Self reliance/
7.	Injustice, deprivation	Inequality-Sarvodaya
8.	To Have/Possession	To be/Self-improvement
9.	Capital Intensive Technology	Labour Intensive Technology with Human face
10.	Centralising	Decentralised/Localism
11.	West-oriented	Endogenous
12.	Exploitative of Nature	Ecological Balance
13.	Quantitative with less	Qualitative/How to do better
14.	Top-down	Bottom-down
15.	Macro-planning	Micro-planning
16.	State-based movements	People-based/Grassroot

References

1. Human Development Report, 1994, Summary. (*U. N. Newsletter,* 4 June).
2. *Ibid.* p. 3
3. *Ibid.* p. 3
4. *Ibid.* p. 1
5. Amlan Dutt, "The Market Economy and Contemporary Crisis", *Beyond Socialism*, p. 20.
6. Sandra Postal, "Carrying Capacity : Earth's Bottom Line Challenge", March-April, p. 12.
   Adopted from *State of the World,* 1994.

Part II

8

Relevance of Gandhian Economics

S. Uma Devi

Recent developments in economics have increasingly brought out the relevance of the Gandhian approach. Among these we may enlist the following:

(a) The realisation of the need to search the ethical foundations of economics.

(b) The emergence of feminist economics and the feminist concept of labour.

(c) The growing concern for the preservation of environment.

(d) The need for decentralization.

(e) The international economic scenario in the context of the establishment of WTO.

The Gandhian philosophy is one package and an integrated whole and his economic philosophy cannot be separated from his total philosophy. Gandhi was much influenced by Karl Marx, John Ruskin and Leo Tolstoy and above all by the Indian philosophy, particularly as epitomized in the *Bhagavat Gita*. Action of means were based on the fivefold path of *Yama* or self control from the *Patanjali Yogasutra* and given in the *Gita* too, viz., Ahimsa (non-violence), Satya (truth), *astheya* (nonstealing), *brahmacharya* (austerity), and *aparigraha* (non-acquisitiveness). In Gandhian economics these principles were concretized in his concept of Swaraj, Sarvodaya, Swadeshi, trusteeship, and decentralization.

Ethics and Economics

Gandhi found that modern Economics ushered in by the industrial revolution was based on exactly the opposite of the five principles mentioned above. It was a violent order, based on stealing acquisitiveness and self-indulgence forsaking the truth.

Recent attempts by economists like Amartya Sen and Rawls to mention a few to incorporate ethics into economics by rejecting utilitarianism and their concept of well-being does not go as far as Gandhian economics in this direction.

The utilitarian concept of well-being, based on hedonism in terms of the amount of goods one is able to command, together with the principle of the greatest good of the greatest number, but it has been found to be a very limited way of looking at welfare of human beings. Sen and others therefore question the utilitarian ethic based on consequentialism, which judges an act or a policy on the basis of its consequences. They point out that man's well-being does not depend merely upon the amount of goods or commodities, he possesses since many a times people are prepared to give up their well-being to achieve a certain goal. In such cases their welfare may not increase even if they get more goods but do not achieved their goal. Even the pursuit of a goal in itself irrespective of achievement may be satisfying. This is called the agency aspect.

Thus, Sen and Rawls base their concept of welfare on value judgements based on rights and freedom of human beings. However, whether it is utilitarianism or the right based theories of moral obligations, both are worked out in the framework of contractarianism. They view society as a contract between individuals in the tradition of Hobbes-Locke and Rousseau.

The post-modernists on the other hand, go further and are sceptical of the view of society as a contract between individuals, since they are sceptical of the rationality of the age of enlightenment. Michel Focault, a post-modernist thinker considers ethics as ascetics. (The latter term has its roots in Greek word aske'sis meaning self-control). Ethics is also seen by him as 'the relation of the self to the self.' This comes close to the Greek Hellenistic way of viewing philosophy as a way of life. Thus ethics has to do with a style of life in contrast with our present day aim of raising the 'standard of living'.

Posting the Gandhian approach to ethics and economics in the light of the developments in economics and post-modernism, one finds Gandhi way ahead.

In Gandhi's own words:

> A votary of Ahimsa cannot subscribe to the utilitarian formula (of the greatest good of the greatest number.) He will strive for the greatest good of all and die in the attempt to realise the idea... The greatest good of all inevitably includes the good of the greatest number and therefore he and the utilitarian will converge in many points in their career, but there does come a time when they must part company and even work in opposite directions. The utilitarian to be logical will never sacrifice himself. The absolutist will even sacrifice himself. (*Young India*, 25.11.1926).

How was this non-violent economic order to be brought into existence? Gandhi's solution lay in the gospel of bread-labour and 'charkha'. He was insistent that man must earn his bread by labouring with his own hands. Which was first stressed by a Russian writer named T. M. Bondaref and later popularised by Tolstoy. According to Gandhi:

> Everyone, who idles away a single minute becomes to that extent a burden upon his neighbours and to do so is to commit a breach of the very first lesson of Ahimsa.

Further he says:

> There is a Worldwide conflict between capital and labour and the poor envy the rich. If all worked for their bread, distinctions of rank would be obliterated; the rich would still be there, but they would deem themselves only trustees of their property and would use it mainly in the public interest... Bread-labour is a veritable blessing to one who would observe nonviolence, worship truth and make the observance of *brahmacharya* a natural act. This labour can truly be related to agriculture alone. But at present at any rate, everybody is not in a position to take to it. A person can therefore spin or weave or take up carpentry or smithery, instead of tilling the soil, always regarding agriculture, however, to be the ideal.

Gandhi knew that the land-man ratio is adverse in India and therefore everyone in India will not be able to achieve the standard of comforts which an average American can enjoy. Moreover, he had no faith in industrialism, mass-production or machinery. As we have seen above, physical labour was very important in Gandhi's thinking.

In his own words:

> I would categorically state my conviction that the mania for mass-

production is responsible for the world crisis. Granting for the moment that machinery may supply all the needs of humanity, we cannot ignore the fact that it would concentrate production in particular areas only, so that you would have to go about in a roundabout way to regulate distribution; whereas, if there is production and distribution both, in the respective areas where things are required, it is automatically regulated, and there is less chance for fraud, none for speculation. (*Young India*, 25.7.1929).

........When production and consumption both become localised, the temptation to speed up production, indefinitely at any price, disappears. All the endless difficulties and problems that our present day economic system presents, too, would then come to an end.

Gandhi feared, justifiably because industrialisation on a mass scale was supposed to necessarily lead to passive or active exploitation of the villagers as the problems of competition and marketing came in.

Categorically, he said:

I do not believe that industrialization is necessary in any case for any country. It is much less so for India. Indeed I believe that Independent India can only discharge her duty towards a groaning world by adopting a simple but ennobled life by developing her thousands of cottages and living at peace with the world. High thinking is inconsistent with complicated material life based on high speed imposed on us by Mammon worship. All the graces of life are possible only if we learn the art of living nobly.

It is for this reason also that Gandhi advocated limitation of wants. Commonly people think Gandhi advocated Ahimsa for the weak and limitation of wants by the poor. First the strong and rich were supposed to practice Ahimsa and limitation of wants. Ethics was thus an art of living nobly. Here Gandhi had drawn much from Ruskin and Tolstoy. The latter in his essay 'what is art'? Elaborates this in terms of a sense of beauty in living.

Feminists' Economics and Gandhian Economics

Economics by defining labour as 'painful exertion' has created the need for payment for labour, gradually. When use value was replaced by exchange value, when production for distant market became the order of the day, paid work came to be attached to a higher value. To add to all this, national income of a country only took account of those goods which were sold in the market. Economic activity also came to be defined as activity for which one is paid. In the process, women who were traditionally engaged in household production for domestic use for which they were not paid came to be marginalists.

The Women's liberation movement has now shown that market and patriarchal forms of domination together exploit women. Slowly the debate whether women should be paid for domestic work weared towards an understanding of the fact that, working is not just the creation of economic wealth. It is also a means of self-creation. It came to be asked; Whether the work done produces the kind of men or women one wishes humanity to be made of ? and; Can people derive a sense of personal identity and social dignity from their work?

Considerations of this kind have led to the evolution of a feminist concept of labour. For example, an analysis of the nature of woman's unpaid work has shown that it is not purely a painful exertion and that if it is a burden, it is an enjoyment too. The same is true with the peasant production which has not totally become commodity production. Periods of harvest are also periods of intense activity, yet these are also a joyful experience. Similar is the case with the artisans's work. Which has not yet become fully commercialized. So also for the tribals, their work is not separated from the production of life.

Those who substitute to a feminist concept of labour consider that labour should be oriented towards the production of life as the goal of work, and not the production of things and of wealth.

Feminist concept of labour also has a different concept of time, in which, time spent on burdensome labour and that spent on leisure are not to be separated but rather the times of work, of rest and enjoyment are to be alternating and interspersed. But there is also a consciousness among this group of thinkers that these concept cannot be implemented in the existing sexual division of labour.

Feminist concept of labour also stresses:

> The maintenance of work as a direct and sensuous interaction with nature, with organic matter and living organism. Here even Marxists' preoccupation with machines and technology, it is pointed, makes them oblivious of the impact on men of their work with computers etc. which have been found to be accompanied

with increasing sexual violence by men.

Such a feminist concept of labour leads to the conception of an alternative economy which is not merely based on competition and greed, where the distance between production and consumption, is reduced and where women's labour instead of being reproduction is turned into production of life including not only production of human beings but also production of subsistence goods in contrast to production of wage goods, production for profit or accumulation. Further, work is to be purposeful and useful.

I have detailed out the feminist concept of labour to show that how similar it is to the Gandhian conception. Thus, in the light of Gandhian economics it becomes clear that emancipation of women or of the poor depends on the type of production we vote for. Industrialism and mass-production also leads to enslavement of women.

This leads us to the question of environmental protection.

Gandhian Economics and Environmental Protection

The present day concern with ecology and the protection of environment is one strong area where Gandhi's perception has been proved to be right. However, sometimes the question of environment and the method of production and mode of living are separated. Gandhi never made this mistake. Inherent in this violent method of mass-production is the destruction of nature. Today, the problems of disposal of urban waste, air and water pollution, denudation of forests, the depletion of non-renewable resources and ecological imbalance, etc., have become catch phrases. But the methods to get rid of these problems are more complicated, unlike the simple remedies suggested by Gandhi.

A new dimension has been added to these discussions by the eco-feminist movement which shows that women and nature together are the victims of industrialization and of the growth of science and technology. However, one must not confuse the ecological and environmental concerns of Gandhi with the recent plea for sustainable development.

Gandhi's solution was simple viz., decentralised household production. His constructive programme detailing out the various village and cotton industries is significant in this context.

Decentralization:

The present Panchayati Raj idea is very much removed from the Gandhian concept of decentralization. Gandhi did not believe in a centralized state. The Panchayati Raj of Gandhi is to be totally based on local finance and should lead to the autonomy of each village. The idea of local-self-government as a political and administrative arrangement was to be combined with a decentralized form of production based on village industries. Today, the sugar lobby in our country is so strong that the mill sugar is finding ways and means of pushing out a village industry like *gur* (jaggery) production. Gandhi had shown the merit of jaggery from the health point of view over sugar. Similar is the case with cotton textiles where the mill sector—cotton or synthetic textiles—is driving out Khadi and handloom. That is why Gandhi made *charkha* his symbol of decentralized household production.

It is claimed in certain quarters that the new information technology with the introduction of electronic mail and PCs in each household factory system is giving way to a decentralised production. In this context it must be mentioned that this is not the Gandhian conception of decentralization because the control is vested elsewhere and not in the person using the technology to produce. In fact, with the new developments of flexible specialization and flexible labour and the need for people to be self-employed, as hunting for markets or jobs constantly throws them at the mercy of the market more and more.

The International Scenario, GATT and Gandhian Economics

In the context of the discussions on the impact of the New Economic policy and the WTO on Indian economy, one witnesses a renewed interest in Gandhi's concept of Swaraj and Swadeshi.

The less developed countries (LDCs) are forced to follow the structural adjustment policies as a result of their indebtedness to IMF and therefore are required to liberalize and open up their economies in a big way to foreign capital. However, the developed countries are not reciprocating by opening up their economies. Instead, they are using tariff and non-tariff barriers to discriminate against the goods exported to them by the LDCs.

The opening up of the economies by the LDCs are likely to drain away their resources to the developed in a bigger way than what happened during the colonial times. Thus, if the LDCs are to maintain their political and economic freedom they cannot follow the path of economic development of the West.

If Gandhi's concepts of Swadeshi and Swaraj were meaningful then, they are more relevant now in the present international economic situation. The only way India and the other LDCs can get out of the debt trap and the unemployment and starvation is by promoting and reviving the village crafts and industries.

Khadi was considered by Gandhi as the sun of the village solar system. In his own words:

> We may profess so graciously the textile, sugar and rice mills, respectively kill the village spinning wheel, the handloom and their product, Khadi, the village cane-crusher and its product, the vitamin-laden and nourishing *gud* (gur or molasses) and handpounder and its product, unpolished rice, whose pericarp which holds the vitamins, is left in fact by these pounders. Our clear duty is, therefore, to investigate the possibility of keeping in existence, the village wheel, the village crusher and the village pounder and by advertising their products, discovering their qualities ascertaining the condition of workers and the number displaced by the power-driven machinery and discovering the methods of improving them whilst retaining their village character to enable them to stand the competition of the mills.

I have quoted Gandhi at length to show that he was not only advocating the revival of village industries to fight the foreign competition but also because he considered them to be superior to the mill-made products in the total sense.

Another fact, which raises alarm for the LDCs is the growing concentration of food in the developed countries. The LDCs are continuing to produce more cash crops and are dependent for food on the developed countries. This started with colonialism and has continued. Gandhi's call for going back to the villages was also to ensure self-sufficiency of the villages, to ensure food and clothing—the basic needs of man.

Thus, be it the green manure of compost in place of chemical fertilizers, *gur* in place of sugar, hand pound rice in place of mill rice, the Khadi in place of mill cloth, neem stick in place of tooth brush;

Gandhi found them superior to the modern alternatives. Poorna Swaraj and Swadeshi was seen to be a superior moral order, superior to the modern economic alternatives based on the utilitarian ethics.

References

1. Amartya Sen, 1987, *On Ethics and Economics,* Oxford University Press.
2. John Rawls, 1971, *A Theory of Justice,* Cambridge M A Harvard University Press.
3. Arnold I, 1994, 'Ethics as Ascetics : Foucault, the History of Davidson, Ethics, and Ancient Thought', in Goldstein Jan, (ed), *Foucault and the Writing of History.* Oxford Blackwell.
4. M.K.Gandhi, 1947, *India of My Dreams* Ahmedabad ; p. 63, Navjivan Pub. House.
5. *Ibid.,* p. 55.
6. *Ibid.,* p. 56.
7. *Ibid.,* p. 29.
8. *Ibid.*, p. 30-31.
9. Sarvodaya in Gandhi's words :

To observe morality is to attain mastery over our mind and our passions. We notice that the mind is a restless bird; the more it gets the more it wants, and still remains unsatisfied. The more we indulge our passions the more unbridled they become. Our ancestors, therefore, set a limit to our indulgences. They saw that happiness was largely a mental condition. A man is not necessarily happy because he is rich or unhappy because he is poor. The rich are often seen to be unhappy and the poor to be happy. Millions will always remain poor. Observing all this, our ancestors dissuaded us from luxuries and pleasures. We have managed with the same kind of plough as existed thousands of years ago. We have retained the same kind of cottages that we had in former times and our indigenous education remains the same as before. We have had no system of life corroding competition. Each followed his own occupation or trade and charged a regulation wage. It was not that we did not know how to invent machinery, but our forefathers knew that, if we set our hearts after such things we would become slaves and lose our moral fibre. They, therefore, after due deliberation, decided that we should only do what we could do with our hands and feet. They saw that our real happiness and health consisted in proper use of our hands and feet".

10. Vandana Shiva, 1990, *Staying Alive, Women, Ecology and Development*, Zed Books.
11. Maria Mies, 1986, *Patriarchy and Accumulation on World Scale*, Zed Books.
12. *Ibid.*
13. Vandana Shiva, 1994, *Eco-Feminism,* Kali.
14. Gali Omoedt, 1994, 'Dependency Theory, Peasants and Third World Crisis', *Economic and Political Weekly*, Jan. 22.
15. M.K. Gandhi, 1967, *The Gospel of Swadeshi* (ed.) Anand T. Hingorani, Bharatiya Vidya Bhavan.

9

Gandhian Socialism
An Ethical Economic Alternative

K. Sreenivasan

Gandhi is modern India's outstanding national leader, who led the country to freedom. Gratefully, we cherish him as the Father of the Nation. The rest of humanity is also beholden to him, because it is he who has highlighted and also helped to evolve an ethically oriented philosophy of life which is the alternative to capitalism and also its camouflaged cousin, Marxian Socialism. Indeed, at this turn of the century, Gandhian socioeconomic thought is gaining more and more approval. It is likely to be the key to the ideology of the future which may help to transform human society, thereby ensuring the survival of the species.

Gandhi's is a complex personality. Some deify him as a spiritual leader, while others are inclined to constrict him as a clever politician. Yet, some others lament that he was blindly anti-West and anti-progress. All these are sectarian assessments. The basic fact is that diverse streams have helped to form his perspective on life. In Gandhi's case there was a continual experiment with truth. As it progressed, more clarity arose. It was an evolutionary process. Ideas underwent metamorphosis. They gathered relatedness. The residue was a galaxy of complementary notions. If they are properly telescoped, they provide the discerning intellectuals with a clear perspective of Gandhian social thought, ethically motivated. Gandhi is not an economist like Adam Smith or Ricardo. Nor was he a prophet of class war and dictatorship of the proletariat as Karl Marx was. He was an uncommon common man who sought to know life as it is lived. This way, he managed to see into the life of things. In fact, Gandhi's views underwent changes as he witnessed and learnt more. There are even instances of *volte-face*. Therefore, he reminded that he should be adjudged by his latest pronouncement. In this sense, he was an empiricist. But, behind it is his firm allegiance to *Satya and Dharma*. Bound by them, he manoeuvres his views. They are found sprinkled in his innumerable random observations in

Harijan and *Young India* and in a succinct form in *Hind Swaraj* (1908). The seminal ideas enunciated in them will help to forge an alternative humanistic philosophy of future.

Is Gandhi's anti-West stance owing to his leadership of the freedom struggle? Not at all. Though he fought British Raj, he admired the people of England for many of their sterling qualities which his own countrymen lacked. Gandhi had imbibed the best in our heritage, which is *Bharatiya*. In our complex but composite culture, there is Ahimsa and Love as preached by Buddha, the Advaita or unity in diversity held aloft by the Upanishadic sages. One who has these values in his blood can hardly stomach the barbarious greed of European imperialism—political, economic and cultural. Gandhi found the Indian National Congress a subservient and slavish forum which begged for favours from our masters. Gandhi urged us to fight for our rights to wrest freedom to shape our destiny in conformity with our ancient heritage. The Mahatma evolved himself slowly though steadily. Gandhi went to England to qualify himself as a lawyer. And there, to begin with, he attempted to become an impeccable English gentleman—in dress, in habits and behaviour and also in perspective. He gave up vegetarianism and even took to dancing lessons. But better sense prevailed, and finally he blossomed into the half-naked fakir, clad only in loin cloth who confronted the British sovereign, on equal terms. This transformation was the offshoot of his self-respect. He chose to uphold the noblest values of his ancient inheritance. Back from England, after his eye-opening travails in South Africa, M.K. Gandhi got sanctified as the Mahatma.

Gandhi's Indianness egged him on to suspect western civilization—the latest as well as youngest among world civilizations—nurtured in the evil syndrome of capitalistic production and distribution. After the industrial revolution, there thrived in Europe a rapid mechanization. It set in motion the capitalistic saga of soulless exploitation, both of human and material resources. Imperialism became the umbrella under which this exploitation flourished as a worldwide phenomenon. Marx and Engels were the most discerning critics of this cancerous growth. However, the scientific socialism they envisaged as a remedy, when implemented by Lenin and his successor, Stalin, turned out to be worse than the disease.

Gandhi in England had his big ears sharp, listening intently to the anticapitalist disillusionment ringing in different spheres. Charles Dickens, for example, through his popular fiction, pictured luridly the engulfing evil. He felt befuddled by the hard times. John Ruskin, the philosopher, sounded his stern warning. In Russia, Leo Tolstoy voiced the spiritual anguish that Mammon worship had unleashed. Thoreau launched civil disobedience in the United States against the encroachment on individual rights. All these had their impact on Gandhi. After groping in the dark, he began seeing light. Thus took shape his epochmaking tract, *Hind Swaraj* (1908). His bitter experiences in racist South Africa led to his forging new weapons—Satyagraha and Ahimsa and collective action—to uphold human dignity. On return to India, Gandhi took over the leadership of the national movement. There ensued a long epoch of struggle and sacrifice which enabled Gandhi to fully grasp the implications of the freedom struggle. This brought about a sea-change in him; he was alerted to the freedom of the species as a whole. And thus evolved slowly as well as haltingly, Gandhian Socialism. Its clarion call is for equality, liberty and fraternity. The end-product is an enriched social and economic stream of thought with a genuine human face.

In Gandhian Socialism, economic change is the key concept and the material aspects are the primary concern. Of course, ethical and spiritual values give momentum to the physical ones and they in turn further mould the former. This is a holistic approach; precept and practice should go arm in arm. Gandhi practised it. In him, there is empiricism and relatedness in an unusual measure. Hence, to compartmentalize his thoughts and concepts is unfair. Yet, certain priorities emerge. That is because of the commitments to the times and to the resultant social prerogatives. That is why opposition to the machine became the vital core of his schedule for change. From it logistically evolved his concepts of decentralization, bread-labour, people's role and village self-rule, trusteeship and social cohesion, and finally Sarvodaya which ushers in a Brave New World where the ideal, 'from each according to his ability and to each according to his need', will be sought to be realized.

Terribly sordid is the scenario the world over at this turn of the century. Mechanization, abetted by consumerism has wrought havoc everywhere. Environmental devastation goes on space. Irrenewable resources are being exhausted with lunatic frenzy. Forest wealth and wildlife are being mercilessly exterminated. Many species have become extinct. *Homosapiens* too are sliding towards the brink. All these are the gifts of advanced technology. Gandhi sensed this danger early. His onslaught on the Satanic inventions, to begin with, was almost fanatical. In *Hind Swaraj*, he condemned machinery as 'a great sin'.

> Books could be written to demonstrate its evils.... It is necessary to realise that machinery is bad. If instead of welcoming it as a boon, we should look upon it as an evil, it would ultimately cease. (Chap. XIX).

This extreme stance he later on sheds:

> I am uncompromisingly against all destructive machinery. But simple tools and instruments and such instrument and machinery to save individual labour and lighten the millions of cottages. I should welcome. (*Young India,* 17-6-1926)

Gandhi insisted that machine had no place as long as there were unemployed persons. He was against high-tech. Production of things which villagers could produce with their simple tools. He was against the large-scale use of machinery which kept millions without work.

> Industrialisation, I am afraid, is going to be a curse for mankind. Exploitation of one nation by another cannot go on for all time. (*Young India,* 12-11-1931)

> I can have no consideration for machinery which is meant to enrich the few at the expense of the many. (*Harijan*, 22-6-1938.)

Gandhi was for conditional acceptance of heavy machinery:

> The heavy machinery for work of public utility, which cannot be undertaken by human labour, has its inevitable place, but all that would be owned by the State and used entirely for the benefit of the people. (*Harijan,* 22-6-1935)

Gandhi insisted on the ethical ordering of economic life. He was against increasing human wants. In fact, he thought, echoing Lord Buddha and conforming to the noblest Indian tradition, that *trishna*, (Desire i.e. greed) is the root cause of *dukh* (human sorrow). He points out:

> I do not believe that multiplication of wants and machinery contrived to supply them, is taking the world a single step nearer

> its goal... I wholeheartedly detest this mad desire to destroy distance and time, to increase animal appetites and go to the end of the earth in search of their satisfaction. If modern civilization stands for all this and I have understood it to do so, I call it Satanic. (*Young India,* 17-3-1927)

> Civilization, asserts Gandhi, "in the real sense of the term consists, not in the multiplication but in the deliberate and voluntary reduction of wants. (*Hind Swaraj*, p. 44-45)

This is the solid base of Gandhi's Socialism—its ethico-economic justification viz limitation of human wants—i.e. a simple way of life. Machine as a tool will be fully subservient to human volition and need. In western civilization, the individual is a hostage of these diabolical factors. The ancient civilization of our land has always upheld simple living and high thinking. The alternative to capitalistic system Gandhi envisages, enshrines more or less, the life-ennobling ingredients of the great River Valley Civilizations of the world, especially that of India.

Inevitably, Gandhi envisages a decentralized economy which anti-mechanization necessitates. In political and social realms also this trend will be dominant. Thus the ideal of the self-sufficient village republic looms large. In his eagerness to emphasize the integrity of the village, Gandhi asserts:

> Under my scheme, nothing will be allowed to be produced by the cities which can equally well be produced by villages. The proper function of cities is to serve as clearing houses for village products. *(Harijan,* 28-1-1939)

It is clear that he anticipated the plague of urbanization which now afflicts the globe and irrevocably destroys the pattern of the clean and tranquil rural life.

Gandhi's humanistic creed extols the need and sanctity of physical effort. To work with hands and feet is a noble idea. It also entails a psychological significance. The balanced person of brawn and brain is envisaged by Gandhi. He said :

> "God created man to eat his bread by the sweat of his brow" (*Harijan,* 16-5-1936.)

> "It is only when a man or woman has done bodily labour for the sake of service that he or she gets any rights to live". (*Young India,* 20-9-1928)

He called it Bread-labour. Such manual labour, if practised by all, brings about in its wake, brotherhood and a sense of equality. Associating only the Sudras with physical labour is the biggest folly of the ancient Indian approach. To Gandhi, work is true worship. Gita extols above all Karma.

Gandhi's economic stance is meant to initiate an alternative to capitalism and its goal is the humanistic well-being of all viz. Sarvodaya. His socialism is distinctly different from liberal democracy and scientific socialism of the West. Gandhi disapproves of private property and the right to possession which is the cornerstone of liberal democracy :

> Possession seems to me a crime. I can only possess certain things when I know that others who also want to possess similar things, are able to do so. But we know that such a thing that can be possessed by all is non-possession, not to have anything whatsoever. (Address at Guild Hall London, Sept. 22, 1931).

Aparigraha (non-possession) and *samabhavana* (equality) are ethical concepts built into the Indian tradition. Gandhi subscribed to the idea of voluntary poverty, reduction of wants and restriction on possession of property to the basic needs of existence.

Gandhi lived up to non-violence and the credo of noble means to noble ends. His difference with the revolutionary socialists was unbridgeable. He shared with the Marxists the desire to end capitalist exploitation, but not through violence and class war. He proclaimed his faith thus : "This, I do say fearlessly and firmly, that every worthy object can be achieved by the use of Satyagraha. It is the highest and infallible means" (*Harijan,* 20-7-1947). Truth and non-violence should inhere in Socialism.

Gandhi did not believe in the annihilation of the affluent. Individual talents being diverse, achievements of wealth and status could vary. To proselytize the rich, he envisaged the trusteeship concept: "And if I would recognize the fundamental equality, as I must, of the capitalist and labour, I must not aim at his destruction, I must strive for his conversion". (*Young India*, 26-3-1931) The rich will be induced to serve the poor and ensure their welfare.

The noted economist, Dr V.K.R.V. Rao, sums up as follows in his Oxford lecture, 'The Gandhian Alternative to Western Socialism' (p. 47, Bhartiya Vidya Bhavan, Mumbai, 1970).

The Gandhian alternative is Sarvodaya, or the welfare of all, a classless society based on destruction of the classes, but not on the destruction of the individuals who constitute the classes, a system of production that does not fail to make use of science and technology for creating an economy of abundance, but does not in the process either kill the individual initiative or freedom for development, not create a psychology of ceaseless striving for more and more of material goods, a system of distribution that will ensure a reasonable minimum income for all while not aiming at a universal equality of an arithmetical kind, will nevertheless ensure that all private property of talent beyond the minimum will be used as a trust for the public good and not for individual aggrandisement, a social order where all will work but there will be no inequality, either in status or in opportunity for any individual, and a political system where change is the result of persuasion, differences are resolved by discussion and conflicts by love and recognition of mutuality of interests.

References

Branson, W.H. (1979) *Macro Economic Theory and Policy* (Universal Book Stall,

Diwan, R.(1985) *'Economics of Love'* in Essays in Gandhian Economics, Romesh Diwan and Mark Lutz (ed), New Delhi. Gandhi Peace Foundation

Duesenberry, J.S. 1978, Income-consumption Relations and their Implications in 'Readings in Macro Economics' M.G. Mueller (ed.) New Delhi Surjeet Publication.

Ganguli, B.W. (1978) *'Indian Economics Thought'* (Tata-McGraw-Hill), New Delhi.

Glahe, F.R. (1985) *'Macro Economics Theory and Policy'* (Harcourt Brace Javonovich).

Huq. A.M. (1985) "The Doctrine of International Trade : A Gandhian Perspective' in *'Essay in Gandhian Economics'.* R. Diwan and M. Lutz (ed.)., Gandhi Peace Foundation, New Delhi.

Nurkse, A.M. (1952) *Problems of Captial Formation in Under Developed Countries* New Delhi. Oxford University Press

Sethi J.D. (1979) *'Gandhi Today',* New Delhi Vikas

10

Gandhian Swadeshi

An Antithesis to Demonstration Effect

S. Muraleedharan

It is pathetic that people have to assemble to rediscover Gandhi. Such a phenomenon has emerged because we have forgotten or neglected Gandhi. Forgetting Gandhi is the consequence of our reluctance to realize and pursue Gandhian Principles.

India formally accepted self-reliance as the basic aim of economic planning. We marched to this end by way of the strategy of import substitution. Still, we could not integrate Gandhian Principles into the generic aspects of economic system. Further, we kept Gandhian ideology aloof from the academic circles, especially from mainstream Economics. As a basic discipline in social science, Economics deals with most of the western origin theories in this country. We even teach certain such principles which were pointed out much earlier by Gandhi. The Duesenberry thesis of consumption function is one such example. An attempt is made in the ensuing sections regarding the comprehensive nature of Gandhian Swadeshi in the context of wide popularity that Duesenberry thesis achieved in these days.

Swadeshi

Swadeshi is one of the core elements in the Socioeconomic organization of Gandhian system. * The central core of Gandhian system consists of six concepts, viz., Truth, Non-violence, Satyagraha, Swadeshi, Equality and Bread-labour. The plain implication of Swadeshi is self reliance. The idea of Swadeshi was evolved from a narrow base and acquired a broad outlook later. Initially it was a part of Swaraj which dealt with Hindu-Muslim unity, removal of untouchability and Swadeshi (Sethi, 1978). Swadeshi, in the narrower sense, connotes boycotting of foreign goods and conserve the interests of handicraft and small-scale industries against the intrusion of imported machine-made goods. The broad implication of Swadeshi is to emphasize on the basic needs of an individual or locality, to

* The central core of Gandhian system consists of six concepts, viz., Truth, Non-violence, Satyagraha, Swadeshi, Equality and Bread- Labour.

care the nearest neighbour rather than the distant, to cooperate and persuade neighbour producer to improve the efficiency of production.

Swadeshi insists on self-reliance both to the individual and society as a whole. In this context, one needs to be conscious of the nature of human wants. The primary attention may be devoted to the fulfilment of basic needs rather than pursuing conspicuous consumption. That is, production is for use initially and later it can be conducted for exchange. This requires the use and service of one's immediate surroundings. Surplus can be exchanged for other village and towns. Thus, Swadeshi conveys the idea of self-reliance and mutual help and disregards enslaving of any form.

Further, consumers in Swadeshi are expected to cooperate with the producer to improve the efficiency of production. If the producer is not on the track of improving efficiency, one can teach him how it can be. Thus consumer and producer are not competing elements in the process of production and consumption but two agents keeping intimate rapport. Diwan (1985) argues in this context that it will reduce the cost of production. He points to five such elements, viz:

(i) Minimum selling cost due to neighbourly relation,

(ii) Skill specialization due to the efficiency criterion,

(iii) Use of local material,

(iv) Service oriented production, and

(v) Intense labour participation if the producer cuts down the cost.

Though, Swadeshi preaches preference to local environment and manufactures, it does not suggest cent per cent closed-door policy. It is not a fetish to show a negative approach to foreign manufacturers due to its alien character. Swadeshi is not in favour of promoting the production of inappropriate goods in one country, as it will be a sheer waste of time and money. In other words, one can attempt to think the international dimension of the concept of Swadeshi. Huq (1982) made an attempt in this direction. It may be remembered that any Gandhian concept is rooted on ethical principles. Naturally this is relevant while extending the concept of Swadeshi in the context of international trade. Gandhi was very much cautious of the prevailing nature of trade between two unequal partners, that is, a dominant industrial economy and a dependent less-developed economy. Gandhi found the element of exploitation which were essentially in two forms (Huq). One is the exploitation of one nation by another nation and another is the exploitation of the rural poor by the urban elite in the dependent country. Huq sees six distinctive features in Gandhian approach to the doctrine of international trade. They are :

(1) It does not consider the principle of comparative advantage as the sole basis of international trade;

(2) Reciprocal demand is replaced by reciprocal need as the determinant of International terms of trade;

(3) International cooperation and understanding of mutual need instead of the free play of market forces;

(4) The notion of service is more important than economic gain;

(5) It is based on the principle of non-violence and non-exploitation; and

(6) It wants to guard against unequal distribution.

In short, Swadeshi advocates to care primarily the immediate surroundings so as to satisfy the basic needs of each individual and village. Later, surplus can be produced and exchanged for other villages and towns. This self-reliant and self-sustaining approach can be extended to the international arena. Whatever may be the coverage and magnitude of the relationship, it should be based on reciprocal need and mutual cooperation. Such relation can eliminate the elements of exploitation, through hegemony at any level—local, national or international.

Corresponding to the evolution of Gandhian Swadeshi, theorising of consumer behaviour, relating to immediate surrounding took place in the western context. It was not a vision like Gandhi had; or the purpose of such theory was not that of Swadeshi. Yet one can see curious similarity in the Gandhian vision and theorizing of actual consumer behaviour in the west. This is very explicit in the Relative Income Hypothesis (RIH) of Duesenberry. Firstly we can discuss briefly the major contents in the RIH.

Relative Income Hypothesis

RIH as formulated by Duesenberry explains the consumer behaviour and their saving habits. It frames the logic that consumption is essentially not related to the absolute level of income but relative position of the consumer in the income distribution. This can be explained in two ways. One explanation is that there is a shadow effect of consumption in the past, on the present consumption. This is very evident in the behaviour of members of erstwhile royal families and landlords in India. Duesenberry argues that consumption depends on the level of present income relative to previous peak income.

The second and important explanation, in this context, is that consumers are not concerned with their absolute level of consumption; but, consumption is relative to the rest of the population. It is well-known that each consumer will try to maximize his utility. It can be argued that the consumer will try to maximize his utility by adjusting his consumption in relation to the weighted average of the consumption of the rest of the population (W). This may be presented schematically as follows:

$$U=f\begin{pmatrix} xo\ldots\ldots\ldots\ldots & xt,\ldots\ldots\ldots\ldots & XT \\ \cdots & \cdots & \cdots \\ wo, & wt, & WT \end{pmatrix}$$

Where 'x' stands for consumption. The relationship shows that consumers will look around them before taking any decision on consumption. To Duesenberry "it means that any individual's desire to increase his expenditure is governed by other items which are demonstrably superior to the ones which he consumes.... The strength of any individual's desire to increase his consumption expenditure is a function of the ratio of his expenditure of others with whom he comes in contact" (Mueller, p. 74). A person's average consumption (C) income (Y) ratio i.e. C/Y depends on his position in the distribution of income in one society. Assume that the average income of an economy is z, and a person's income is below z, then he will have a high C/Y ratio. This is the result of the consumer's behaviour to emulate the lifestyle of the neighbouring rich people. Duesenberry calls this as demonstration effect. If the particular consumer is above average, he will have a lower C/Y ratio because the share of income is devoted to acquire typical group of consumer goods. They do not follow the consumption pattern of the low income groups, but of the higher.

The concept of demonstration effect was developed by looking into the consumption pattern of different income groups in USA. This was later extended to the international context by Ragnar Nurkse (1952) while discussing the problems of capital formation in underdeveloped countries. Nurkse argues that individual consumption functions are interrelated through demonstration effect. The propensity to consume will shift upwards when they get information about the so called superior goods or superior patterns of consumption. This generates new temptations and desires in the mind of consumers of low income groups.

Technical progress paves the way for the emergence of new products which, in turn, modify ways of life. The trouble with the poorer countries is that they get most of these commodities through imports. Imports further raise the propensity to consume. Advertisements add new dimensions to this phenomenon. Global network of information technology facilitate the reach of new ideas to the remotest corner of the world at a faster rate.

The demonstration effect in the international scene is pictured as the luring effect of consumption patterns of the developed world. The international inequality in real income and consumption levels is one of the determinants of this effect. Yet another factor is the extent of people's awareness of them. Another significant factor is education which acts as a stimulant of early new desires rather than improving productivity in the third world.

The ideas of Duesenberry and Nurkse can be schematically presented in Fig. 1.

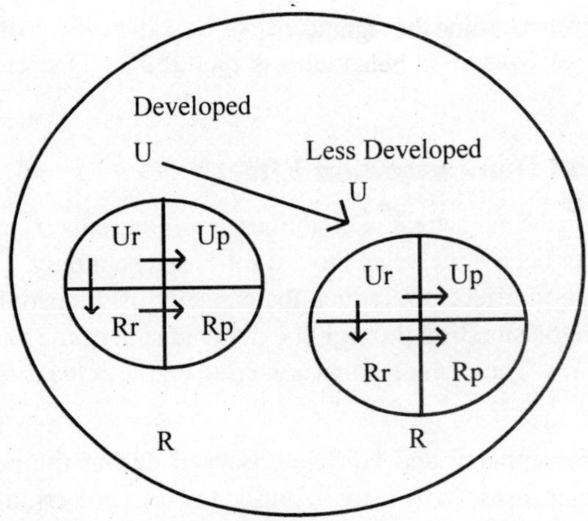

U -Urban R -Rural

Ur-Urban rich Rr-Rural rich

Up-Urban poor, Rp-Rural poor

Fig. 1. Extent of Demonstration Effect-National and International.

There are three circles in Figure 1. The big one represents the world and small ones shown inside the big one represent the developed and less developed worlds. The arrow mark from Ur to Up shows that the consumption pattern of the urban rich influences the consumers belonging to the urban poor. The arrow mark from Ur to Rr display the fact that 'well off' group of the rural follows the behaviour of the rich urban consumers. This, in turn, reflects in the consumption pattern of the rural poor. The irony of the situation is that both urban and rural poor eventually dissave as a result of demonstration effect. Though the relative positions of the rich and poor consumers may change in the developed and less developed worlds, the emulation or imitation habits of the poor consumers are generally visible in both the worlds. This is the fundamental principle of Duesenberry's Relative Income Hypothesis.

The long arrow mark pointed to less developed convey the idea that countries of the less developed worlds try to achieve the standard of living of the advanced world. This may be at the cost of the productivity and balance of payments in the poor world. Thus, the imitation of the less developed world is simply a logical extension of the urban poor-rich relationship or rural-urban connection. This is the fundamental idea of Nurksian version of demonstration effect in the international plane.

Now we can examine the significance of Gandhian vision of Swadeshi in the context of consumer behaviour as pictured by Duesenberry and Nurkse.

Swadeshi and Demonstration Effect

Just like in the mainstream Economics, both Duesenberry and Nurkse depict consumer behaviour related to a want-based economy. They argue that demonstration effect can reduce the capacity of the people to save. They approach the situation through the demand side of the national and global economies. Their conclusions are based on the actual behaviour of the consumers.

What Duesenberry and Nurkse observed during the post-World War II period was foreseen by Gandhi during the interim period of the two world wars. Gandhi advocated Swadeshi to resist the evil effects of international trade emanating from the exchange of two unequal powers. Nurkse also based his argument in the domain of international disparity. Therefore, Swadeshi demands international exchange on the basis of mutual needs, rather than wants linked to money power.

Gandhian Swadeshi contains both demand and supply side of the economy. It advises the consumers to use locally made goods. While demonstration effect oozes out poor consumers' income, Swadeshi assures the flow of resources within a locality and does not encourage rural to emulate urban, poor to imitate rich or a poor country to follow the advanced ones. Thus, it discourages demonstration effect both at the national and global levels. In Swadeshi, consumption is based on needs and production is linked to consumption. Swadeshi primarily demands the interdependence between the consumers and producers. Duesenberry - Nurkse explain only the interdependence among the consumers.

Demonstration effects in the international plane assumes world centre (advanced countries) for consumption pattern and others are tempted to follow. Swadeshi visualizes an integrated and self-sustained village system which can eventually be extended to other villages firstly, to towns next and international level at the end. The interests of both consumers and producers need to be adhered to in the system of Swadeshi. Thus, Swadeshi is an integrated system from below that can assure equality. But Nurksian version exhibit the defacto world which dominates from above. It is only a description unlike Gandhian Swadeshi which is a prescription against exploitation and inequality. The Swadeshi scheme is presented in Fig. 2.

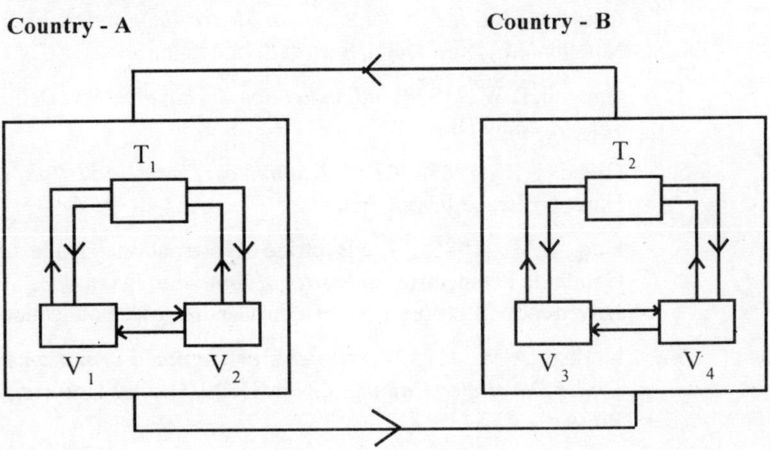

V - Village, T - Town

Fig-2. Gandhian Swadeshi Scheme.

Swadeshi is based on the principle of self-reliance and self-sustainability. Hence the economic system evolves from individual units which have strong mutual relations with the local surroundings. Here, poor man does not look for the lifestyle of the rich or the rural for the urban as in the demonstration effect. Interdependency exists not only among the consumers but also among the producers and between consumers and producers. This is perceptible in each village based on their primary needs. Even then a village cannot become self-sufficient; so it produces surplus and exchanges with other villages based on their mutual needs. Hence there is flow and counter flow between V_1 and V_2 in country A and between V_3 and V_4 in country B. Similar relationship exists between rural and town areas. Same logic is extended to show the connection between two countries.

References

1. Branson, W.H., 1979, *Macro Economic Theory and Policy*, New Delhi, Universal Book Stall.
2. Diwan, R., 1985, 'Economics of Love' in *Essays in Gandhian Economics*, Romesh Diwan and Mark Lutz (ed.), New Delhi, Gandhi Peace Foundation.
3. Duesenberry, J.S., 1978, 'Income-consumption Relations and their Implications' in *Readings in Macro Economics*, M.G. Mueller (ed.), New Delhi, Surjeet Publication.
4. Ganguli, B.W., (1978) *Indian Economic Thought,* New Delhi, Tata-McGraw-Hill.
5. Glahe, F.R., 1985, *Macro Economics Theory and Policy,* Harcourt Brace Javonovich.
6. Huq., A.M., (1985), 'The Doctrine of International Trade : A Gandhian Perspective' in *Essays in Gandhian Economics*, R. Diwan and M.Lutz (ed.), New Delhi, Gandhi Peace Foundation.
7. Nurkse, A.M., (1952), *Problems of Capital Formation in Under Developed Countries*, New Delhi, Oxford University Press.
8. Sethi, J.D., (1979), *Gandhi Today*, New Delhi : Vikas.

11

Ethical Basis of Gandhian Economic Thought

S. Arunkumar

Gandhi was not an economist in the conventional sense of the term, but he was very much concerned with applying economic ideals and principles that became a part of his life. Gandhian economic ideals are scattered throughout his vast and voluminous literature, consisting of occasional journals, popular writings, platform speeches and letters. His economic ideals were a part of his general crusade against poverty, exploitation, socioeconomic order and deteriorating moral standards. He said, "The economic constitution of India and for that matter, that of the world, should be such that no one under it should suffer from want of food and clothing. Everybody should be able to get sufficient work to enable him to make both ends meet. And this ideal can be universally realized only if the means of production of the elementary necessities of life remain in the control of masses. They should be freely available to all, as God's air and water are or ought to be...their monopolization by any country, nation or group of persons would be unjust...the neglect of the simple principle in the cause of the destitution that we witness today not only in this unhappy land but in other parts of the world too''. Such economic norms cannot be found in any text book, whether capitalist or communist. Gandhian economics is based on a paradigm that is fundamentally different from that which forms the basis of prevailing economics. Addressing a college economic society as far back as in 1916, Gandhi asserted :

> I venture to think that scriptures of the world are safer and sounder treatises of laws of economics than many of the modern books.

Unlike the dominating economic system which limits itself only to the material welfare of the individuals and their society, the Gandhian economic thought is concerned with total welfare of the integrated individual, inseparable from its society. He drew no distinction between economics and ethics. According to the Gandhian approach, the pursuit of truth gives rise to certain ethical values like non-violence, fearlessness, non-stealing, non-possession, bread-labour, Swadeshi, trusteeship, etc. Gandhi suggested that the adoption of these values emanating from truth would serve as principles of life to guide human conduct and relationships. These ethical values bearing upon economics, lead to profound changes in certain basic concepts, economic 'ends' and 'means' which form 'the wrap and weft' of economic thought. It is impossible to think of Gandhian economic thought without ethics. Ethics permeates his economic ideas all along the line. The economic laws must be consistent with moral laws. To quote Gandhi:

> I do not believe the spiritual law works on a field of its own. On the contrary it expresses itself only through the ordinary activities of life. It thus effects the economic, the social and the political fields.
>
> Gandhian economics takes self-annihilation to be the basic driving force of human behaviour. In this respect, Gandhian economics stands in sharp contrast with modern economics which upholds the pursuit of self-interest as being the prime psychological drive in man. Self-interest according to modern economics is deemed not only rational but also desirable. Pursuit of self-interest for the sake of pleasure leads to certain economic values like acquisition, competition, protection, assertion of sensual indulgence. But they are not valuable according to Gandhian economics. Hence, in 1921, he wrote,"I must confess that economics that hurts the moral wellbeing of an individual or a nation is immoral and therefore sinful.

Economics that makes bodily welfare its sole objective, ignoring moral and spiritual welfare is fragmentary and therefore disastrous. Economics that violates morality was in no way acceptable to Gandhi. So he repeated his belief in 1924:

> That Economics is untrue which ignores or disregards moral values.
>
> "The extension of the law of nonviolence in the dominion of economics means nothing less than the introduction of moral values".
>
> In 1927, he wrote:
>
> "Economics to be worth anything must be capable of being reduced to terms of religion or spirituality".

Writing ten years later, in 1937, he put more content to his concept of economics, he wrote:

> True economics never militates against the highest ethical standard just as all true ethics to be worth its name must at the same time be also good economics. An economics that inculcates Mammon worship, and enables the strong to amass wealth at the expense of the weak, is a false and dismal science. It spells death. True economics on the other hand promotes the good of all equally, including the weakest and is indispensable for decent life.

This profound concern for the ethical ordering of economic life led him to pronounce a number of criteria in the economic field. Thus, contrary to all accepted economic thinking Gandhi denounced the principle of unlimited character of human wants as the determinant of economic activity and its satisfaction as the index of economic progress. He wrote:

> I do not believe in the multiplication of wants and machinery contrived to supply them in taking the world a single step nearer its goal ...I wholeheartedly detest this and desire to destroy distance and time, to increase animal appetites and go to the ends of the earth in search of their satisfaction. If modern civilization stands for all this and I have understood it so, I call it Satanic.

Gandhi was all in favour of an economic system that gave to all beings the means to satisfy their minimum material requirements. But, he was not prepared to accept the thesis of the need for satisfying increasing human wants with its concomitant machinery, industrialism and urbanism. He observed:

> The mind is a restless bird. The more it wants and still remains unsatisfied. Therefore, the ideal of creating an unlimited number of wants and satisfying them seems to be a delusion and a snare.

He further said,

> Truth requires that wants should be scientifically explored, pruned and regulated in the light of wholeness.

They cannot be taken for granted blindly, as they arise, in the mind due to the operation of self-interest. An alert bright and sensitive mind which is rooted in wisdom puts a deliberate restriction on wants. A mechanistic mind which is enslaved to the dictates of self-interest gives rise to the multiplicity of wants. The quest for truth makes man 'need -

oriented', whereas the pursuit of self-interest makes him 'want-oriented'. The purpose of consumption is not pursuit of pleasure, arising out of satisfaction of unlimited wants but the fulfilment of 'needs' which are essential for the maintenance of body and development of mind, so that man may become an effective instrument of service to mankind. Gandhi therefore denounced the unlimited character of wants and advocated fulfilment of needs. Voluntary restriction of wants is different from forced poverty. It is not a negative activity. It is a positive expression of love for fellow beings. Gandhi also denounced modern civilization based on materialistic pursuit of self-interest leading to multiplicity of wants. He asserted:

> Civilization in the real sense of the term consists not in the multiplication of wants but in the deliberate and voluntary reduction of wants.

According to Gandhi the scope of economics lies in helping man to maximize his moral well-being with the help of necessary material requisites. In the words of A.M. H:

> Maximisation of moral and to the extent necessary, material welfare may be stated as the principle welfare criteria in Gandhian economies.

Material advancement is acceptable to Gandhi, only so far as it provides spiritual interest. Economics, thus must never be allowed to cut across the path of morality. In a lecture, delivered to teachers and students of economics Gandhi had raised the question, "Does economic progress clash with real progress"?

He had explained:

> By economic progress we mean material advancement without limit and by real progress we mean moral progress, which again, is the same thing as progress of the permanent element in us.

Answering the question he said:

> "I held that economic progress in the sense I have put it is antagonistic to real progress. Hence the ancient ideal has been the limitation of activities promoting wealth... that you cannot serve God and Mammon is an economic truth of the highest value".

Gandhi has vehemently criticized that kind of economics which makes 'bodily welfare' the object of life. The hunger of wealth and the greedy pursuit of worldly pleasures results in "life corroding competition". It leads to the creation of an economic order in which inequality, exploitation, oppression and poverty prevails and human dignity is mutilated and destroyed. Regarding the degradation of life, in this connection, he writes:

> Formerly, men worked in the open air only as much as they liked. Now, thousands of workmen meet together and for the sake of maintenance work in factories and mines. Their condition is worst than that of the beasts. They are obliged to work, at the risk of their lives at most dangerous occupations, for the sake of millionaires. Formerly, men were made slaves under physical compulsion, now they are enslaved by temptation of money and of the luxuries that money can buy .

He further asserts:

> This civilization is irreligious and it has taken such a hold on the people in Europe that those who are in it appear to be half mad. They lack real physical strength or courage. They keep up their energy by intoxication. They can hardly be happy in solitude.

This civilization takes note neither of morality nor of religion being based on a fragmentary world view. Gandhi therefore, forcefully condemns, ''This civilization is such that one has only to be patient and it will be self-destroyed. According to the teachings of Mohammed (PBH) this would be considered a satanic civilization. Hinduism calls it Blockage... It must be shunned". Gandhi is, therefore, in favour of ancient Indian civilization which sets a limit to our indulgence, dissuades us from the economic philosophy of more and more and thus contributes to our moral welfare which is the source of true happiness. In 1938, Gandhi wrote in *Hind Swaraj* :

> The tendency of the Indian civilization is to elevate the moral being, that of the western civilization is to propagate immorality. The latter is Godless, the former is based on belief in God. So understanding, so believing, it behooves every lover of India to bring to the old Indian civilization even as the child clings to the mother's breast.

In conclusion, it may be said that Gandhi was an economist of the masses. His approach was entirely empirical. His economic philosophy is the result of innumerable experiences which he had shared with his fellow beings. His pragmatic touch gave a new solution to the existing socioeconomic problems in the international sphere. The fluid international conditions fraught with ideological tensions in the economic dominion demanded a fresh approach to economic philosophy, with emphasis on ideals of democracy, economic freedom and social justice. Gandhism as a socioeconomic philosophy did not only fit in the higher ideals of democratic freedom and socialism, but it was also thoroughly developed to meet the challenge of national and international focus of communism and capitalism. Gandhi was not a doctrinaire economist in the true sense of the term. But he has formulated a number of novel concepts to bring about an equitable economic order in society. As a pragmatic thinker, Gandhi felt that without a sound economic basis, a society cannot prosper. So, his economic theory provides a new and realistic approach to contemporary problems of poverty, hunger and degradation. He tries to uplift the economic condition of every man in his ideal state by introducing the concept of trusteeship, bread-labour and Swadeshi. Dr V.K.R.V. Rao observe :

> Gandhi's ideas are beginning to command increasing attention in a world that is disillusioned by the working of both capitalism and communism and attracted by the possibility that the circle can be squared with economic growth, social justice, full employment, economic and social equality, political democracy, and individual freedom all forming components of a harmonious new social order.

References

1. *Young India*, 15 November, 1928.
2. This was on 22nd December 1916 in Muir Central College, Allahabad.
3. *Young India*, 3 September, 1925, 'The Collected Works of Mahatma Gandhi', (CWMG) New Delhi, Publication Division Vol. 28, 1968 p. 148.
4. CWMG, Vol. 21, 1966 p. 290.
5. *Young India*, 13 October 1924.
6. N.K. Bose, *Selections from Gandhi*, Navajivan Publishing House, Ahmedabad, 1948, p.41.
7. *Young India,* 15 September 1927.

8. 'Harijan', 9 October, 19......., N.K. Bose, 'Selections from Gandhi', Navajivan Publishing House, Ahmedabad, 1945, p. 39.

9. *Young India*, 17 March, 1927.

10. M.K. Gandhi, *Hind Swaraj*, Navajivan Publishing House, Ahmedabad, 1938 p. 45.

11. M.K. Gandhi from *Yervada Mandir*, Navajivan Publishing House, Ahemedabad, 1932, p. 16.

12. A.M. Haq, 1985, 'Welfare Criteria in Gandhian Economics,: New Delhi : (ed.) Ramesh Diwan and Mark Lutz, p.72. Gandhi Peace Foundation, Essay in Gandhian Economics.

13. CWMG, Vol. 13, 1962, p. 311.

14. *Ibid*, p. 314.

15. *Hind Swaraj*, op. cit., p. 61

16. *Ibid*, p. 36.

17. *Ibid*, p. 34.

18. *Ibid*.

19. *Ibid*, p. 63.

20. V.K.R.V. Rao, 1982, p. 80, *Indian Socialism*, New Delhi,: Concept Publishing Company.

12

Nation-Building Through Rural Organisation

A Study of Gandhi's Concept of Cooperative Movement

P.N. Sankaran

Introduction

Though Gandhi's views on mass mobilization, trusteeship, Sarvodaya, non-violence, Satyagraha, Gramswaraj, etc., are widely understood, yet, his approach to cooperative form of rural organization has not received proper emphasis in mainstream Gandhian thought. However, now interest in Gandhian thought has been reinforced by new problems of world economy, the alarm over the exhaustion of nonrenewable resources, the ecological and environmental imbalance affecting the quality of life, the widening gap between rich and poor nations, the consequences of consumerism and above all the growth of violence and the threat of nuclear holocaust troubling the entire mankind (Joshi, 1987). The present ills of cooperative bodies such as the mounting defunct, dormant and sick organizations, politicization or officialization etc., may be cured in part with the adherence to Gandhian emphasis on purity of means in cooperative endeavours. This is a big challenge that the leadership of cooperative has to encounter if they are to emerge as healthy, democratic and vibrant organizations especially in the emerging economic scenario of liberalization, globalization and privatization.

The ongoing dismantling of the regulated marketing and pricing system in countries like India, accentuates the need as well as the potential for cooperatives. The need originates from the ability of cooperatives and farmer groups to serve as a counterveiling power to other private sector enterprises and thereby to safeguard farmers and weaker sections against unfair economic practices (Hussi, 1993). Again democratic power to the people and grassroot functionaries in matters of self-operatives as peoples' organisation. Therefore, Gandhi's concept of cooperative movement has to be evaluated against the background of the national economy going global on one hand and the process of decentralization gaining momentum at the ground level. The present paper is a modest attempt to highlight the relevance of Gandhi's vision on the cooperative movement.

Approaches to Cooperation

Cooperation not only plays a major role in the economic machinery of the world but also a vital role in the minds, the characters and even the hearts of men and women of many lands, colours and cultures, to whom it is a unifying bond subsisting through great wars and deep political cleavages (Digby, 1948). Cooperation has been looked upon as a distinct 'form of organization' and is a 'way of life'. The idea of cooperation as a way of life owes its origin to Robert Owen, who pioneered the cause of weavers 'in early 19th century in England. In India, however, cooperation was introduced in 1904 as an instrument— a form of economic organization — for providing stability and longevity to the empire and not so much as a peoples' movement for economic and social development. In other words it lacked what may be called the 'social basis' of cooperatives. In fact the cooperative development in British India was marked by the absence of spontaneity, democratic element, social objective, business efficiency and genuine leadership — a pseudo-cooperative edifice (Sinha, 1970). It may be remembered that an obvious, but often disregarded condition for the formation of a sustainable cooperative is that it should be based on the felt need of its members. Formation of the initiative for outsiders and as mere 'conveyor-belts' for goods and services has not proved to be a successful way to promote cooperatives (Hussi, 1993). According to Kalelkar, the British administration had ignored the moral aspect of cooperation (Sinha, 1970).

Gandhi was in fact the champion of cooperation as a way of life; his concept of cooperation has theoretical linkages with thrust areas in his philosophy and an intellectual appeal which renders the whole outlook a moral and human touch. Conceptualizing of cooperation on Gandhian lines may also be noted from foreign authorities on cooperation. The cooperative economy will be essentially decentralized, providing for control by the people 'from within and below'. It will also provide for balances between individual freedom and self-imposed controls. It will thus integrate self-interest and social responsibility. Because it provides these 'goods', it will be a truly human system. Cooperative economic institutions appeal to the normal sense of individuals. They provide social arrangements that enable the best tendencies within us to flourish. The cooperative plans provide the charters, even the 'Magna Cartas' of economic freedom and thus help to insure all other freedoms. The cooperative economy is thus one of the chief corner stones of the free society (Landis, 1943).

Gandhi's Concept of Cooperation

A comparison between the mainstream and Gandhian economics shows that the latter, because of its interdisciplinary dimension is more sociological in content and method, whereas the former is more a social and non-sociological in content and method (Rao, 1987). Therefore a moral overtone permeates Gandhi's concept of cooperation which, in turn also provides a well-knit intellectual support for the ultimate end, he has visualized, namely, trusteeship as Sarvodaya. Gandhi assigned a positive role to cooperative initiatives in his scheme of political independence, economic freedom and social justice. He maintained that if the will to cooperative effort is created, there is surely ample opportunity for cooperation, division of labour, saving of time and efficiency of work (Tendulkar, 1961). His views on cooperation remain obscure, scattered and mostly mixed up with his letters and public lectures. Records of the 'Champaran Satyagraha' in Bihar during 1917 and a paper on 'The Moral Basis of Cooperation', contributed to the Bombay Provincial Cooperative Conference, held on 17th September, 1917 contain explicit exposition of Gandhi's theory of cooperation.

According to Gandhi, the love for others generates the desire to cooperate. It is a philosophy, an ideology, a way of life and is universal in character. In the stupendous task of economic independence, he visualized a great role for the cooperative method of working in the field of agricultural products, utilization of land, village and small-scale industries, organization of industrial workers, distributive trade, utilization of manpower including women workers, animal husbandry, dairying, etc. Cooperation was a means for the attainment of ideals of 'trusteeship' and 'Sarvodaya'. Hence, the basic objective of trusteeship and cooperation was the same.

Gandhi was generally averse to the growth of credit cooperatives (which in fact were the first to develop) as they were interest-oriented. Cooperative banks do not pry into the borrower's moral character, if they are satisfied that he meets his overdrafts and promissory notes punctually. It is necessary that a movement which is fraught with so much good to India should not degenerate into one, for merely advancing cheap loans.

The cooperative movement will be a blessing to India only to the extent that it is a moral movement, strictly directed by men, fired with religious fervour. He was not interested in cooperation as a relief work, but as a part of nation-building. Therefore some of the persons who could have been utilized for cooperative development were assigned Khadi work which was also an experiment in cooperation and an important activity in the attainment of 'Swaraj'. Khadi, in fact, provided a forum for producers' and consumers' cooperation. With regard to the structure of membership in cooperatives, Gandhi wanted to restrict it among people similarly placed. It was so in the South African context (where Gandhi started with his ideas of cooperation, Satyagraha, social service, fight against untouchability, etc.). Some modern development practitioners have also concluded that cooperatives can only effectively help weaker members of society if they are made up of participants with the same socioeconomic background (Baverman et al., 1991).

According to Gandhi, we should not measure the success of the movements by the number of cooperative societies formed (as it is sometimes understood) but by the moral conditions of the cooperators. Again cooperative leadership has turned out to be the most handy springboard for entry into different hierarchies of political leadership. Gandhi, on the other hand wanted those responsible for the proper conduct of cooperative societies, to see to it that the money advanced did not find its way into the toddy sellers' bill or into the pockets of the keepers of gambling dens. His vision of cooperatives, centres round the following :-

a) The Government should not control the cooperative movements, though it should be financed by the governments.

b) There should be a group of national and cultural leaders to give advice and guidance to the cooperative movement.

c) The formulae for cooperative growth should not be prescribed.

Conclusion

Cooperative movements in underdeveloped countries—among people generally illiterate and without business experience — are a special case. In India, quite early it was visualzed that the cooperative sector was to emerge as a strong balancing sector between the private and public sectors. Later, a 'Cooperative Common Wealth' was established and ultimately, the cooperation became a common thing for people in India (GOI, 1991). Gandhi gave the message of cooperation as a weapon for achieving political independence, economic freedom and social justice. His idea of the movement was a part of his wider programme of nation-building and sustenance, rather than an institutional device, usually state sponsored and many a time class dominated. Perhaps, Gandhian vision of genuine cooperation alone can provide a partial remedy to the ills of the movement and transform the cooperatives into agents of socioeconomic development.

References

1. Baverman et al., 1991 'Promoting Rural Cooperatives in Developing Countries : The Case of Sub-Saharan Africa', World Bank Discussion Papers, The World Bank, Washington, DC. p. 13.
2. Digby, Margaret, 1948, *The World Cooperative Movement*, p. 177, 186, London, Hutchinson University Library.
3. Gandhi, M.K., 1917, The Moral Basis of Cooperation, Paper Contributed to the Bombay Provincial Cooperative Conferences, 17th Sept.. See Appendix I in Sinha, B.K. (1970) Mahatma Gandhi and the Cooperative Movement, p. 155-62.
4. GOI, Report of the Committee on Model Cooperatives Act, Planning Commission, p. (i) (1991).
5. Hussi, Pekka et al., 1993 'The Development of Cooperatives and Other Rural Organizations : The Role of the World Bank', World Bank Technical Paper No.199, Africa Technical Department Series, The World Bank, Washington, D.C., p. 19.

6. Joshi, P.C., 1987 'Gandhian Economics Today : Issues for Discussion Awasthi (ed.) *Gandhian Economic Theory*, Papers presented at the 68th Conference of the Indian Economic Association, held at Ahmedabad, p. 2.
7. Landis, N.Y., 1943 *A Cooperative Economy : A Study of Democratic Economic Movements',* p. 172, New York Harper and Brothers Publishers.
8. Rao, S. Srinivasa, 1987, 'Some Aspects of Gandhian Economic Theory' In Awasthi (ed.) *Gandhian Economic Theory*, Papers presented at the 68th Conference of the Indian Economic Association, held at Ahmedabad, p. 55-56.
9. Sinha, B.K., 1970, *Mahatma Gandhi and the Cooperative Movement*, p. 67, NCUI, New Delhi.
10. Tendulkar, D.G., 1961, *Mahatma*, p. 4-5, Vol. IV, Publications Division GOI.
11. Tendulkar, D.G., 1951, *Gandhi in Champaran*, New Delhi, Publications Division, GOI.

13

Gandhi's Strategy for Nation-Building

Ranbir Singh

The national movement was dominated by the moderates like Gopal Krishan Gokhale and Mahadeo Govind Ranade, during the period 1885-1905. Their use of liberal ideology, constitutional approach, modern idiom and English language resulted in confining it to a microscopic minority of educated Indians in the urban centres. But the extremists, like Bal Gangadhar Tilak, Bipin Chandra Pal and Lala Lajpat Rai who eclipsed them in 1905 could not convert it into a mass movement in spite of using the ideology of Hindu revivalism, agitational approach, traditional idiom and vernacular language. They did succeed in spreading its influence over the upper caste Hindus of urban centres and the Sikhs, rural masses, women, peasants and other sections of Indian society during the national movement. As a result, the national movement could not be converted into mass movement and the process of nation-building could not gather momentum. However, Gandhi who took over the leadership of the Indian National Congress in 1919 after the First World War succeeded in galvanizing the freedom struggle and converting the national movement into a mass movement by innovating an alternative strategy of nation-building which was based on his deep understanding of historical, social, cultural, economic and political milieu of India at that juncture of colonial rule.

First of all, he decided to project himself as a 'Mahatma' or a saint by adopting a lifestyle and political behaviour required for achieving that status. His resolve to discontinue the western, as well as the Indian dress and to cover his body with a loincloth, the way it is done by the ascetics, was to get recognition as a 'Mahatma'. His decision to remain a teetotaller and a vegetarian, to discontinue sex and practise 'Brahmacharya' were also influenced by that objective. His determination to lead a religious life and present himself before the masses as a selfless, sacrificing and spiritual leader, who had denounced worldly desires for wealth and power had been motivated by the same aim. In this manner, Gandhi was able to acquire a charisma which could enable him to command respect from sections of Indian society in general and the Hindus in particular. It was this charisma, having its roots in Indian tradition that made it possible for him to convert the national movement into a mass movement and in accelerating the process of nation-building.

As a highly articulate student of Indian society, Gandhi was able to take into account the multi-nationality character of India, while framing his strategy of nation-building. He decided to build a broad coalition of various nationalities, by advocating the promotion of regional languages and by lending support to the demands for linguistic reorganisation of provinces, so as to enable, every nationality to achieve a distinct administrative status. Instead of forming Provincial Congress Committees on the basis of administrative provinces created by the British, he constituted these on linguistic basis and set up a Provincial Congress committee for each linguistic group. It was owing to his influence that the Indian National Congress demanded linguistic reorganization of provinces. This success of Gandhi in building a broad coalition of various nationalities proved very useful for nation-building.

Owing to his deep understanding of the psyche of the majority community, Gandhi made full use of the precepts of Hindu religion. He extensively utilized the Hindu concepts of 'Satya', 'Ahimsa', 'Ram Rajya', 'Aparigraha', 'Varat' and 'Brahmacharya' in his political discourses. He also made use of the concept of 'Ashram' to designate the places of his operation. He liberally used Hindu scriptures like the *Ramayana*, the *Mahabharata* and the *Bhagavat Gita* to lend religious sanction to political actions. He utilized the name of Rama, Sita and Ishwar, used 'Bhajans', prayers, prayer meetings and religious places for mobilizing the support of Hindu masses. Even his plea for Hindu-Muslim unity had the sanction of Hindu religion as it was based on the belief of Hindu religion in 'Vasudeva Kutambakam' and 'Serva Dharama Sambhava'. This subtle use of Hindu religion enabled Gandhi to aggregate Hindus of all sects, castes, linguistic groups, regions and classes in national movement. But we can not, overlook the fact that the large-scale use of Hindu religion by Gandhi did contribute to the isolation of a larger segment of Muslims and other religious minorities from the national mainstream.

However, Gandhi did try to mobilize the support of the Muslims and the Sikhs by pleading for the unity and communal harmony between the Hindus and the religious minorities by pleading that all religions have common objectives and a common God with different names. He also extended full support to the Muslims when they launched the Khilafat Movement to protest against the injustice done by Britain and her allies to their religious leader, the Khalifah (Sultan of Turkey) after his defeat in the First World War. Gandhi also gave wholehearted support to the Gurudwara Movement, launched by the Sikhs in the 1920's, to liberate their religious institutions from the control of corrupt Hindu Mahants who had the support of colonial administration. These gestures of Gandhi did succeed in uniting all the religious communities against the British imperialism for sometime. But in the long run, these movements promoted separatism as these resulted in religion-based political mobilization. However, Gandhi must be given due credit for recognizing that only 'accommodation model' can be functional for nation-building in India's multi-religious society in which religion based identity is very strong in all the religious communities. That is why he agreed to give due weight to the wishes of leadership of the Muslims and the Sikhs in matters pertaining to these religious communities. However, Gandhi failed to persuade the Muslim leaders and the masses not to insist on partition. But his party did succeed in convincing the Sikh leaders and masses to opt for India by assuring them that they would be able to enjoy the glow of freedom in northwestern India. Moreover, it has to be recognized that the Sikhs took an active part in freedom struggle. However, it is difficult to say how far the Gandhian strategy of nation-building was instrumental in it.

The tactics adopted by Gandhi also proved useful for keeping the depressed sections of Indian society in the national mainstream. His vehement opposition to the practice of untouchability and his programme for the uplift of the depressed sections of the Hindus proved useful in defeating the British design of driving out the depressed classes from the national mainstream by providing them separate electorate, through Communal Award, in the same manner as had been done for the Muslims in 1909 and for the Sikhs in 1919. The British had also done the same, in case of the depressed castes among the Hindus, following a demand of the leader of these castes, B.R. Ambedkar. But the fast unto death by Gandhi persuaded Ambedkar to drop his demand to save Gandhi's life and to accept reservation of seats in the legislature out of the general seats meant for the Hindus. This can be described as the success of Gandhi's strategy of nation-building by moral persuasion based on self suffering. This shows how Gandhi could successfully use the traditional means or methods for nation-building. Here it is pertinent to point out that Gandhi succeeded in retaining the depressed castes in the national mainstream without offending the high caste Hindus. He pacified the upper caste Hindus by accepting the legitimacy of the concept of 'Varna Ashram Dharma' which not only provides the religious sanction to the fourfold division of Hindu society into the Brahmins, the Kshatriyas, the Vaisyas and the Shudras but also makes it obligatory for every one to perform the function of the 'Varna' of his birth. However, Gandhi reinterpreted 'Varna Ashram Dharma' by according equal status to all 'Varnas'. He expressed the view that the function of a 'Shudra' was as important as, and as honourable, as, that of a 'Brahmin'. This reinterpretation was done by Gandhi to improve the status of the depressed castes of the Hindu society whom he designated as the 'Harijans'. It was also part of his strategy for nation-building by keeping the depressed castes of the Hindus in the national mainstream. In this way, Gandhi was able to mobilize the support of the upper castes as well as the depressed castes of the Hindus in the struggle for the liberation of India.

Gandhi started the programme of rural uplift in mobilizing the rural masses who had remained till then out of the fold of national movement. He had the vision to grasp that nation-building could not be possible unless the rural masses—who constituted at that time, more than four-fifth of India's population—joined the national movement. Hence he declared that real India comprised the villages. He gave priority to rural development for nation-building. Gandhi expressed the view that India should be a commonwealth of villages. Every village should be politically independent and economically self sufficient. For ensuring political independence to villages, he advocated 'Gramswaraj' and for making them economically self-sufficient, he pleaded for the promotion of cottage and village industries. This stance of Gandhi proved very useful for enlisting the support of the rural masses in the struggle for freedom. He used political idioms based on the great tradition of the *Ramayana*, the *Mahabharata* and the *Gita* for communicating with the rural people who could not understand the modern idiom of western political discourse of liberalism and Marxism.

As a part of his strategy for nation-building, Gandhi also mobilized the women. He encouraged them to participate in the national movement. For the mobilization of women, Gandhi took up the cause of improvement of their condition. He not only laid stress on the education of women but also pleaded that they be accorded a status of dignity. As a master strategist, he adopted those programmes which directly affected the women. For instance, the issue of tax on salt was taken up by him in the Civil Disobedience Movement of 1930s as salt was an item of daily use by women in every household for cooking food. Likewise, the issue of prohibition was adopted in that movement as it was of direct concern for them because the male members would spend their earnings on the consumption of liquor and cause great hardship to women who had to run the household. Besides, they abused and beat them after getting intoxicated. Gandhi knew that nation-building would remain incomplete if women, who constituted about half of the population of India, continued to stay out of the national movement. Moreover, they could play a vital part as agents of political socialization for transmitting the values of nationalism to the children. Further, they could act as a source of inspiration and encouragement for motivating the male members of their families. Thus, Gandhi's concern for women was influenced not only by his gender sensitivity but also by the objective of nation-building through their active involvement in freedom struggle. Gandhi also advocated democratic decentralization for nation-building. His plea for decentralization of political power was motivated not only by his deal of a polity based on truth and non-violence but also by his conviction that nation-building cannot be achieved through centralization of power in a continental sized country marked with cultural plurality, linguistic diversity and social heterogeneity. In such a policy, the nation-building could be done only by giving maximum powers to the political authority at the apex. That is why Gandhi wanted that 'Gram Panchayat' be given maximum powers and 'Mandal' level political institutions could perform those functions which the village level bodies found beyond their capacity to discharge. Similarly, the district level bodies could be given the role which 'Mandal' level bodies found difficult to be undertaken. Likewise, the provincial level political authority be delegated the functions that the district level bodies could not perform and the national level government be assigned the remaining powers. Thus, Gandhi suggested the creation of a genuine multi-tiered federation for nation-building in India. He had the foresight to visualize that a centralized polity could not be functional for national integration and would only promote separatist tendencies.

His plea for partyless democracy and elections through consensus too was based on his perception that these were essential for nation-building. He apprehended that political parties would sacrifice the national interest at the altar of partisan interests. These would play a disintegrating role instead of an integrative one and lead to fragmentation of Indian polity. Therefore he suggested the disbanding of the Indian National Congress and its conversion into 'Lok Seva Sangh' before his death in 1948. He also feared that a democracy based on election of those who got highest number of votes or majority of votes would also not be conducive for nation-building as it would not be a representative democracy in the true sense. Such representatives would promote the interests of only those who voted for them and could work against the interests of others. Hence, he pleaded for the election through consensus. Besides, Gandhi was in favour of indirect elections of representative institutions at the 'Mandal', district, provincial and national levels for establishing an organic line between the authorities at all the levels and for keeping the political parties at bay. Here it may be mentioned that Gandhi's idealism made him overlook the evils of indirect election system. Moreover, he could not visualize that partyless democracy could not be possible in a nation-state and it was likely to get degenerated into an authoritarian system. Furthermore, his plea for election through consensus was bound to establish the hegemony of the dominant communities, the dominant castes and the dominant classes. The system of indirect elections could be easily manipulated by them by using money and muscle power, as the case might be. We can not suspect that Gandhi was motivated by their interests to make these suggestions. Instead, his scheme of partyless democracy, election through consensus and indirect elections was based on his commitment for nation-building.

Gandhi also decided to build a united front of all classes for nation-building by mobilizing their support for the national movement. He secured the support of the capitalist class by continuing the programmes of the 'Swadeshi' and the boycott initiated by Tilak. This programme was not only meant to fight against British imperialism but also sought to promote indigenous industries of the Indian capitalist class. To enlist the support of the working class, Gandhi advanced the theory of 'Trusteeship of Property'. This theory on one hand assured the capitalists that their private property would not be confiscated or taken over by the State, on the other it impressed upon the capitalist class to treat their private property as a trust assigned to them by God for management. He asked them not to use it for exploitation of the working class or for leading a luxurious life. He advised the capitalists to use their private property for the welfare of society as a whole. Besides, he lent support to the strikes of the workers for their just demands. Similarly, he was able to woo the zamindars, who had been traditional supporters of the British imperialism by assuring them that the Congress governments which had come to power in most of the provinces as the result of the 1937 elections would not abolish Zamindari system. But at the same time he was able to retain the support of the peasantry by supporting its struggles against unjust rent and unreasonable hikes in land revenue. He won over the artisan class by advocating the cottage and village industries. The landless agriculturist labourers from the depressed castes were mobilized by him through his opposition to untouchability by his attempts to enhance their social status by designating them as 'Harijans' and by undertaking programmes for their welfare.

Gandhi developed the technique of 'Satyagraha' or non-violent political struggle not only because he realized that the Indians could not afford to launch armed struggle against British imperialism, (which was powerful enough to suppress the same), but also for removing fear from the Indian mind by giving the national movement a moral or ethical colour. The use of moral force for fighting the British regime helped Gandhi in inculcating the spirit of nationalism among the Indian masses. They began to perceive participation in the national movement as 'Dharma' or duty. The movements launched by Gandhi, the Non-cooperation Movement of 1920's and the Civil Disobedience Movement of the 1930s were exercises in nation-building. These transmitted the values of fearlessness, sacrifice and nationalism to the Indian people.

Besides, he made skilful use of certain symbols for nation-building. For instance, his emphasis on the use of 'Khadi' by the Indians in general and the Congressmen in particular aimed at inculcating the spirit of nationalism among the masses and creating the feeling of brotherhood by removing the distinction in the quality of cloth used by them for their dress. Similarly, the popularization of 'Khadi' cap—also known as the Gandhi cap—by him could also be described as a successful effort to use it as a symbol of nationalism. His insistence that every Congressman must religiously ply 'Charkha' for sometime, everyday, not only aimed at promoting dignity of labour, but also at strengthening the spirit of nationalism in them. Here it may be mentioned that 'Charkha' was successfully identified by Gandhi with the national movement. He selected this symbol because 'Charkha' was used in most of the middle and lower class Indian households during those days. For the same reason Gandhi got it inserted in the flag of the Indian National Congress also.

Lastly, Gandhi used institution-building as a device for nation-building. Before he took over the leadership of the party, the Congress had no organizational structure worth the name. There were only annual sessions of the party for passing resolutions. Gandhi converted the Congress into a very powerful political instrument by constituting the Congress Committees at the village, 'Mohalla, 'Mandal', district, provincial and the national levels. In this way he developed a network for political communication which linked people at grassroot level with the national leadership of the party. Besides, he created a cadre of whole time Congress workers for participation in the movements launched by him. During the intervals, these workers remained engaged in the constructive programmes. Moreover, Gandhi developed a set of leadership in the Congress party at all the levels. He converted the party not only into a mass organisation but also a fighting machine. For maintaining discipline in the party, Gandhi not only created a High Command, a volunteers force— the Congress Seva Dal but also built up front organizations of the party for mobilizing the youth, women and peasants.

This strategy of institution-building played a significant role in nation-building during the pre-independence period.

Thus, it may be concluded that Gandhi used a fairly successful multipronged strategy for nation building by taking into account the historical, cultural, economic and political context, existing at that time. In spite of his failure to avert partition for reasons beyond his control, Gandhi has been legitimately recognized as the 'Father of the Nation'. But, the strategy of nation-building innovated by him during the colonial period as such may only be partially relevant in the changed domestic and international context of present times. However, it would be wrong to infer that Gandhi's strategy of nation-building has no relevance today. Our political leadership can learn a lot from it for facing the internal and external threats that have now assumed alarming proportions.

Part III

Part III

14

Sarvodaya, Swaraj and Panchayati Raj

Ramashray Roy

Sarvodaya, Swaraj and Panchayati Raj, these three terms constitute three different but organically linked aspects of Gandhian thinking. Without realizing the importance of these terms in individuals' lives and relations, on the one hand and in social institutional arrangements, on the other, sociopolitical system of Gandhi's conception will not be possible to be realised. It does not need to be stressed here that without realizing the Gandhian vision of individual and collective life, the civilizational crisis that mankind faces today cannot be averted and overcome.

But, why should one prefer Gandhian panacea for overcoming civilizational crisis when there exist numerous tried and untried panaceas? Since the beginning of civilization, numerous philosophers and thinkers have tried to understand the nature of this crisis and have suggested or actually acted upon ways and means of overcoming this crisis. What makes Gandhian perspective on man and his world so distinctively beneficial? What is it about Gandhian solution to civilizational crisis that it should be preferred to other possible solutions?

The answer to this question is necessary in order to facilitate turning around from those factors that have brought about the onset of the contemporary crisis and engaging into the creative act of reconstruction. However, space does not permit a detailed answer except to say that other solutions, whether at the level of idea or institution, either make man subservient to the system or expose the system to the ravages of individual self-aggrandizement. No matter which way one inclines, there is always the danger of conflict between individual well-being and collective good. It is this conflict that Gandhian perspective on man and his world seeks to completely terminate or, at least, minimize.

But, why do the private and communal order of man's existence collide and come into conflict? To answer this question, we must raise another question to seek an answer to it. It can be asked : What constitutes a political community, which, through institutionalizing a primordial insight into the structure of order, makes possible the reconciliation between the claims of the private and the public orders of man's existence ? A society is composed of diverse aspirations and interests which provides it with an arena where private concerns are pursued. This marks society with diversity and heterogeneity. Self-interested pursuit of these concerns creates and, in many cases, provokes and produces an actual conflict, the war of one against all others. As such, sociopolitical order is always disturbed making individual well-being and collective good hard to safeguard and promote.

In creating the 'city in speech', i.e. the Republic, Socrates addresses precisely to this problem. A political community, because it serves the purposes of human living, necessarily embraces an abundance and multiplicity of human goods. But, because we neither know what is the greatest of the goods nor have a basis upon which to choose reliably among the multiplicity of apparent goods, we tend to be engrossed in our own private goods and vigorously, even aggressively, seek to realize them. This shatters the 'wholeness' or 'completeness' of the political order. This is so, for the simple reason that, generally speaking, we are unable to discriminate among goods. We have therefore no alternative but to welcome them all and then try to determine in what manner and to what extent they might fit together (Utilitarianism is the best example of this).

Thus, for ensuring the 'wholeness' or 'completeness' of the political community, one must consider the possibility of order among the multiplicity of human goods. This possibility can be made actual, only when the capacity of what Socrates calls 'synopsis' is cultivated and used in arranging the institutional structure of the political community. By 'synoptic vision' Socrates means not only the capacity to judge which goods must be preferred and sought to be realized in life. Also, it includes discernment for organizing them in such a way that higher goods do not suffer at the hand of lesser ones. But, how can the synoptic vision be cultivated and institutionalized, when this vision becomes a reality?

We need not go into the details of the answer to this question here. What needs to be pointed out, however, relates to Platonic distinction between appearance and reality and the need to attune one's soul, through dialectics, to that reality in order to gain sharp-sightedness that permits one to have the synoptic vision. In order to institutionalize this synoptic vision into the institutional arrangement of the political community, certain other factors are necessary. For one thing, not all can hope to have the sharp-sightedness necessary for cultivating synoptic vision. It is therefore necessary to instal the rule of the philosopher-king and devise certain institutional mechanisms, such as, censorship, etc., for ensuring general conformity to the vision of order yielded by philosophy.

Also necessary in this connection is to see to it that, on the one hand, the size of the political community is kept very small (Plato suggests a population of 5046) and on the other, no one should desire or have anything beyond the plain necessities that life itself demands. Also, the rule of one person-one art must be strictly followed. But, does not all this—it can be asked, as Glaucon does ask—suppress 'spiritedness' and render the city 'fit for pigs' only, not for human beings. But, to recognize the claim of 'spiritedness' is to admit into the city, unnecessary desires, that is, desires what Glaucon calls 'relish' as a supplement to the indispensable staples of human life. He insists upon the inclusion of the full array of goods and services, commonly accepted as pertaining to an elegant lifestyle.

To satisfy the demand for 'relish' is, however, not only to give primacy to technical expertise but also to encourage territorial expansion, a large army, complex production system, consumerism, etc. As a result, no hierarchy or order among the myriad of consumer goods and services that the city permits can be contemplated or maintained. Like the inflamed appetite, it is obliged to admit that the political order itself becomes limitless. It does not possess or it soon loses if it begins with a principle according to which its order or even its own completion may be determined. Thus, to satisfy the demand for 'relish' produces nothing more than a 'promiscuous heap, stuffed and multitudinous' (Plato, 'Republic' 373 b 3-4).

Needless to say that political communities responding to the demands of inflamed appetites, have—as Gandhi's *Hind Swaraj* amply demonstrates—been reduced to promiscuous heaps engaged in the difficult and thankless task of satisfying ever-growing and ever-proliferating demands for material goods and services. It is to save the political community from such a dismal and dismaying fate that both

Plato and Gandhi lived and toiled. However, Plato's solution is not efficacious for various reasons which it is not possible to go into here except to say that for him, only a rare few of men are capable of cultivating the capacity of synopsis. As a result, many have to be 'forced to be free' so that the wholeness of the political community can be safeguarded. If Plato fails, his modern day counterparts, advocating varieties of liberalism too, must fail because they prescribe more of the same medicine that has induced the disease in the first place. The degeneration of a political community 'into a promiscuous heap, stuffed and multitudinous' does not simply mean the incapacity of either envisioning or sustaining order that can hold diverse elements together, lend them coherence and inspire them to rise above their own petty self-interest and promote collective well-being. This is symptomatic of a situation from which shareable commonality has been drained out. This means that individuals and groups have their own private dream worlds which not only divide them but also frequently pit them against one another. In the lack of a shareable commonality, order is drained of its substantive, normative, and regulative significance. It also gets separated from the sense of justice. If it does commit itself to securing justice, its commitment becomes very difficult to honour.

It is, therefore, no wonder that politics has, in recent times, been defined as 'who gets what, when and how'. There is no doubt that this is characteristic of modern politics. This is so for the simple reason that privileged access to and control over material resources hold the key to individual happiness, personality development and civilisational progress. Given the centrality of access to and control over material resources for individual well-being and collective good, of course, in the modern sense of the terms, it is not surprising that intense and harsh competition for these resources ensues making politics a process of reciprocal resistance. Further, in the grim battle for occupying privileged positions in society, power plays a major role in deciding who gets what, when and how. Not to say that power, as is well known, respects no values and moral laws.

With power, becoming the primary determinant of who gets what, when and how, inequality, exploitation and oppression become constant features of society. Inequity and injustice are tolerated even while the political system commits itself to eradicating them. This is so, for the reason that acquisitiveness is—especially in modern time—the engine of progress and to suppress it, is to suppress the one factor that endows contemporary societies with their dynamism. But the economics catering to the impulse of acquisitiveness, as already pointed out, institutes the politics of interest. These two taken together, drain social life and relations of what Gandhi calls affection. And when affection, true and ennobling affection, gets eroded, sociopolitical order becomes shaky, unsteady and fickle.

A society, lacking order exacerbates the conflict between the private and the public orders of man's existence. This conflict gets externalized and pervades the whole society. This conflict erodes human values, blunts human development, and cuts at the source of personal and collective welfare. As long as inequality, exploitation, domination and oppression characterize social life and relations, harmony, peace and welfare will elude.

It is in this context that Gandhi's insistence on Sarvodaya as the highest human ideal can be appreciated. Sarvodaya, or the well-being of all, does not refer to the promissory note that the dominant paradigm of development benefits all. This promissory note projects the hope that everybody's desires (of every sort) will be satisfied. Needless to say that this note adds to inflamed appetites referred to earlier. Also, the earth, as Gandhi underlines, possesses only that much which can satisfy the needs, but not the greed of all. Physical and social limits to growth put this beyond the range of possibility. Perhaps, redistribution of wealth following the dictates of equality, particularly in its modern-day version, can conduce to the well-being of all. However, equality cannot be maintained even if it is instituted. Nor can the continual change in the external social environmen help in encashing the promissory note.

The promissory note has to be rejected. This signifies what Gandhi calls minimization of wants. But, easy as it appears in words, its practice is not that simple. Decision to minimize wants, involves on the one hand, conscious and active consideration for the good of others and, on the other, the ability to control imperious and wayward appetites and passions as a precondition for forcefully and effectively following the course, one has charted for oneself. A little deliberation makes it clear that what appears to be a part of man's external behaviour is intimately linked with his interior world; this behaviour will not have durability if the interior world of man lacks the order it requires for supporting, directing and regulating will power.

It is against this background that we can, appreciate Gandhi's insistence on changing man's interior. He argues that change in man's interior cannot come from any external source or circumstance or through any categorical imperative of Kantian variety. "It is an inward change......it is the transformation of heart....and that absolute transformation can only come by inward prayer and a definite and living recognition of the presence of the mighty spirit residing within." (*Collected Works of Mahatma Gandhi*, 34:506).

> Once, this internal transformation occurs, the outward forms automatically change. What one should be concerned with, therefore, is a radical change more in inward spirit than in outward form. If the first is changed, the second will take care of itself. If the first remains unchanged, the second, no matter how radically changed, will be like a whited sepulchre (*Collected Works of Mahatma Gandhi*, 55:62).

This inward change, as Gandhi insists, is consequent upon "a definite and living recognition of the presence of the mighty spirit residing within". To put it differently, unless the soul is irrevocably attuned to the divine ground of being, the change in the interior of man—change that is supportive of the individual effort to reconcile the private and the public orders of his existence—cannot take place. Soul's attunement to the divine ground of being engenders the awareness not only of the openness of the horizon of man's destiny but also of the relatedness of all conditioned beings. This is, in short, the awareness of a shareable commonality which becomes the seed bed of the feeling of fellowship and brotherliness. It is also this attunement that yields the synoptic vision making it possible to visualize the right order among different constituents of his being. This right order consists in accepting overlordship of the mighty spirit within one's own soul and then, letting the soul keep appetites and passions under tight leash so that they do not become wayward, rebellious and self-aggrandizing. It is this self-mastery that Gandhi calls Swaraj whose origins go back to 'Brihadaranyak Upanishad'(4.4.23) and 'Chhandogya Upanishad' (7.25.2).

Swaraj in the sense of inward transformation based on the soul's attunement to the divine ground of being is a necessary condition for appreciating and accepting the idea of Sarvodaya. It is not, however, a sufficient condition for giving effect to the idea of Sarvodaya. What is additionally needed is self-rule in the political sense, not in the sense of deliverance from any alien rule but in the sense of managing the affairs of the community one belongs to. As was indicated earlier, Plato suggests a very small political community as the most appropriate arena for the successful functioning of any system of self-rule. There are several reasons for it, only two of which need to be mentioned here. In the first place, vitality and vigour of any democratic system depends on the capacity of the citizen to rule and to be ruled. It requires to have the experience and the confidence of the citizen who rises above his own self-interest and identifies himself with the collectivity, he is an integral part of safeguard and promotes collective good. In the second place, as the size of the political community increases, divorce between active community political life and collective power and authority occurs. As a result, the equation between community needs and state action becomes malign, legitimacy of the political system becomes fragile and denies the right to participate. People do not come forth to the rescue of the system when in crisis.

But, States today are very large. As such, centralization of power and authority, especially in a situation of sociocultural diversity, allows the nation as a country, distinct from different areas and sociological groupings to emerge prominent, suppressing all others in importance, resources and authority. Losing their distinctiveness, these communities also lose their voice in managing their own affairs as well as the affairs of the nation which, in any case, is remote, daunting and cognitively opaque. With the segregation between politico-administrative decision-making and the legitimation process of political will, as is the case with 'representative democracy', substantive democracy is reduced to market-mode democracy, transforming politics into business. This also reduces the role of the citizen to that of acclaiming the selection of 'ruler-managers' in the open market of electoral politics.

For all these reasons, the common man, denied any role other than occasionally selecting the 'ruler-managers', grows either apathetic or highly exuberant. He becomes apathetic because he cannot find any basis to meaningfully relate himself to the larger political process. Similarly, he becomes exuberant when his hopes and aspirations, given a fillip by the political system itself, are continuously frustrated because of the inability of the system to perform. Becoming dissatisfied and frustrated, he expresses his anger in outbursts of violence and destruction. In any case, as a passive citizen, he has no opportunity to actively participate in community political life, he is prevented from learning and performing essential citizenship roles. Needless to say that in and through political life, men's true individuality can be cultivated within an ensemble of responsibilities (sharing in tasks of deliberation and executing public decisions and so on) that encourages them to see what is good for themselves and desirable for others in general.

The present system robs the people of such an ensemble of responsibilities and then expects them to become perfect citizens. It is this paradoxical situation that erodes political responsibility and responsiveness and breeds tyranny. Gandhi therefore insists on the need for the people to develop the capacity to resist tyranny. This is possible only through self-rule in the framework of a decentralized polity, exemplified by a full-fledged Panchayati Raj with full powers of decision-making and execution, pertaining to the totality of local affairs. Such a Panchayati Raj offers the people ample opportunities for training themselves in accepting and carrying out the ensemble of responsibilities that self-rule implies.

Needless to say that the Panchayati Raj, even in its recently enacted form, falls far short of the Gandhian idea of Panchayati Raj.

15

Sustainable Development, Good Governance and Gramswaraj

B. Mohanan

The much talked about concept of sustainable development can not comprehend properly Gandhi's holistic approach to life. Sarvodaya is the appropriate term to be used while discussing Gandhi's views on well-being of all and sociopolitical organisation to ensure it. Even a cursory look at the origin and growth of the term 'sustainable development' and the way that it has been currently used by the apostles of the dominant paradigm of development would give a clear idea about the nature and extent of differences between sustainable development and Gandhian vision of well-being of all.

Sustainable Development

As is well-known, the concept of sustainable development surfaced as an important theme of discussion in 1987. The Brundtland Commission Report on environment and development exhorted that all development initiatives and activities should be sustainable. The Commission wrote:

> In order for development to be sustainable, it must meet the needs of the present without compromising the ability of future generations to meet their own needs.

However, its prescriptions for the future did not deviate a little from the framework of the dominant paradigm of development. Crass materialism which is at the centre-stage of western thinking about development has not been questioned by the commission in its prescriptions for the future. Making money and accumulating more and more goods are the central aspects of development in its western formulation. Unfortunately, many of those advocating sustainable development, appear not to be able to get out of this mindset, so all they are rooting for is a continuous growth in material wealth, albeit in a sustainable manner (Ashish Kothari, 1993).

It is to be noted that the principal trustees of western notion of development, sideline all the aspects of 'sustainability' from the concept of sustainable development. Thus, the term which originated from the fierce debate generated by environmentalists lost all its content and meaning. In its co-opted form it is part of a well designed strategy of the World Bank and other international institutions to construct a global capitalist order. A look at the development strategies now advocated by the bank alongwith good governance and infrastructure for development, would reveal the intention of the bank.

Co-opted Ideas

As has already been noted, the World Bank has co-opted ideas and themes of alternative ideologies and movements. Greening of Development, Gender Hierarchies in Development, Citizenship Empowerment and Development are some of the samples of such co-optation. Also at the same breath the bank is talking about 'privatization and deregulation'. One may wonder how this greening of development and privatization and deregulating go together.

In the aftermath of the collapse of the Soviet Union and the east-European political systems, new ideas and strategies have been floated to strengthen the capitalist global order. It is in this context that the World Bank came out with its idea of good governance. The term first appeared in 1989 in the report of the World Bank on Africa.

> "Underlying the litany of Africa's development problems is a crisis of governance", the report said.

The bank defined good governance as 'the exercise of political power to manage a nation's affairs'. The features of good governance as identified by the bank are the following: an efficient public service, an independent judicial system and legal framework to enforce contracts, the accountable administration of public funds, an independent public auditor responsible to a representative legislature, respect for law and human rights at all levels of government, a pluralistic institutional structure and a free press. This initial formulation of good governance became a definitive statement in a publication of the bank entitled, 'Governance and Development' (1992). In this publication good governance has been treated as sound development management.

It should also be noted that between 1989 and 1991, all the western governments issued a number of statements on governance and democracy and the relationship of either or both to development. These pronouncements of western governments were supported by major international institutions. Thus, from the pronouncements of western governments and the reports of the World Bank emerged the concept of good governance. It appears that the concept of good governance is wider than government. Governance denotes the structures of political and economic relationship. It also denotes the rules by which the productive life of a society is governed. In short, it refers to a regime. Thus, in current usage, good governance means a democratic capitalist regime presided over by a minimal state which is also part of the new world order (Leftwich, 1993). He adds further :

> And clearly the barely submerged structural model and ideal of politics, economics and society on which the contemporary notion of good governance rests is nothing less than that of western liberal (or social) democracy—the focal concern and the logical terminus of much modernisation theory.

According to Leftwich, this is the new orthodoxy (that) dominates official western aid policy and development thinking. This new orthodoxy does not assert simply that good governance and democracy are desirable in themselves and the likely outcome of development (roughly the view of modernization theory in the 1960s), but that democracy is a necessary prior or parallel condition of development, not an outcome of it.

Infrastructure for Development

Alongwith the above formulation of good governance and development, the concept of infrastructure for development is required to be analysed. The text of the 1994 World Development Report discusses the importance of infrastructure for development. The report has noted that the developing countries invest $ 200 billion a year in infrastructure. According to the report the result of it is a dramatic increase in infrastructure services—for transport, power, water, sanitation, telecommunication and irrigation. The report further says that during the last fifteen years the share of households with access to clean water has increased by half and power production and telephone lines per capita have doubled. Such increases do much to raise productivity and improve living standards. The same report continues to say that there is no room for complacency: "One billion people in the developing world still lack access to clean water and nearly 2 billion lack adequate sanitation. In rural areas especially, women and children often spend long hours fetching water. Already inadequate transport networks are deteriorating rapidly in many countries. Electric power has yet to reach 2 billion people and in many countries unreliable power constrains output."

The argument of the World Bank is that infrastructure can deliver major benefits in economic growth, poverty alleviation and environmental sustainability. But, the bank is critical of the system which is inefficient. To ensure efficient and responsive delivery of infrastructure services the bank suggests that incentives need to be changed through the applications of three instruments—commercial management, competition and stake holders involvement. The concept of stake holders involvement is very important. The report says: Involving users more in project design and operation of infrastructure activities where commercial competitive behaviour is constrained, provides the information needed to make suppliers more accountable to their customers. Users and other stake holders can be involved in consultation during project planning, direct participation in operation and monitoring. Development programmes are more successful where service users of the affected community have been involved in project formulation. User participation creates the appropriate incentives to ensure that maintenance is carried out in community based projects.

Further, the Bank talks about new forms of public-private partnerships to provide infrastructure and to manage common property resources. It further states: "Infrastructure services that help the poor also contribute to environmental sustainability. Clean water and sanitation, non-polluting sources of power, safe disposal of solid waste and better management of traffic in urban areas provide environmental benefits for all income groups". One can notice a new emphasis on the role of institutions and institutional incentives in promoting sustainable development. Institutions are being set up for the participation of local people (Corbridge, 1995).

A Democratic Capitalist Order

Current approach of World Bank to Development has been discussed in detail with a view to show that the intention of World Bank is the construction of a democratic capitalist order with a minimal state. Either 'good governance' or 'infrastructure for development' can in no way contribute to poverty alleviation and environmental sustainability. It points to the fact that the brand of sustainable development advocated by the supporters of the dominant paradigm of development is not at all desirable due to the simple reason that it is unsustainable.

Thus, the whole concept of development with its emphasis on industrialization and urbanization is required to be rejected. Nonetheless it has prefixed the word sustainability. The reason is that greed and fierce competition are the hallmarks of such development. There is no place for cultural, spiritual and other aspects of human existence in it. The promoters of this branch of development have themselves realized the limits of economic growth and disastrous environmental effects. Even then they are not prepared to abandon the emphasis on material growth. Instead, the attempt has been to devise ways and means to sustain capitalist developmentalism by minimizing ecological and environmental disasters. The hard reality is that within the framework of capitalist developmentalism the civilizational crisis mankind faces and the environmental catastrophe can not be averted. That is why it has been argued that the dominant paradigm of development has to be rejected totally. Then what kind of development is desirable? In fact, any development should be in tune with the central organizing principle of that society. Thus, it is the duty of the development strategist to identify the central organising principle of the society concerned and devise a mode of development accordingly. In this context, Ramashray Roy writes:

> It can be argued that every society has at its core a central organising principle which gets progressively actualized in its institutions and cultural life in the process of social development. Like Aristotelian entelekheia, the central organising principle represents at one and the same, the genius of the people of a particular society and constitutes the guiding principles which shape their ways of looking at and doing things. This organising principle informs their cultural as well as material life. Given this central tendency of growth implanted in all societies, it is only the question of identifying this tendency and then devising a mode of development that not only conforms to it but also becomes its accomplice in directing development of society in a way that makes progressive realization of this tendency possible. Such a development will eminently suit the genius of society and will, therefore, be quite sustainable because it is compatible with the basic 'nature' of society (Ramashray Roy : 1993).

Here lies the importance of Gandhian thought system. Gandhi could identify the central organizing principle of the Indian society and could suggest a development philosophy that would suit to the genius of the society.

A Unique Vision

Gandhi had a unique vision of a self-sustained village society. It is very simple and at the same time very complex in its structural aspects. It is composed of innumerable villages in ever-widening circles. Gandhi observes:

> Life here will not be a Pyramid with the apex sustained by the bottom, but it will be an oceanic circle whose centre will be the individual, always ready to perish for the village, the latter ready to perish for the circle of the villages, till at last the whole becomes one life composed of individuals, never aggressive in their arrogance, but ever humble, sharing the majesty of the oceanic circle of which they are integral units". The idea of the circle stands for integration, fullness and self-sufficiency. He wrote that independence must begin at the bottom. Thus, every village will be a republic or Panchayat having full powers. It follows, therefore, that every village has to be self-sustained and capable of managing its affairs even to the extent of defending itself against the whole world.

Here Gandhi rejects the western concept of power and the kind of political organization based on it. He thus provides an alternative to capitalism. In the Gandhian alternative, villages are the primary units.

> The villages should be self-governing entities interacting among themselves in a spirit of cooperation and love. Such a system will give no quarter for domination of any kind. This communitarian model of village democracy is expected to be a healthy blend of individual freedom and social responsibility.

Gandhian concept of Gramswaraj is not only different from western concept of local government but also from Nehruvian model of Panchayati Raj. Nehru considered Panchayati Raj institutions as the local delivery system of the State sponsored developmental activities. On the contrary, Gandhian notion of Gramswaraj is firmly rooted in his distinct understanding of Indian villages. It is based on the bottom-up view of power. People will have to manage their affairs at the village level itself. In other words the bottom-up view of power postulates a situation in which people govern their affairs at the primary level itself, organised into large number of village republics with absolutely no use to expand their area of operation. Thus, the essentials of Gramswaraj are neighbourhood, self-reliance and self-regulation.

Gandhi wanted villages to be self-sufficient republics. His idea of self-sufficiency was that:

> The village must be self-sufficient in regard to food, cloth and other basic necessities.

It is to exercise legal, executive and judicial functions. It is in this sense that the village is a circle, full and self-contained. This concept of self-sustained village society is the integral component of Gandhi's holistic approach to life, his philosophy of truth, non-violence and love. Therefore, his political philosophy can not be separated from his economic philosophy.

In this context it should also be mentioned that Gandhi's Gramswaraj can not be established by merely amending the Constitution of India. In fact, we need the support of a circular constitution in the place of the present pyramidal, one for the realization of Gandhi's Gramswaraj.

In the light of the above, it has become clear that Gramswaraj is a comprehensive term which encompasses the economic, political, social and educational dimensions. The principles such as trusteeship, Swadeshi, full employment, bread-labour, self sufficiency, cooperation, equity and nationalism are organically linked to it. Gramswaraj is the basic organizational requirement for the realization of Sarvodaya, the well-being of all by means of truth and non-violence. Unlike other thinkers of modern times, Gandhi approached political and economic problems from a highly ethical and humanistic point of view. According to him, the acute economic disparity between the rich and the poor is the product of the capitalist industrial civilization of west as embodied in big machines.

Conclusion

The above analysis underscores the fact that the concepts of good governance, infrastructure for development and even sustainable development can not be used as a substitute to Gramswaraj and Sarvodaya owing to the reason that these terms originated in the context of western developmentalism which Gandhi rejected in toto.

16

Gandhian Approach for Development

T. Kalyani, C. Gnanapragasam

Development means a change which may be either upward or downward or a cyclic process, that is, a spiral one. Several yardsticks have been designed to measure the change. In modern times, everything is measured by appropriate tools. The development of human being is measured by the way of life from the ancient period to the modern. The economic development is measured by per capita income and expenditure as well as the amount of consumption of electricity. In rural India a man leads a life in the traditional way, he will perhaps never join the club of development. In the same manner, Gandhi is not an emperor or a war hero but he is remembered for his philosophy. In the words of Professor Toynbee:

> The Power and creative suffering must be evident to any one of my age, for the generation into which I happen to have been born, has not only been Hitler's generation in the west and Stalin's in Russia; it has also been Gandhi's in India and it can already be forecast with some confidence that Gandhi's effect on human history is going to be greater and more lasting than either Stalin's or Hitlers.

What was Gandhi's idea of India which he was setting out to mould according to his own wishes and ideals? He said :

> I shall work for an India in which the poorest shall feel that it is their country, in whose making they have an effective voice an India in which there shall be no high class and low class of people, an India in which all communities shall live in perfect harmony.......There can be no room in such an India for the curse

> of untouchability or the curse of intoxicating drinks and drugs......Women will enjoy the same rights as men........ This is the India of my dreams.

A country can be developed only with the cooperation of all especially the involvement of the economically disadvantaged people, namely poor. Poverty is a kind of violence, which kindled and mobilized the rebel attitude against political system. So the commitment of the poor to the nation is a real patriotism and works for the development of the nation.

The society is a cohesive one and the division of society either hierarchically—rich and poor, high and low class—or good and bad or on the basis of sexual discrimination, etc., leads to the division which loosens the social cohesiveness and harmony of society. Gandhi therefore wanted to work for perfect harmony of the society.

Today, our full efforts are concentrated only to achieve a social cohesiveness. Of course, equality is ensured to all, discrimination of any kind is debarred in our constitution. Gandhi's dream of equality is only through the self-realization of people and he did not try to impose it and never sought the organizational support, namely through Congress.

Gandhi was of course, essentially a man of religion. His attitude towards other religions was, "All religions are almost as dear to me as my own Hinduism". He tried to give Hinduism a kind of universal attire and included all religions within the fold of truth. Truth and non-violence appeared to him to be the same. Gandhi termed the Indian culture neither as Hindu nor Islamic nor of any other religion, wholly. For him it was a fusion of all. Again he said, "I want the culture of all lands to be blown about my house as freely as possible. But I refuse to be blown off my feet by any. I refuse to live in other people's houses as an interloper, a beggar or a slave. The religion is in no way a trouble maker but the trouble shooter".

The way to freedom was through organized non-violent resistance, which ultimately blessed both the Indian people and the foreign rulers. It is realized today that the significance of the moral basis of Gandhian campaigns lay in their efforts to fight for their rights. In short, truth always prevailed. Gandhi had launched three movements in a span of 23 years, namely Noncooperation Movement, Civil Disobedience Movement and Quit India Movement. The time-gap between one movement and the other was of several years. The gradual degree of intensification of resistance increased from one to the other. Normally, any civilized and conscious people could never continue to rule in the midst of such agitations, they might have voluntarily left India. But, after 1942, the problem of two nation theory arose, which retained the Britishers till 1947. The role of Mahatma Gandhi in our freedom struggle is a role model for the freedom movement of any nation and of non-violence. In fact, Gandhian non-violence is an instrument to maintain peace both for the individual and the nation.

Gandhi was working out for a socioeconomic pattern of society. According to him equality was the essence of socialism. Gandhi wrote in 1947, "Socialism is a beautiful word. So far as I am aware in socialism all the members of society are equal—none low, none high". Even in analysing socialism, Gandhi's view was truthful and non-violent. The non-violence is embedded in truth. Thus, the socio-economic approach of Mahatma Gandhi has many good aspects.

To establish socialism, Gandhi basically wanted village development. Gandhi liked the micro level development, because he was in favour of self-sufficiency. He opined that each person should contribute something for his own living and happiness. The best way of life according to Gandhi was simple living and high thinking. According to him poverty led to social disorder and dehumanization, whereas opulence led to exploitation and degradation of man.

Gandhi's thought revolved around the village life, and village oriented economy. His emphasis was on simple way of life. Apart from this, Gandhi stressed upon the cooperative techniques at all levels. He felt that the welfare of all developed only through cooperation and not through competition.

The Sarvodaya concept of Gandhi includes all. It does not stress on number, or segment. Gandhi wished this concept of development to take practical shape through villages. He wanted the village to be democratically organized.

Democratic decentralisation of Gandhian model is very much in vogue in the modern society. Gandhi's socialistic pattern of approach is also followed in the working of the Indian Constitution. Gandhi was for eradication of poverty and uplift of poor in the villages. Even today, our government is stressing upon the eradication of poverty, employment opportunity to all and the extension of all facilities to the villages. In fact, development from below is the concept followed in the world today the basis of which was totally laid down and supported by Gandhi. Gandhi was able to bring out the peasants from their nest. The peasants of the modern era must thank Gandhi for rural reconstruction and community development programmes.

The credit of abolition of untouchability also goes to the father of the nation. He described the untouchables as children of God. It was Gandhi's influence only which made the present leaders to work for abolition of untouchability.

Gandhi holds that a real development can only be achieved through our own efforts, that is sell-reliance. The so-called development of industries has made the human beings dependent on them and may be described as pseudo-development. India is an agricultural country. Imposing alien or industrial culture on India may lead to deviation of values and people may be confused in identifying the real development.

In order to achieve Gandhian goals, Vinoba Bhave started the Bhoodan Movement and later he tried to achieve Sarvodaya. He succeeded to a great extent but not fully. After some time, the Sarvodaya Movement was conducted by Jayaprakash Narayan. But, he was also only partially successful. Truly speaking, these two followers of Gandhi have contributed a lot by their efforts to achieve the ultimate goal of development the Gandhian way.

17

Gandhian Way of Development
The Indian Experience

S. Muraleedharan

It is well known that the core elements in Gandhian ideology are truth, non-violence, Satyagraha, Swadeshi, equality and bread-labour. Of these, the last three are analysed here to comprehend Gandhian vision of development. The intention of the present work is not to transcribe what Gandhi told us, but to make an humble attempt to highlight the significance of Gandhian vision of development in the light of India's experience. The purpose is to link Gandhi's ideas on rural India and technology with the three core elements referred above.

Regional Dispersion of Industrialization and Agricultural Development and removal of social Inequalities

India is still an agrarian economy. Because agriculture is the second main contributor to national income and more important, two-third of the population adopts agriculture as their prime means of living. It is well acknowledged that urban India is non-agricultural while, rural India is pronged to agriculture. The greatness of Gandhi may be understood in the context that the soul of India lies in our villages. In other words, Gandhian view on development emphasizes the purpose of the same rather than a higher quantified rim of growth.

Here, one may understand the traditional culmination of rural society in India. It was one of self-reliant rural economies (Kurien, 1978). Full- fledged village economy was the hallmark of Chola dynasty (Kurien, 1978 & Majumdar, 1978). Such economies were need-based and not want-based. The former one was natural and biological in form and the latter was a carved out or generated one. The first one could not be avoided while the second one could either be minimized or eliminated. The traditional rural societies were able to satiate the requirements of the inhabitants when these were minimum in nature.

The very feature of Indian agriculture was that it was subsistent and not commercialized (Kurien 1978). A self-reliant village economy is the true reflection of Gandhian Swadeshi.

One may raise his eyebrow with the doubt whether Gandhian development visualizes a stagnant economy. One needs to understand the quality of the argument rather than the quantum of development. The real achievement by pursuing the so-called modern development is not in favour of the masses. Any development paradigm that neglects the masses is only a pocketed growth and not real development. This can be understood by looking into the sheer fact that the extent of poverty and inequality continues to be unabated (Ahluwalia 1985, NCAER, 1985).

The extent of inequality is discernible mainly in three dimensions, viz, income distribution, land distribution and expenditure pattern. It is argued that our public sector undertakings, which were moulded with the intention of socialist outlook can only share loss and create a new elite group among the working class (Bagchi 1982; Ahluwalia 1985). It implies that current trends in development violate the principle of both Swadeshi and equity.

The true spirit of Swadeshi and equity will be sabotaged, once we consider the regional dimensions of growth and poverty. For instance, the per capita income of Punjab at current prices was Rs. 8281 in 1990-91. Meanwhile, poverty is registered more in Bihar than in Punjab.

We have been blindly following the footsteps of western type of industrialization. As a result, the country adopted a growth pole-strategy without giving much attention to the regional dispersal of industrialization and agricultural development (Shekhar 1982, Singh 1995, Tewari 1988, Alagh 1983).

The orientation was that certain States industrialized faster and others lagged behind. A striking feature is that the States with higher per capita income (Punjab and Haryana) are not as industrially progressed as Maharashtra and Gujarat which are relatively industrialized but have less per capita income than the first category. Meanwhile, Punjab and Haryana are advanced on the agricultural front. This further signifies the Gandhian idea of rural development. In addition, the regional concentration of growth, i.e., industrialization in Maharashtra and Gujarat and agricultural growth in Punjab and Haryana negates the Swadeshi principle of local development. The contention is that

Gandhian development underscores decentralized local development in place of higher growth concentrated in a few hands and spaces. Because western style of development marks greater numerical strength with less 'trickling down effect'.

Apart from the regional dispersion, there is the question of social inequality. If we try to identify people with low income and high incidence of poverty, they belong to the group of Dalits (Economic Survey). The extent of poverty is more among the Scheduled Tribes than the Scheduled Castes (Prabhu 1994).

It may be heartbreaking to note that the percentage of dalits is higher in States like Bihar, Orissa, MP and UP. These States, except MP are normally ranked at the lowest bottom among the major States and MP is placed in the middle. It implies that one of the contributing factors of backwardness of these States is the presence of downtrodden classes in large numbers. It is also equally notable that the incidence of poverty is very high among these groups. Thus, backwardness of India is concentrated spatially and demographically. Gandhi was able to judge this lacuna in Indian economy due to which emphasized upon the programmes for the upliftment of the dalits. In short, Gandhian concept of development pursued and underlined the need for the social and economic emancipation of the downtrodden classes.

The argument in the above section is that Gandhian mode of development doesn't consider industrialization as the only way out to end backwardness. Modern development disregards self-reliant village economies. As a result, poverty and inequality also persist spatially and demographically.

In the following section the nature of technology is examined.

Technology for Development : Gandhi's Perception?

Perhaps the most misunderstood aspect in the whole Gandhian system is his view on technology. Technology is commonly defined as the application and skill of scientific knowledge. There are two elements of technology, on the basis of its role in growth and development. They are disembodied and embodied forms of technology (Solow, 1957; Nelson, 1966). Growth contribution will take place in two ways. One is the increased and better use of inputs like labour and capital and the other is the growth in the output without any change in the used quantity of capital and labour. The former is known as embodied form of technology. Embodied technology can further be subdivided into labour-embodied and capital-embodied technology. Here, technology does not directly contribute to growth and development, instead it enters into the inputs to upgrade skill and efficiency. This, in turn, enhances the volume of output.

The categorization made above is very much essential to judge Gandhian view on technology and its impact on development. The common criticism against Gandhian view on technology is that it is neither progressive nor tuned to the writings on the walls. Once we make a survey through *Young India* and other marked writings by Gandhi, it would become clear that he was against labour-saving technology or capital intensity. In other words, he favoured a technology that would foster employment and output rather than output as such. That is why we argued early that Gandhian style of development disregards mere numerical exercise in growth. He, in fact, wanted a technology with a human face.

Let us make a quick look at the reality in Indian economy. India opted for the import of technology immediately after the independence. Reserve Bank of India (RBI) surveys on foreign collaboration show that flow of foreign technology continued till the mid-sixties and later declined till the late 1970s. The flow further enhanced in the 1980s and became extensive by 1990s (Subramanian, 1995). As a part of the policy for self-reliance which is the cornerstone in 'Swadeshi idea'—government fostered import substitution through direct investment in the R and D front. Government also inspired other agencies to adapt foreign technology. Import substitution was a success up to 1965, but slowed down after that period (Ahluwalia, 1985; Pitre, 1977, 1979).

At present India has no sound policy on import substitution and her investment on R and D has been declining since 1990. It implies that the urge for self-reliance (Swadeshi) will persist only if there is selective flow of foreign technology and the parallel provision for more R and D expenditure (Subramanian, 1987). The policy on import substitution also needs to be stream-lined more effectively. In short, our overall technological policy is not in tune with the Gandhian perception of development.

Foreign collaboration caused excess flow of capital and technology to India (Kidron 1965; Balasubramaniam, 1971). It implies that we have been importing capital embodied technology which was unable to accommodate the locally available labour force and other resources. The essence of Swadeshi is to rely on local resources and thereby to reduce cost and foster self-reliance. Empirical studies show that capital intensity increased when there was free flow of technology and it reduced when import of technology was regulated (Ahluwalia, 1991; Raj, 1984; Subramanian, 1987). It is further found that employment in the organized manufacturing sector was either stagnant or less when the economy was decontrolled. Thus, we imported more capital-embodied technology than labour-embodied technology. It may further be noted that employment generation did not increase at the same rate as the rise in capital formation. Capital formation increased from 14.3 per cent during the first plan to 24.1 per cent at the end of the seventh plan while employment rose form 3.3 million to 2.8 crore during the same period. The latent rise in labour force was absorbed to agricultural, small-scale and informal sectors (Patric, 1996). These sectors have very high local linkage and labour absorption capacity and require less capital. Gandhi was against development which substituted capital for labour and had no safeguards for labour. He was against labour displacing technology and not technology as such. Thus, Gandhian perception favours disembodied and labour-embodied technologies and disregards capital-embodied technology, if it displaces labour and local resources. This underlies the principle of Swadeshi on one side and equity on the other side, through the preponderance for labour employment.

Swadeshi as a mass movement can resist the unnecessary flow of capital and technology in any country. This is not only a historical fact but can be used as a shield through demand side. It is well accepted that there exists a strong international market for technology. Demand for technology comes from the investors of the host country. The official policy may sometimes be in favour of such agreements but may be against the larger interest of the country. Then the public can resort to many methods to shield it. One of the fruitful and peaceful way is to foster the use of locally made commodities. As we know, the exchange of a commodity does not take place, if demand is absent. Here, Swadeshi advocates that consumers will refrain from the consumption of foreign goods, if they are locally available thereby giving preference to goods which are manufactured with inappropriate technology. Even if public pressure or debate fails, each consumer can individually resist the aggressive nature of foreign technology or commodity-embodied technology.

Conclusion

Industrialization-oriented modern development disregarded self-reliant village economies. This lopsidedness reflected in the flow of foreign technology which was capital-embodied and less employment oriented. This also contributed to the high incidence of poverty and inequality spatially and demographically. What Gandhian way of development suggests is the village economics. We may opt for a labour friendly technology so that poverty and inequality can be minimized. Above all, Swadeshi can be used as a shield against the intrusion of foreign products and technology via the forces of demand.

References

Ahluwalia, I. J., 1985 *Industrial Growth in India*, New Delhi : Oxford University Press.

1991, 'Productivity and Growth in Indian Manufacturing', New Delhi : Oxford University Press.

Bagchi, A.K., 1982 'Public Sector Industry and Quest for Self-Reliance in India', *Economic and Political Weekly*, May, 24.

Balasubramaniam 'V.M., 1971 'Foreign Collaboration in Indian Industry', *Economic and Political Weekly*, November, 27.

Kidron, M., 1965 'Foreign Investments in India : A Review', *Economic Weekly*, August, 27.

Kurien, C.T., 1978 *Poverty, Planning and Social Transformation*, Oxford Publishing House.

Pitre, V., 1977 'A Study of Factor Intensities in Indian Manufacturing Set up with Reference to Import Substitution', *Artha Vinjana,* Vol. 19, No. 2.

—, 1979 'Import Substitution in Machinery and Transport Equipment Sector–1960-70', *Economic and Political Weekly*, July, 21.

Raj, K.N., 1984 'Economic Growth in India, 1952-53 to 1982-83', *Economic and Political Weekly*, October, 13.

Shekher, A.U., 1982 'Trends in Interstate Disparities in Industrial Development in India, 1961-75', *Indian Economic Journal*, Vol. 30, No. 2, October-December.

Singh, P., 1995 *Regional Aspects of Industrialisation in India*, New Delhi, Deep and Deep Publication.

Solow, R.M., 1957 'Technical Change and the Aggregate Production Function', *Review of Economics and Statistics*, 39.

Subramanian, K.K., 1981 'Towards Technological Self-reliance : An Assessment in Indian Industries, in the Development Process of Indian Economy', Brahmanda and Panchamaki, (eds.) New Delhi, Himalaya Publishing House.

—, 1990 'India's New Approach to Multinational Corporations and Technology Transfer', *Asian Journal of Economic and Social Studies*.

Tewari, R.I., 1983 'Inter-regional Pattern of Industrialisation in India', *Indian Economic Journal,* Vol. 36, October-December.

Alagh, Y.K., 1988 *Regional Dimension of Indian Agriculture in the Indian Economy : Recent Development and Future Prospects*, Robert, E.B. Lucas and Gustav, F. Papanek (eds.), Oxford University Press.

Patrick, M., 1977 'Emergence of Entrepreneurship and Linkage in Informal Sector in Kerala', unpublished Ph.D thesis, Cochin University.

Prabhu, P., 'Tribals in Alternative Interest Research Survey 1933-94', Public Interest Research Group, April, 1994.

Economic Survey, Govt. of India (1995-96).

18

Sarvodaya As a Strategy for Development

Midatala Rani

"If man is to survive, if civilization is to survive and flower in freedom, truth and decency, the remainder of the twentieth century and what lies beyond must belong not to Marx or Lenin, Mao or Trotsky, but to Mahatma Gandhi".

Louis Fischer
(Well known Biographer of Mahatma Gandhi.)

It is very ironical that Mahatma Gandhi is commonly regarded as a great political leader and not much of a social leader. Political importance is attached to Gandhi as he was closely associated with India's freedom struggle. But very few, however, know that he was a great social leader.

Gandhi and Social Revolution

Change and growth are the conditions of life in this world. All prophets of mankind have helped in this change to better our life and help in the process of all round evolution. Gandhi is a unique revolutionary leader, who emphasised upon the need for change in both the individual and society. He believed that this change should be brought about simultaneously. To him, change should not come through external pressure but through inward change. He succinctly said:

If inward change is achieved, the outward change takes care of itself".

Social Change

In order to achieve social change, Gandhi advocated three phases of change. Firstly, there should be a change in the thought structure of the people. Secondly, there should be a change in the life of the people. Lastly, there should be a change in various relationships in life. All these changes should be brought together for all round revolutionary transformation of an individual. Thus Gandhi's idea of social change may be described as the ideological combination of two schools of thought namely, 'pacifism' and 'social revolution'. Elements of these two traditions converged to produce the 'Nonviolent' revolution.

Social revolution to Gandhi was a continuous process. But he rejected the idea of violence to bring about a social revolution. Gandhian social revolution was a two sided one. One, he termed as 'Satyagraha' or civil resistance and the other side being 'Sarvodaya' which is the essence of social reform. In 1931, he stated that his work of social reform was not subordinate to political work and that social work was impossible without political work. Hence, he maintained that he had taken to the latter only with the hope that it will help to achieve the former.

The Gandhian concept of Satyagraha rejects the biological concept of the struggle for existence and survival of the fittest. It rejects Hobbe's conception of human life as 'the struggle of all against all'. It rather believes in mutual cooperation as the basis of social intercourse and human progress.

The concept of Sarvodaya means universal upliftment or welfare of all men and not just the welfare of the greatest, happiness of the greatest number as believed, but the Utilitarians, or with the modern view of judging an affluent society with the yardsticks of Gross National Product.

The objectives of social change for which Gandhi strove have been clearly laid in his writings and speeches. His views greatly inspired the political and social leaders of the times. It was therefore natural that when the Constitution of India was drafted, the views of Gandhi were reflected in it. The ideas of Gandhi with regard to social change can be understood within the general framework of his ideas of non-violence and democracy. He claimed that his ideas of social change have come to him naturally and have not emanated from any book but from his innate belief of non-violence.

Global Grassroots Development

Development is a very attractive concept and in recent years, it is assuming increasing importance. As an American scholar, T.H. Brann has rightly noted:

> The whole world is caught up in the concept of development—there seems to be no escape from it.

Reflecting on its use, eminent Indian sociologist, Dube writes:

> During the last three decades, development has occupied the centre of the stage in reflection and action, concerning man's present and future. Prodigious industry has been invested in it.

The development debate began with concentration on economic development. Gradually, it has moved towards an emphasis on human development. To further human development, it is moving on one hand from national development to global development as 'global village' is fast becoming a reality at the hands of modern technology. The logic of development coupled with the logic of democracy, has high potentialities of humanizing, globalizing and at the same time localizing or grassrooting of the development process. This logic is contributing to the growth of a new ideology called 'Developmentalism'.

In the postwar period when the concept of development began, focus was on the social, economic and political spheres of human life, ideologically moulded in the 'westernization' or 'modernization' model. But, the West-oriented development process proved to be inadequate. Doubts were expressed whether it was leading to development or only development of underdevelopment or dependence on the west. The big gap between promise and performance of the traditional model and between the resulting growth and social justice led to a more humanistic (man-centered) and universal understanding of development.

The very concept of 'social justice' is not very new. Several political philosophers have given attention to it. J.S. Mill pleaded for reforms in liberalism to achieve it. Karl Marx advocated for a political revolution for the purpose. T.H. Green favoured positive freedom to realize it. Fabian socialist like H.J. Laski stood for it. The postwar planning in Europe, the New Deal Programmes and attempts for a welfare State were all efforts in this direction. But, the gap between growth and social justice proved the inadequacy of these calls and therefore the cry was towards social justice.

In the seventies and eighties of this century, the value of social justice in development came to be reiterated. In early seventies, a Brazilian scholar, Dennis Goulet defined development more humanly. He considered development as a total social change of a responsive and responsible nature from a less human condition to more human condition. This was followed by the 'Cocoyoc Declaration' of 1974. It emphasized that the purpose of development should not be to develop 'things' but to develop 'man'. Rejecting the gaps in development, the declaration noted:

> The goal is not to 'catch up' but to ensure the quality of life for all with a productive base, compatible with the needs of the future generation.

On strategy for development, the Cocoyoc Declaration highlighted, 'increased national self-reliance.... trust in people and nations, reliance on the capacity of people themselves to invent and generate new resources and techniques, to increase their capacity to absorb them, to put them to socially beneficial use, to take a measure of command over the economy and to generate their own way of life' Further, 'the growth with justice' slogan in India in mid-seventies is an example of humanistic concern in development. The development debate is gradually coming closer to Gandhian concept of Sarvodaya, through Antyodaya.

Gandhi's Preseription of Sarvodaya through Antyodya

The Gandhian ideas and model have not been precisely stated. In fact, Gandhi never believed in starting any 'ism' including Gandhism. For him, 'truth' was never final and he believed that life was a continuous 'experiment' with truth. He reposed a lot of faith in truth and his was a kind of scientific openness. One has to infer his ideas from his experiments with truth in action and a vast body of Gandhian literature, and in a continuous dialogue with life.

In his younger days, Gandhi was greatly influenced by Tolstoy and John Ruskin. John Ruskin influenced him in developing his philosophy of 'Sarvodaya'. Ruskin's Book *Unto the Last* had a profound impact on Gandhi. He translated the book into Gujarati and called it *Sarvodaya* or welfare of all. The book defined the three basic principles of Sarvodaya. They included the following :

(i) The good of the individual is contained in the good of the society.

(ii) The lawyer's job is as good as a barber's work.

(iii) The life of the tiller of the soil and the artisan is worth living.

Development is a complex task and involves growth with justice. Obviously, a complex task needs a number of complex and comprehensive strategies. Some of them are, mixed economy strategy, liberalization, debureaucratization, sustainable development strategy etc. The concern of this chapter is on Sarvodaya as a strategy for development.

The basic prerequisites of the Sarvodaya strategy are as follows :

Sarvodaya

Etymologically, 'Sarvodaya' means the well-being and development of all people. It believes in transforming the individual on the one hand and changing the social setup on the other. This is because a good social structure can be achieved only when there is a proper development of individual morality. Sarvodaya visualises the creation of a new society, based on non-violent social order. The Sarvodaya strategy does not repose faith in class struggle or domination. On the contrary, it emphasizes on harmony and ethical virtues of life. Humanism is the basis of Sarvodaya, because it does not differentiate man from man.

In short, the principles of Sarvodaya are as follows:

(a) Moral and human values must reign supreme in our economic and social reconstruction from the grassroot levels.

(b) Natural life based on agriculture is the most appropriate basis of livelihood planning.

(c) Basic unit for a Sarvodaya society is a small face to face community structured on principles of cooperation and collective endeavour.

(d) An educated, morally upright, non-violent individual is the central focus in Sarvodaya.

(e) Sarvodaya visualizes the goal of a simple, self-restrained life style in its campaign for constructive revolution, based on non-violence.

Antyodya

One of the crucial question in the entire development debate is 'whose development?' The answer to this lies in Antyodaya or the development of the hindermost. Antya or the weakest in society, if developed obviously leads to Sarvodaya. Hence, 'Sarvodaya' through

'Antyodaya' assumes importance. Protection of the being and promotion of the becoming of the Antya could certainly lead to a more humane development. At the macro level, 'Antya' can be identified by the poverty line (economically) and backward classes (socially). This work may be entrusted to committees and commissions. At the micro level, identifying 'Antya' is the function of Gramsabha or locality. Indian experience clearly shows that 'Antya' experiments are quite old and many.

Aparigraha

The meaning of Sanskrit word 'Aparigraha' is non-acquisition in excess of need. As per the Gandhian model, the goal of economic life of each individual in society is not maximization of wants and acquisition and consumption of material things. Sarvodaya demands that each individual must adhere to Aparigraha at some reasonable point and make way to others to get their minimum share. If this is not done, the social benefits will not be sufficient for everybody to share to promote Sarvodaya.

Trusteeship

The Gandhian concept of 'Trusteeship' is related to the property system. Under it, property belongs to all and the holder manages it and takes care of it only as a socially responsible trustee. It paves way to an economic system, based neither on private property nor on State property or profit motive but on trusteeship.

Man-centered Appropriate Technology

In a society, where labour is in abundance, the 'Technology' should be man-centered and labour-intensive. Man should become the producer and it should lead to mass production. It calls for such technology that would decentralize power to the village or locality, based on surplus human labour, small machine and appropriate technology.

Decentralization and Consensus Decision Making

Gandhian model emphasizes upon decentralized social, economic and political system starting with village republics (Gramswaraj) organized upwards in a loose confederation from Gramsabha to Loksabha.

Consensus decision making is another principle of Gandhism. It rejects the idea of majority rule and party system as the basis of democracy in order to avoid majority tyranny and division of society on party lines.

Lokniti or People's Policy

Walter Lipman terms 'Lokniti' as 'Public Philosophy'. Politics is looked upon as an agency of service and not as an instrument of power. 'Raj' and 'Rajniti' (State and State Policy) will be replaced by 'Lok' and 'Lokniti' (Public and Public Policy). People in the local communities will have to find policy solutions to all their problems.

It may be noted that the Gandhian model of development is an autonomous one. After the country attained independence, Jawaharlal Nehru incorporated the Gandhian ideas in the Constitution. Further, socialist policies and programmes were also initiated in the country. Thus, Nehru's experiments have retained a Gandhian touch in India's developmental process. The Gandhian model of Sarvodaya is unparalleled in its universal, human and moral values. It is the forerunner in the growth with social justice concerns of the Cocoyoc Declaration, human touch of Dennis Goulet and the emerging human theme in economic development. The greatest challenge in human development today is to go back and experiment towards Gandhian dream of Sarvodaya through Antyodaya.

Evaluation of the Gandhian Model

India is still an agriculture oriented economy. Agriculture is the second main contributor to national income and more importantly two-third of the population finds agriculture as their primary source of living. The importance of Gandhi must be understood in this context.

Today, when there is a crisis in our national character, Gandhism becomes all the more pertinent. The Gandhi bashing should not be a mere rhetoric in the battle for votes. As rightly said by Atal Behari Vajpayee way back in 1978, "We may all become fashionable Gandhians tomorrow ... nothing will be worse than paying lip service to Gandhi's ideals and not applying them".

Development is of great concern to the underdeveloped countries consisting of new nations. Now, development is the movement of people from a less human condition to a better human condition. It has a universal and humane connotation. Development is not of one person or few people but of all people i.e. Sarvodaya. As such, a global effort at Antyodaya would lead to a balanced growth and a better world order for all. 'Think Globally and Act Locally' is an age-old adage. Even though Antyodaya demands this, global thinking must be followed by global action always.

Finally, development as a 'just change' basically involves change of values, change of context, change of instrument. The change of values needed is from 'Selfishness' to 'need' and 'war' to 'peace'. The change in context needed is from exploitation to democracy and sharing. The change of instruments needed is from centralized national bureaucracy to a decentralized one, participating management of all local, regional and global concerned. This is the dream of Gandhian humanism and logic of developmentalism too, which has been growing into an ideology of a 'just change' i.e. Sarvodaya through Antyodaya. If this ideology is effectively handled, perhaps it will solve the economic crisis that confronts mankind both at the national and global level today.

It remains to be seen to what extent the new coalition Government in India will live up to its twin promises of thrust on 'Swadeshi' and 'Human Face' in economic development. A new human civilization needs to be built by using the Gandhian legacy in the best possible manner.

References

1. B.N. Asthana, 1977, 'Social Change via Village industries' in, J.S. Mathur and P.C. Sharma, *Non-violence and Social Change*, p. 9. Ahmedabad : Navajivan Publishing House.
2. *Collected Works of Mahatma Gandhi*, Vol. 34, p. 506, Publications Division, Government of India, New Delhi.
3. *Ibid,* Vol. 55, p. 62.
4. R. Achuthan, 'Gandhi and Social Change'. In J.S. Mathur and P.C. Sharma, (eds.) *Non-violence and Social Changes,* p. 228, *op. cit.*
5. *Gandhi Marg*, Vol. 18, No. 1, April-June 1996, p. 91.

6. J.B. Kripalani, 1970, *Gandhi : His Life and Thought*, p. 345. New Delhi, Publications Division, Government of India.
7. Glyn Richards, 1991, *The Philosophy of Gandhi*, p. 56. New Delhi, Rupa and Co.
8. Morarji Desai, 'Gandhi and the Destiny of Man', in *Mahatma Gandhi - 100 years*, p. 65.
9. *Harijan*, April 20, 1940, p. 96.
10. Norman D.Palmer, 1977, 'Development : The Need for an Affective Dialogue', in S.K. Sharma (ed.), 'Dynamics of Development', Vol. 1, p. 65, New Delhi, Concept Publishers.
11. S.C. Dube, 1983 'Development Perspectives for the 1980s ', p. 1. New Delhi, Abhinav Publishers.
12. M. Umapathy, 1994, *The Development Debate: The Missing Questions*, Preface., p. ii., Mysore, Manu Publishers.
13. For more details on the defects of the Western model read, *Ibid,* p. 10-13.
14. Dennis Goulet, 'Notes on the Ethics of Development Assistance '(unpublished paper), cited in Norman D. Palmer, *op. cit.,* in S.K. Sharma (ed.,) *op. cit.,* p. 97-98.
15. The 'Cocoyoc Declaration', is a statement adopted at the International Symposium on 'Patterns of Resources Use, Environment and Development Strategies', sponsored by UNDP and UNCTAD, held at Cocoyoc in Mexico in October 1974.
16. Norman D. Palmer, *op. cit.* in S.K. Sharma (ed.), *op. cit.,* p. 97-98.
17. Loc. cit.
18. Loc. cit.
19. It may be noted that during Mrs. Indira Gandhi's period, particularly during the emergency period, popular slogans like 'growth with justice' and anti-poverty programmes were started.

20. *Collected Works of Mahatma Gandhi*, Publications Division, Government of India, New Delhi. Also read Raghavan Iyer, *The Social and Political Thought of Mahatma Gandhi*', Cambridge, (1973).

21. M.K. Gandhi, *Sarvodaya (Welfare of All),* Ahmedabad : Navajivan Publications.

22. S.N. Sinha, 1990 *Gandhian Philosophy of Sarvodaya*, p. 129. New Delhi, Classical Publishing Company.

23. Read K. Zelinsky's Article, 'The Intellectual and the Revolution, Culture and Life', *Moscow Journal*, November, 1957, Preface, p. iii.

24. Based on lecture, delivered by K.S.Narayanaswamy, Secretary, Gandhi Peace Foundation, Bangalore Centre, at Academic Staff College, Mysore, on, 'Development - The Gandhian 'Perspective'.

25. M. Umapathy, *op. cit.,* p. 55.

26. G. Thimmaiah, 1993, *Power Politics and Social Justice*, New Delhi, Sage.

27. Noshir Bilpodiwala, 1963, *The Social Order and the Sarvodaya*, p. 58, Rajghat, Varanasi.

28. For a detailed discussion read K.S. Narayanaswamy, 'Lokniti or People's Policy', in *Gandhi Margs*, Vol. II, No. 3, p. 121-131.

29. Economic Survey, 1995-96.

30. Anita Joshua, 1994 'A Return to Gandhi'. In., *The Hindu,* 2 October.

31. Cited in *Star of Mysore* (a local newspaper), 19 March, 1998.

32. M. Umapathy, *op. cit.,* p. 71.

33. Based on Prime Minister A.B. Vajpayee's interview to press reporters at New Delhi. As reported in Delhi Doordarshan News Bulletin., on 18 -19 March, 1998.

Acknowledgement

M. Umapathy, 'The Development Debate : The Missing Questions', Manu Publishers, Mysore (1994). This book has been extensively used by this writer, for which she expresses her gratitude to the author of the book.

19

Relevance of Gandhian Social Order

N. Durairaj; Kala Rani Rengasamy

> "We, who follow Gandhi Maharaj's lead, have one thing in common among us; we never fill our purses with spoils from the poor nor bend our knees to the rich."
>
> *Rabindranath Tagore*

In a world where the rulers of nations are relying more and more on brute force and the nations trusting their lives and hopes, to systems which represent the very denial of law and brotherhood. Gandhi stands out as an isolated but most impressive figure. He is a ruler, obeyed by millions not because they are afraid of him, but because they love him, not as the master of wealth and secret police and machine guns, but holding that spiritual authority which, when it dares assert itself, seems to reduce the values of the material world, almost to impotence.

Gandhi was a social reformer. Perhaps he was first among those who had identified a close correlation between social processes and political emancipation. It was Gandhi, who rightly felt that so long as Indian society did not emancipate itself from the age-old social disabilities and evils, it would not be possible for it to build a collective conscience, necessary to liquidate the vast British Raj. Gandhi stood for the abolition of such disabilities and practices which had created social distances, differentiation and socially damaging rankings by fortifying all opportunities for social cohesion and solidarity. By this, he referred to the removal of untouchability, poverty, dowry, inequality and exploitation which had eaten the vitals of Indian society.

Gandhi has conceived a social order in which there is no stratification based on ascription; no exploitation between the propertied and the peasant classes and it would be a society in which the assigned roles could be performed on the idiom of moral-ethical normative structure. Further, in such a society there is an equality of men and the institution of dowry and polygamy have no place. By all means Gandhi wished to emancipate Indian society from evils.

Way out of the Present Crisis

We are living in a world of material abundance and intellectual power, yet, peace is in peril. The crisis, faced by us is neither material nor economic. It is not an intellectual crisis either. It is a moral and spiritual crisis. We cannot decide and choose between the pleasure that is immediate or the joy that comes after travails. The modern man is not properly adjusted to this new world of immense scientific knowledge and great technological powers. Instead, there is a feeling of discontentment, of anxiety and even despair. Nations do not trust nations, individuals suspect each other. It is in this context that faith must be recovered.

Sarvodaya makes that attempt of reorienting human mind and reconstructing human society. Sarvodaya means the welfare and prosperity of all. All must progress together with collective interest. Prosperity is not beneficial in vacuum. In mundane life, it is concerned with the availability of the essential materials for its continuance - food and a home. These are obtained through money. Hence, money too has to be obtained or acquired, but there is a warning 'wealth earned without moral and spiritual considerations leads to animality.' When man becomes acquisitive, he cares for no frontiers and it leads to social imbalances. Sarvodaya prescribes checks against these imperfections of human mind and soul and endures to put men on the track which may lead him to real social happiness.

Mahatma Gandhi makes it clear in one of his speeches that Sarvodaya is not his innovation. It is rather a stream of thought from ancient times. He has only arranged man's conscience to that great reality—a way of life, which once was and now should be. The Vedas and Upanishads have proclaimed the life of equality in ancient times so also all the scriptures of the world. He, therefore induces people to come round to help the *daridranarayana* to eliminate the difference between rich and poor.

Romain Rolland rightly observes:

> To understand Gandhi's activity it should be realised that his doctrine is like a huge edifice, composed of two different floors

and grades. Below is the solid ground work, the basic foundation of religion. On this vast and unshakable foundation is based the political and social campaign. This is quite natural, for Gandhi believed that only properly chastened men and women would bring nearer the goal of Sarvodaya.

Instead of rights, Gandhi taught the importance of acknowledging duties. Instead of possession and rightful claim, he taught people about Aparigraha or non-possession and non-hoarding. He was a Socratic, a Buddhist, a Jain, a Christian, a Sufi and a Vedic sage on this account.

To have such a nice character, Gandhi believed in the goodness of human nature and that human nature is never beyond redemption. Man is derailed by evil, presented in a beautiful garb. It has been noted that Gandhi did not divide life into spiritual and material or secular sectors. To him spiritual is practical. Hence, the formula of self-purification to see the universe and all-pervading spirit of truth and unity, speaks for itself and the person who aspires after that, must be able to love the meanest of creation as oneself.

As Gandhi believed, all global problem could no doubt be resolved through moral and spiritual consciousness.

When Gandhian scheme of social order is followed—authority, compulsion, exploitation, etc., have no place; because he never advocated the change of social order through the force of State but pleaded for spontaneity in which the ethical soundness was a driving force.

20

Gandhi's Concept of Social Change

Padma Ramakrishnan

With the advent of British rule in India and the western impact in general, the superstructure of political, social and economic institutions underwent a radical transformation, whose outward expression was the nationalist movement. Gandhi became the symbol and the moving spirit behind this movement. Some of the socio-religious movements of the earlier period like the Brahmo Samaj, the Arya Samaj and the Ramakrishna Mission had highlighted many ills and evils pervading society, especially Hindu society, and they had sought to eradicate and eliminate them and thus create a new reformed society. These movements also created the proper atmosphere, climate and background for the national movement by championing individual liberty and social equality. In 1920, when Gandhi emerged as the most important champion of Indian nationalism, he became heir to this rich legacy. He continued and carried on the efforts for a political, social, economic and religious change.

It is difficult to analyse and assess Gandhi's concept of social change since it was part of his total programme of a political, social and religious change. Gandhi functioned as a political leader, a social reformer and a religious reformer. He was also a saint, a prophet and a philosophical anarchist. This combination of many and varied roles in the same man, makes it difficult to isolate his role in one field from another. At times, it is almost impossible to reconcile his one role with the other. For example, his role as a Hindu religious reformer almost clashed with that of his role as a national leader. To many Muslims, he appeared as a Hindu leader and they were critical of his style of functioning in public life. Also many of his followers, both Indian and western were perplexed by his inconsistent (to them) utterances and actions.

But to Gandhi, there was no doubt or controversy about his multiplicity of roles. He would function simultaneously as a religious and social reformer and as a nationalist leader. This is because he conceived of society as a whole integrated unit, in which social change could not be accomplished without corresponding political and economic change. Therefore Gandhi's concept of social change is part and parcel of his concept of political, economic and religious transformation.

Gandhi's ideal of a society was one that was based on truth and non-violence. These were the twin pillars to prop up a just and human social order bereft of inequities and inequalities. But Indian society was far removed from this ideal. It was cast, class ridden full of contradictions and disparities. These fissures were horizontal, vertical, political, social, economic, religious and cultural. First of all, the rulers were the British masters and Indians were a subject people. Racial bitterness poisoned the relations between the two. Secondly, Hindus and Muslims were antagonistic to each other and this inherent contradiction was almost irreconcilable. Therefore change was required on all these fronts and Gandhi had to tackle all these problems simultaneously.

Gandhi was a reformer, a revivalist and a revolutionary. He was a creative reformer who sought to change society by precept and example, by words, deeds and action. He tried to reconstruct Indian society by concentrating his attacks on feudalism, superstition and other corrupt practices. He was a revivalist because he worked within the framework of the Hindu Philosophical tradition. In India as is well known, any social question affecting the Hindu community is bound up with religious consideration. This is a deep-rooted instinct. Therefore any social reformer has to fight against religious and semi-divine forces, resting upon traditional instinct and reinforced by religious convictions. Like Chaitanya before him, Gandhi encountered the same difficulty when he tried to reform Hindu society. Gandhi was a revolutionary but minus violence. His tactic of change was through non-violence. Gandhi made non-violence a practical method of action. He translated an idea into a technique and developed it, step by step over a span of forty years. With this single weapon, Gandhi could organise effective social and political action. Thus, Gandhi's approach shunned violent measures as a medium of change. From the days of Hind Swaraj he had been advocating the reordering of social relationships but without resort to violence.

Gandhi's approach to social change was diametrically opposed to that of the Marxists. Many Marxist thinkers considered Gandhi to be a leader of the Indian bourgeoisie. But they also agreed that Gandhi did not always function as a representative of that class. Gandhi's sympathies lay with the poorer classes and masses. Gandhi never justified the violence and nor he deviated from the non-violence. He strictly adhered to certain basic moral values. The change that he desired to bring about, was a moral and psychological change. His style of functioning was both liberal and democratic. He had no faith in violent outbursts nor revolutionary overthrow of existing social order. Unlike the Marxists, he did not think that class struggle was inevitable. He repeatedly affirmed that his non-violent technique could be invoked for social transformation and as well as for anti-colonial struggle.

Like any other creative philosopher, Gandhi struggled for a radical social transformation and emancipation. Gandhi wanted to free individuals from oppressive political and social systems. But the uniqueness of Gandhi's concept of social change lies in the fact that his method—non-violent as it was—disarmed the enemy and evoked no ill will towards the forces and agents of change. That is to say, Gandhi's Satyagraha or soul-force did not aim at destroying the foe; rather it sought to effect a change in him and in his mental outlook. In the 1930s, Gandhi advised and begged the rulers of princely States to divest themselves of their riches and pomp and undertake democratic reforms in their domains. What he sought to achieve, was an escape from the vicious circle of violence and exploitation and not the substitution of one set of oppressors by another. Gandhi's concept of social change—the non-violent method—is not a withdrawal from or resignation to oppression. He wrote:

> Non-violence is not a resignation from all real fighting against wickedness; on the contrary, the nonviolence of my conception is a more active and real fight against wickedness.

Gandhi contemplated a mental and therefore moral opposition to immoralities. He saw the impracticality of any attempt to reform society through violent methods. Gandhi's counsel against the violent strategy of revolutionary action was not a counsel of futility; rather it was a counsel for a practical, effective and emancipatory technique of action. For bringing about the liberated society of his conception, he held that the entire social order had got to be reconstructed. According to him, what was needed was a method or technique of action that would eliminate not only social evils but political, economic and moral evils also. In Gandhi's view, violent methods would not end the system of oppression; on the contrary, violent means perpetuated and strengthened the oppressive system. "What was required", he said, "was not a method of elimination or destruction but a programme of transformation of relationships". The Satyagrahis, according to Gandhi, should seek to transform oppressive social relations, by :

(a) persuasion

(b) reasoning

(c) self-suffering and

(d) through noncooperation and civil disobedience.

Satyagraha, therefore excludes the use of violence in any shape or form. In this context, Gandhi attached the greatest importance to the Constructive Programme—the promotion of inter-communal unity, the removal of untouchability, adult education and the removal of social and economic inequalities. This novel technique of transforming oppressive social relations seeks to root out the deeper, inner, psychological sources of oppression and subordination. "The oppressed", Gandhi said, "must overcome their psychology of submission, which acts as the enemy within oneself. According to Gandhi, in the application of the method of non-violence, one must believe in the possibility of every person—however deprived—being reformed under a human and skilled treatment.

Gandhi followed the democratic method of bringing about social change. It was a method of 'civilised conflict resolution' whether in the political or social arena. He modified the liberal constitutional methods, so that he could creatively apply them to Indian situations, in his efforts to set in motion a social reform movement or initiating a political action. By insisting on the purity of means and ends Gandhi provided the moral framework for right action, whether political or social. He had conceived of a stateless and classless society which was consistent only with a decentralized economy and polity. This was the socialist society of his conception, a Sarvodaya society. He was opposed to violence as a means for bringing about any change or for that matter, for maintaining peace. He therefore, attempted to operationalize and perfect the instrument of non-violent action, based on truth. To fight injustice and oppression, he invoked the concept of trusteeship. To end exploitation, he prescribed the instrument of Satyagraha.

In a non-violent social order as envisaged by Gandhi, there is no room for : .

(a) poverty,

(b) exploitation,

(c) inequality,

(d) industrialism,

(e) unrestrained individualism,

(f) centralization.

Such an ideal-type of social order could be realized only through a process of social change which invoked truth and non-violence and more positively, was imbued with the spirit of love and brotherhood. As far as the Gandhian concept of social change is concerned, there could be no compromise with these principles.

21

Gandhi and Social Revolution

P. Gopinathan Pillai

Gandhi, like all prophets, gave to the world a vision of life based on truth and non-violence, which necessarily involved immediate suffering but the ultimate supremacy of the moral values of human life, as well. Gandhism, as an ideology emerged from the Indian social realities. The 'Gandhi Yug', which lasted for nearly three decades in India, transformed our whole country and also influenced the ideology of many millions throughout the world.

We, the people of India, follow his teachings and many of us call ourselves his disciples or followers in social life. Our present government is said to be run on Gandhian lines. It is an ideology patterned on Gandhian lines which helped us in righting the wrongs of our country by non-violent means and that has gone a long way towards making India a political nation, earning the respect of many unprejudiced countries for its rapid democratic progress on the basis of coexistence.

Gandhi and Marx

Since the French Revolution, the modern world has produced two great revolutionaries, Marx and Gandhi. The former believed in a violent revolution to end an unjust, inequitable and antisocial order, while the latter believed that a real revolution to end the tyranny and oppression of the weak by the strong could only be carried out through resisting evil without deviating from the fundamentals of moral law and its cardinal principles of truth and non-violence.

Gandhi was basically a humanist, who was spiritually rich enough to be eclectic in choosing what he found to be good, yet realistic enough to be particularistic to the society, he lived in expressing and justifying his position through an unflinching commitment to practice. He was much influenced by Hindu scriptures, especially the *Gita* and by western thought—Christ, the Theosophists, Ruskin and Tolstoy.

Truth and Non-violence

The basic tenet of the Gandhian outlook is its supreme emphasis on the ethical side of life. He equated religion with Truth and Ahimsa. Gandhi explained that truth and non-violence were not virtues closed within themselves, but were just as applicable in court and legislation itself or in the marketplace. Spiritual and moral values did not form an independent field of action but were apparent and realizable when applied to practical problems in society. Thus, Gandhi's ideas about politics and national economy may in principle be studied as the fields of application of self-realization and morality. Gandhi says that he approaches political matters and everything else in a religious spirit. Truth is his religion and non-violence is the only way to realize it.

According to Gandhi, real democracy is free of violence. Gandhi, called himself a 'nonviolent communist' several times. His differences with communism were not so much concerned with ends as with means. In fact, they meant a different morality. The material well-being of the majority did not, in Gandhi's view justify a violent social system.

Vision of Society

Gandhi's vision of society was based on his innate love of equality, unflinching support of individual freedom and his consistent plea for bringing about a just social order that recognized no barriers of sex, religion, language and culture. He wanted to create a classless and casteless society with decentralized system of political and economic freedom based on truth, equality and non-violence.

State and Gandhi

Gandhi, very firmly believed that the State was an instrument of coercion and thereby it was likely to sacrifice the individual at the altar of state aggrandizement. He believed that violence was an inevitable concomitant of the State and it would lead to the distortion of the objectives of the State. He visualized a society where there was a total absence of state and thereby the role of power was to be a destiny within the framework of social good.

> I value individual freedom but you must not forget that man is essentially a social being. He has risen to his present status by

learning to adjust his individualism to the requirements of social progress. Unrestricted individualism is the law of the beast of the jungle. We have learnt to strike the mean between individual freedom and social restraints. A willing submission to social restraint for the sake of wellbeing of the whole society enriches both the individual and the society of which one is the member, he observed.

Gandhi and Caste

Gandhi considered that the caste system as it existed in his own time was the antithesis of the just order of life and he was willing rather to destroy it than accept it as it stood. Gandhi's idea of the caste system differs in some respects from it original nature. The worst fault in his view was the idea of untouchablility and he devoted a large part of his life for correcting it. It is a consequence of non-violence that untouchability must be removed.

Abolishing untouchability means removing the barriers between people. We find such barriers, in one form or another, all over the world. It is not possible to abolish it with violence, it requires a change of heart and complete purification.

Another great defect in the caste system is the different valuing and rewarding of different positions. Gandhi departed completely from tradition and wanted to make all the castes of equal value. Physical work must be respected as much as the mental work of a teacher. Gandhi wanted to destroy respect for professions as a 'high and low level' and make them all equal. He said that if everyone did physical work, value differences would disappear.

Social Equality

Gandhi explained that one basis for equality was the fact that all Varnas need one another, even though it was his opinion that respect for equality was an essential consequence of the norms of natural right and non-violence. It was in the non-violent 'peace army', for example, that we could see an evident attempt to ignore caste differences.

To obtain equality, it is indispensable to raise the economic status. Economic equality is a major factor to wipe out other discriminations and to bring about equality in other spheres. The foundation of economy, especially in India, rests on land. The untouchables are all sturdy labourers. Hence, they are made to be slaves under selfish high caste people who are exploiting them. Secondly, untouchables should be given proper training, capital, tools and machines to start various industries along with credit facilities through cooperatives and nationalized banks. Thus, economic equality will go a long way to solve the social problem of untouchability and bring about social equality.

Education for Liberation

The progress of any community depends on the nature of education system. It is through the forces of both formal and non-formal education that human standards and ideals are raised. Educational development, therefore, is the essential prerequisite to the all round development of any community. If the untouchables are to be educated and made to realize their own strength and importance and stand on their own legs, proper education should be imparted to them.

Temple Entry

Once the untouchable is allowed entry into Hindu temples, the stigma attached to his community will no more be there. About this Gandhi says:

> Temple entry is the one spiritual act that would convey the message of freedom to the untouchables and assure them that they are not outcastes before God.
>
> If all that there is in the universe is pervaded by God, that is to say, if the Brahmin and the Bhangi, the learned man and the scavenger, the Ezhava and the Pariah—no matter what caste they belong to—all these are pervaded by God. In the light of this mantra there is none who is high and none who is low, all are absolutely equal, because all are the creatures of one Creator....... It enunciates an eternal truth which admits no reduction and no palliation. So, how can anyone dare to arrogate superiority to himself or herself over any other human being? I tell you therefore, that if this mantra holds good, if there is any man or woman here who believes that the temples are defiled by those (who are) called Avaranas, that person I declare, would be guilty of grave sin, he adds.

Gandhi set up an organisation, the Harijan Sevak Sangh, which worked for the removal of all the disabilities and disparities. He blessed all the marriages taking place between Harijans and caste Hindus.

Gandhi and Women's Equality

With his belief in non-violence, Gandhi was against all inequality in any walk of life—political, economic or social. He held that inequality ultimately led to exploitation, which to him was violence. Also, he held that all work, socially useful, was of equal worth, whether that of a scavenger, a doctor, a lawyer, a merchant or a minister. Hence work should get, if not equal, at least equitable remuneration. In his Ashram, all the inmates, engaged in physical or intellectual work, were treated as equal and everyone was provided with facilities, according to his or her need. Gandhi made no distinction between men and women.

Gandhi was against the pernicious system of child marriage. He considered such marriages abnormal and void and as such, no marriage at all. A child widow was not, therefore, in reality a widow but a maiden and must be treated as such.

He was against all social and religious barriers to widow remarriage. Gandhi held that if a widow could not or did not wish to live alone, she had every right to remarry and society must not look down upon such marriages.

He was against the purdah system, as it crippled not only the free movements of women but interfered with their advancement and their capacity for doing work, useful to society. Gandhi said, "To call women the weaker sex is libel, it is men's injustice to women. If by strength is meant brute strength, then indeed are women less brute than men. If by strength is meant moral power, then women are immeasurably men's superior".

Gandhi was against the evil practice of dowry system. For the middle and poor classes it was a nightmare. It was also on this account that, while there was joy on the birth of a male child, there was evident or silent mourning on the birth of a female child. Gandhi said, "Invidious discrimination against the female sex is an anachronism. I fail to see any reason for jubilation over the birth of a son and for mourning over that of a daughter. Both are God's gifts. They have an equal right to live and are equally necessary to keep the world going".

He was also against heavy expenditure in connection with marriages. He wanted to simplify marriage ceremonies.

Gandhi invited the women of India to participate in the Satyagraha movement not only because they were equal to men but also because they possessed virtues which made them superior to men in a non-violent fight which required infinite patience and uncomplaining and silent suffering.

Gandhi and Prohibition

In consonance with his idea about the simplification of life through the limitation of wants, necessary for a healthy, cultural and moral life, Gandhi wanted India to be free from the evil of the use of intoxicating drinks and drugs.

Gandhi said:

> In no part of the world is prohibition as easy to carry out as in India, for with us it is only a minority that drinks. Drinking is generally considered disreputable and there are millions, I believe, who have never known what drink is.

Constructive Programme

Gandhi took up the constructive programme and created great national movements through it. He took the educated classes, including the leaders, into the villages and among the masses through the Khadi and village industries programme. The goal of constructive work is not to provide economic relief to the unemployed or to distribute some wages to the poor but to build up a non-violent social order. The constructive works according to Gandhi are communal unity, removal of untouchability, prohibition, Khadi village industries, village sanitation, adult education, basic education, upliftment of women, health and hygiene, Rashtra Bhasha (national language), economic equality and upliftment of farmers, labourers, Adivasis, lepers, etc. Gandhi also offered the concept of Shanti Sena to organize a non-violent force—to intervene in the conflicting situation— to root out the causes of violence and peacelessness and to establish a society dominated by peace, characterized by truth and non-violence.

Gandhi spearheaded a silent social revolution in India and the world. The road that Gandhi travelled from his early life in South Africa to the liberation of India—which he achieved through his non-violent movements and assisted by the march of events in the world—is perhaps the most significant in the history of mankind. He was like Buddha, a champion of the freedom of human mind. He gave us ideas, methods and the outlines of great ideals of human society. It is for us to understand and then accept or reject what he gave. Gandhi was the greatest gift of history to mankind. As Dr Radhakrishnan observes:

> The greatest fact in the story of man on earth is not his material achievement, the empires he has built and broken, but the growth of his soul from age to age in its search for truth and goodness.

References

Grover, V. (ed.), 1970, *Political Thinkers of Modern India*, New Delhi : Deep and Deep Publishers.

Bharathi, K.S., 1991 *The Social Philosophy of Mahatma Gandhi,* New Delhi : Concept Publishers.

Kripalani. J.B., 1991, *Gandhi: His Life and Thought*, New Delhi : Publication Division, Govt. of India.

Tahtinen Unto, 1979, *The Core of Gandhi's Philosophy*, New Delhi : Abhinav Publications.

22

Mahatma Gandhi's Attitude Towards Women

P. Chinnathurai

Mahatma Gandhi's attitude towards women was essentially evolved through his lifetime experiences. Though, he was inspired by his mother, yet, he revolted against her practice of untouchability. He pointed out the inconsistency in her philosophy—"God is everywhere" and her segregation of the scavenger - Uka. He greatly trusted Rambha (an old servant of Gandhi family and a nurse as well) and he shared with her his deep fear of ghosts and spirits and she came out with her 'Ram Raksha' as a way out. Though he did not like this, his faith on Rambha motivated him to take up this path of 'Mantra Yoga' (repeating a sacred name of God relentlessly over a period of time as a way of spiritual evolution). This happened when he was 13 years old.

Gandhi was married at the age of 12 and like any other man of his place, time and setting, he wanted to play the role of a dominating husband. Kasturba, though, innocent and not well educated, was courageous and she could not be subjected.

Gandhi loved Kasturba passionately. Though, he had occasions to have sexual contact with other women, he was saved at the last minute and remained a faithful husband throughout.

With the rise of Gandhi in other spheres, including education, profession, public life, spiritual development, etc., there was a simultaneous rise in his relationship with his wife. He, without hesitation, took his family to South Africa. His home slowly emerged into a small community—a world in miniature with persons of different castes, languages, nationalities, religions and other diverse backgrounds. As time went on, his home became a real community—Phoenix Settlement and later on Tolstoy Farm. Then, till the end of his life, he was either in prison or in a community home.

The Gandhi-Kasturba relationship passed on from a 'dominating husband model' to that of friends, co-pilgrims, co-constructive workers, co-nonviolent fighters and a model devoted to the 'welfare of all, uplift of the least and holistic development'. This transformation did not take place in one day, rather it took more than twenty years. There were difficult moments, stresses and conflicts but ultimately there was the dawn of progress.

Gandhi acknowledged his indebtedness to Kasturba and said that he learnt non-violence from her. Kasturba's courage to enter the Satyagraha campaign in South Africa for racial justice opened up Gandhi's eyes. This was a turning point in the South African Satyagraha movement. Kasturba remained a non-violent activist and constructive worker till her last moment. She died in detention. Along with Kasturba, a number of Indian women participated in the Satyagraha campaign in South Africa. M. Valliammal, a sixteen year old Tamil girl was released from a South African jail (she was arrested for her participation in the above campaign) after she became seriously ill. Gandhi met her on her death bed. He was deeply touched by her courage and determination even at the verge of her death. Gandhi realized that women could play a better and effective role in non-violent action. Thereafter all his campaigns had considerable women participation.

Gandhi, with his increasing role in public life, converted his home into an Ashram. Before his first Ashram (Phoenix Settlement) was established, his home itself took almost all the characteristics of an Ashram. There was a personal change taking place in him as well. He was moving towards a Brahmacharya lifestyle.

Brahmacharya may be regarded as sexual restraint or abstinence from sexual activity and self-control of sense organs. But in its literal sense it might be termed as realization of Brahma—God realization. Here Brahmacharya is shown as a way to realization of God.

When Gandhi proposed the Brahmacharya vow, Kasturba without any hesitation accepted it. In fact, they were moving in that direction for quite a few years. They took this vow in 1906 and kept it up till the end.

In the Brahmacharya tradition, usually men keep away from women. The latter are considered to be drawing the former into sex. This is however a partisan vision. But in Gandhi, there was no question of avoiding or isolating or alienating from women. He never ran away from the company of women. He always had a healthy and positive relationship with women. This was further enriched by his Brahmacharya. In the absence of sexual desire and possessive instinct, man-woman relationship reached new heights of friendship and mutual trust. The wall separating them was broken.

The radical feminists today take a stand very similar to this. For them as long as sexual activity persists, real equality cannot be achieved. To Gandhi, lust separates and alienates man and woman.

Gandhi's Brahmacharya vow is not a negation of body, earthly life and women. But it is a new vision of body, life and women.

Now let us examine Gandhi's Brahmacharya experiments during his last phase. There is criticism against Gandhi's long baths, massage and placing his hands on the shoulders of young women (his 'walking sticks') while walking. Further, Gandhi was engaged in experiments 'to test his mastery of celibacy' by allowing young women to be close to him. [This needs a detailed examination and it may become a subject for separate research work.]

There was no secret about these experiments as Gandhi remained an open book. Gandhi was involved in such experiments mostly when there was a storm outside, his non-violence was challenged and there was bloodshed and demonic forces of violence, hatred and revenge were taking the upper hand. Was he seeking light, energy and vision from such experiments? Was he involved in new experiments relating to human body? Was he testing his bisexuality i.e. his being a mother to those women?

Mahatma Gandhi after a certain point in his life, had reached a new level of existence. He was a true Mahatma and to understand him, one needs a different scale. It appears that the Mahatma had ascended to new heights in the last phase of his life. Various aspects of his life will remain a mystery for years to come. Only with greater understanding of human body, we may be able to better explain some of these.

Gandhi remained friendly as an affectionate mother and father to his close associates (men and women) till his end. He had the remarkable ability to link up with women without any inhibition and blocks.

Gandhi's Brahmacharya experiments in his last phases explain his remarkable courage and originality even in the evening of his life. He wanted to live for 125 years but, the assassin ended his life abruptly. Had he lived for a longer period, he would have explained his experiments.

References

1. Erikson, Erik H., 1970, *Gandhi's Truth on the Origin of Militant Nonviolence*, London : Faber & Faber Limited.
2. Gandhi, M.K., 1927, *An Autobiography or Experiments with Truth*, Ahmedabad : Navajivan Publishing House.
3. Gandhi, M.K., 1928, *Satyagraha and South Africa*, Ahmedabad : Navajivan Publishing House.
4. Mehta, Ved., 1977, *Mahatma Gandhi and his Apostles*, New York : Viking Press.
5. Prema M., 1994, *From Wife to Friend*, unpublished manuscript.

Newspapers

(a) *Young India* (b) *Harijan*

Government Publications

Collected Works of Mahatma Gandhi, Publication Division, Govt. of India, New Delhi.

23

Untouchable by Choice
Gandhi's Crusade Against Untouchability

K.C. Sreekumar

Fundamental social change emanates from imminent individual change. Transforming the age-old belief systems and practices of people is easier said than done. Changing the beliefs and behaviour patterns of religious nature, of a people of great numerical strength and a tradition of millenniums, through non-violent means is like watering an asphalt pavement with the confident anticipation that lillies will reward the labour. Nevertheless, whatever changes a violent revolution will bring about in these fields will only be superfluous and momentary. These facts point toward the magnitude of the work of eradication of untouchability undertaken by Gandhi. An evaluation of this becomes possible only after acquainting oneself with facts concerning the history of untouchability in India, the rationale of Gandhi in considering this as important as securing political independence, the religious content of the programme, the application of the programme as a tool for social mobilization, the measures adopted by and under the supervision of Gandhi to tackle the question, and last but not least, the opposition faced and the support received by Gandhi in his work.

History of Untouchability

The Aryans brought in a system of class division. These class divisions hardened when they began to settle down among the darker aboriginals, because of the former's emphasis on purity of blood. As a result, the Dasas, who had earlier a place on the fringes of Aryan society and those Aryans who ventured to intermarry with the Dasas and adopt their ways were excluded. Their social status was the lowest[1]. By the end of the Rig Vedic period, the fourfold division of society, named as Varna, was firmly established. This type of stratification on society was not prevalent in the early Dravidian South. The earliest

Tamil literature gives the portrait of a society divided into tribal groups with little sense of the precedence of one over the other. However, the Aryan Varna system crept into the Dravidian system in the succeeding centuries.

It is interesting to note that the outcastes themselves had developed a caste hierarchy and had their own outcastes by the beginning of the Christian era. Instead of waning with the advancement of time and civilization the system only got more and more rigid and by the time of the struggle for independence, it posed the most serious threat to national unity.

The Rationale of Gandhi's Crusade Against Untouchability

A.R. Wadia opined that it was due to Gandhi's consummate love for humanity that he strived for the abolition of untouchability. There is no need to disagree with this. But one can go a step further and look at the whole issue from a different perspective. Gandhi was a very wise politician whose entire social reform activities were connected with the political aim of uniting the people of India to make them stand as one man against the mighty empire, in the struggle for securing independence. Arun Shourie recently observed :

> The British saw that the main movement against them would come from (and) that it was arising from within the Hindus. From the late 19th century to the time they left, British policy was directed towards dividing the Hindu community, to hacking sections away from it, to propping up groups in other communities who would proclaim that India was not one country (and) that the movement for freedom from the British did not speak for all Indians".

Gandhi was aware about the imperial designs. This is clear from his words :

> In fighting this battle against untouchability, I am fighting for unity not only among the Hindu touchables and Hindu untouchables, but among Hindus, Muslims, Christians and all the other different religious communities.

Gandhi also believed that truthful and non-violent means should be adopted for winning Poorna Swaraj or Complete Independence. It was for this that he devised his well known

'Constructive Programme'. It was designed to build up the nation from 'the very bottom upward'. Gandhi had no doubt that complete independence through truth and non-violence meant the independence of every unit, be it the humblest of the nation, without distinction of race, colour or creed. Gandhi once declared:

> ... so long as the Hindus wilfully regard untouchability as a part of their religion, so long as the mass of Hindus consider it a sin to touch a section of their brethren, Swaraj is impossible of attainment.

The colonial masters knew very well the power of Gandhi's vision. So, they wanted to pitch his own people against him, for this they got an opportunity in 1931. That year, in the Round Table Conference, Ambedkar demanded separate electorate for the Depressed Classes and he was supported by other minorities except Sikhs. This was exactly what was required by the British Government to follow the notorious colonial policy of divide and rule. Gandhi was farsighted enough to understand the implications of the demand.

Commenting on the demand, he said :

> I can understand the claims advanced by other minorities, but the claims advanced on behalf of the untouchables is to me the unkindest of all. It means the perpetual bar sinister. I would not sell the vital interests of the untouchables for the sake of winning the freedom of India. I claim myself in my own person to represent the vast mass of untouchables.... We do not want on our register and on our census untouchables, classified as a separate class. The Sikhs may remain as such in perpetuity, so may the Muslims, so may the Europeans. Will untouchables remain untouchables in perpetuity ?..... Therefore, I want to say with all emphasis that I can command that if I was the only person to resist this thing, I would resist it with my life.

Later, he wrote to the British premier that in the establishment of separate electorate, he sensed the injection of poison that was calculated to destroy Hinduism and to do no good whatsoever to the depressed classes. So, as per promise, he started to resist it with his life on September 20, 1932, with a 'fast unto death'.

The Religious Content of the Programme

Even before Gandhi started his crusade against untouchability, social workers and spiritual leaders like Dayananda Saraswati, bitterly criticized the inequities associated with the caste system. The former recognised the latter's contribution in these words :

> Among the many rich legacies that Swami Dayananda left to us, his unequivocal pronouncement against untouchability is undoubtedly one.

Both these social workers emphasised the need for social reforms. While most of Swami Dayananda's activities were directed towards the regeneration of the Hindu community, Gandhi gave importance to the Hindus as well as other communities. Once he said :

> The Harijan work is essentially religious from my standpoint. It is my firm conviction that, if the Hindu heart is completely purged of the taint of untouchability, the event will have its inevitable influence not only on all the communities in India but also on the whole world.... The very act of the Hindu heart getting rid of distinctions of high and low, must cure us of the mutual jealousies and distrusts of and among other communities.

He further observed :

> Untouchability was there not only in Hinduism. In South Africa, East Africa and Canada, Musalmans, no less than Hindus, came to be regarded as pariahs.

In fact, Gandhi considered untouchability as the greatest blot on Hinduism. He wanted the people to know that it never was a part of original Hinduism. In his speech at Mayavaram, he asked :

> Is it (untouchability) a part of Hinduism? I do not know. I have now to learn what Hinduism really is. In so far as I have been able to study Hinduism outside India, I have felt that it is no part of real Hinduism to have in its fold a mass of people whom I would call untouchables. If it was proved to me that this is an essential part of Hinduism, I for one would declare myself an open rebel against Hinduism itself.

Many believed that it was from Christian religious literature that Gandhi derived the idea of fighting against untouchability. But this was not correct. The idea dawned on him even before he was twelve years old. He emphasized that the western influence had nothing to do with his views about untouchability. They were the deliberate convictions of a man born and brought up in a purely orthodox Hindu atmosphere and tradition, of a man who had practised the Hindu religious teaching by actually imitating his orthodox parents, of a man who had tried to study the human body as much as the dweller of that tabernacle, of a man who had given years of study to the 'Shastras' in perfect faith and devotion, of a man who had wandered throughout the length and breadth of India, discussing the matter with 'shastris' and 'pundits', and who was more confirmed in his views as a result.

The logic of Gandhi's conviction that the evils of Hinduism should be fought against not from without but from within is appreciable. By rejecting Hinduism, Gandhi would have reached nowhere. A religion lives not in the worshipping places or in the rituals but in the minds of its followers. Endeavours to uproot it from there and implant some foreign idea of nationalism instead would have been catastrophic. The religious content of Indian nationalism is now a well-researched topic. Anyway, one can not mould the destiny of a nation by denying its past.

Untouchability : Eradication and Social Mobilization

A very important effect of Gandhi's social reform movement was large-scale social mobilization of certain sections of the India population, which were not brought to the national mainstream up to that time. This created an awakening all over the country which had a profound influence on the anti-colonial struggle of the Indian people. Millions took part in storming the bastille of Hindu orthodoxy and in liberating the enchained untouchables. It created a sense of dignity and awareness of their rights among the downtrodden millions. Their liberation from the tentacles of the octopus of superstition and orthodoxy enabled and emboldened them to be mobilized for the cause of Indian independence. Their increased participation in the politics of the country itself is a proof of the increase in their political awareness. Further, it won't be out of place here to mention that the roots of contemporary Indian 'dalit awareness' could be found in Gandhi's anti-untouchability programme. It should also be mentioned here that cruel distortion of history is being made today to project Gandhi as a person who played key roles in recreating 'upper caste hegemony'.

The magnitude of the social mobilization that took place in the country at that time is manifested in the following facts. First, nearly ten thousand women were present at the Soitra Conference. This kind of large-scale participation of Indian women in a social reform movement was unprecedented till that time. Second, millions of people fasted on the day of the commencement of Gandhi's 'fast unto death' against the award of separate electorate to the depressed classes. His very decision to fast resulted in the dawn of wisdom as far as the orthodox sections of the Hindus were concerned. They threw open the doors of hundreds of temples for the untouchables. Third, thousands and thousands of meetings were held all over the country. Many leaders of the depressed classes like M.C. Rajah condemned the Communal Award and requested all to save Gandhi's life. Fourth, Gandhi's Harijan Tour attracted thousands and thousands of people everywhere. In Madras (now Chennai) city over a lakh of people attended the meeting. This was the largest gathering that the city had ever witnessed.

Measures Adopted by Gandhi

It goes without saying that Gandhi used only non-violent methods to wipe out untouchability. He never tried to organise the untouchables and pitch them against the touchables. Instead, he used a number of measures like changing the hearts of the upper caste people, making the untouchables economically self-reliant, wiping out the fear of untouchability from their minds, affecting a change in their style of living, educating them, enabling them to enjoy religious, socioeconomic and political rights, etc. For these, he used many techniques like Satyagraha, organizing awareness campaigns, Padyatras, huge meetings and rallies, constructing village temples, forming the Servants of Untouchables Society, publishing a weekly to project the issues connected with untouchability and even causing legislative action. A quick look at some incidents and utterances connected with this gives us the picture of a committed dynamic man.

Everywhere, a section of the Hindu population found it difficult to assimilate the revolutionary ideas of Gandhi regarding social reconstruction. In meetings, whenever Gandhi found the untouchables being forced to sit in a separate corner, he revolted against that and asked the orthodox people to leave instead. His efforts to enable the untouchables to enter into the temples were continuous and ceaseless.

He even raised money to construct a temple for them. Participating in the Vaikom Satyagraha Gandhi said :

> The prejudice we have to fight against, is an age-long prejudice. The struggle for the opening of the roads around the temple, which we hold to be public, to the unapproachable, is but a small skirmish in the big battle.... The end is to get all such roads throughout the Travancore State to be opened to the unapproachable; and not only that, but we expect that our efforts may result in amelioration of the general condition of the untouchables and unapproachables.

Gandhi's fast unto death against the British decision to create separate electorate of the untouchables was a powerful move that opened the eyes of orthodox Hindus. They opened the temples to the depressed classes in many parts of the country. Millions in India offered fervent prayers and fasted on September 20, 1932, the day of the beginning of Gandhi's fast. His fast resulted in the signing of the Yeravada Pact. The resolution drafted by him was adopted by all including Ambedkar, M.C. Rajah and representatives of caste Hindus, The resolution stated :

> This conference resolves that, henceforth, among Hindus, no one shall be regarded as an untouchable by reason of his birth and those who have been so regarded hitherto, will have the same right as other Hindus in regard to the use of public wells, public schools, public roads and other public institutions. This right will have statutory recognition at the first opportunity and shall be one of the earliest acts of the Swaraj parliament, if it shall not have received such recognition before to secure, by every legitimate and peaceful means, an early removal of all social disabilities now imposed by custom upon the so-called untouchable classes, including the bar in respect of admission to temples.

Under Gandhi's direction an 'Untouchability Abolition Week' was observed from September 27 to October 2, 1932. The occasion was used to organize large public meetings, where the pact was explained and appeals were made to abolish untouchability and to hold large inter-caste dinners. More temples and wells were thrown open to the *Harijans* during this period. To carry on the anti-untouchability move, an All India Anti-untouchability League with a network of provincial boards was set up. Earlier, an organisation called the 'Servants of

Untouchables Society' was created on the directions of Gandhi. On his request the society started the publication of *Harijan* weekly on February 11, 1933. The commendable service it rendered for spreading the message of abolition of untouchability is well-known. Gandhi offered the Sabaramati Ashram to the society to make use of it for the Harijan cause.

As a part of the abolition of untouchability programme, legislative measures were also adopted. In order to enable the depressed classes to enter the famous Guruvayoor temple, two bills were framed by the reformers, one for presentation in the Madras Legislative Council and the other in the Central Assembly. The Assembly Bill proposed that no custom or usage based on untouchability should be recognized by any court of law. The other bill sought to empower the Hindu residents in any locality, to secure an alteration by a majority vote, in the established practices regarding the admission of untouchables in the local temples.

Earlier, a plebiscite was conducted in Guruvayoor by C. Rajagopalachari in which 27,465 adults were approached to vote. Of these, 56 per cent were in favour of the temple entry. Only 9 per cent opposed it. The neutral ones consisted 8 per cent. Those who abstained from voting consisted 27 per cent. This provided an opportunity for intensive propaganda against untouchability. Anyway, the abstention of 27 per cent pointed towards the need for more work.

Commenting on the Viceregal decision to sanction the introduction of the Untouchability Abolition Bill in the Assembly Gandhi said :

> The movement for temple entry now broadens from Guruvayoor in the extreme South to Hardwar in the North.

Gandhi's three week fast in May 1933, for the cause of the untouchables further enabled the champions of orthodoxy to open their eyes towards the truth. In a statement issued before the commencement of the fast, Gandhi said that the evil of untouchability will not be eradicated by money, external organization and even political power for the Harijans, though all these were necessary. More than all these, inward organization, inward power in other words and self-purification was required.

Gandhi started his famous 'Harijan Tour' on November 7, 1933. He travelled the length and breadth of the country and millions of people were enlightened by his talks. The effect of it could be measured from the fact that on the eve of Gandhi's entry into Thiruvananthapuram, on January 20th, the Travancore State declared all public roads, wells, *chatrams* open to all classes of people. At Puri, on May 8, 1934, Gandhi renounced the use of conveyances for the rest of the tour in Orissa. This Padyatra enabled him to meet more and more people and convey the message. During the tour, he opened many temples for the untouchables. The tour was concluded by a fast on August 2, 1934.

During the time of elections in 1937, Gandhi said that Harijan workers could utilize the opportunity of the elections for educating the voters on the question of untouchability. Thus, he left no opportunity unused for the purpose of the emancipation of the Harijans. Even Bhajans and processions were used to enlighten the masses. For example, at Kanyakumari, Gandhi passed through the streets leading to the temple, accompanied by a large party of Harijans who were singing Bhajans.

Opposition and Support

When Gandhi founded his Satyagraha Ashram in Ahmedabad in 1915, he received much help from many corners. But when he permitted an untouchable family to join the Ashram, all of a sudden there were oppositions. The orthodox sections of the Hindu society stopped all monetary help. There were even rumours of social boycott. But Gandhi took the firm decision to stick to his stand and if necessary, to shift the Ashram to the untouchable quarters and to live by manual labour. Soon help came from supporters.

Babasaheb Ambedkar was the most vehement critic of Gandhi's crusade against untouchability. He held the view that the untouchables were not a part of Hindu society and that they were a separate group just like the Muslims or the Christians. Keeping the untouchables down was, according to Ambedkar, the very essence of Hinduism. He predicted that this mentality of the Hindus would never change. He considered Gandhi, the Indian National Congress and all those untouchables who were associated with Gandhi's programme of the emancipation of the untouchables and with the Harijan Seva Sangh as enemies of the untouchables. About the latter he said they were just unemployed loafers who were seeking to make politics a source of their livelihood. Ambedkar could influence a section of the untouchables and accordingly the Depressed Class Conference adopted a resolution, recommending severance of the depressed classes from the Hindu fold and embracing any other religion. At Nasik, on October 13, 1935, a gathering of 800 Harijan youths burned the *Manu Smriti*.

Ambedkar and the British government always tried to counter the Congress claim that it represented the Harijans as much as any other section of Indian society. They were dealt with a humiliating blow and the Congress claim was supported by the results of the elections of 1937. The Congress did extremely well in the seats reserved for Harijans. In the Madras Presidency the seats reserved for Harijans were 30. The Congress won all the seats it contested. In Bihar, out of the 24 reserved seats the Congress bagged all the 23 seats it contested. In Bombay the reserved seats numbered 15. The Congress candidate was returned unopposed in one seat. Out of 8 candidates fielded by the party, 5 got elected. In the United Provinces, out of the 20 reserved seats, the party contested 17 and won 16. In Bengal, there were 30 reserved seats. The Congress contested 17 and won 6 seats. In the Central Provinces the party fieleded 9 candidates and won 5 seats. There were 19 reserved seats.

The progressive sections of the Indian society extended all kinds of support to Gandhi. Ordinary village folks as well as Maharajas stood with him. Great leaders like Rajendra Prasad even suggested ways to tackle the problem. Thinking men all over the world praised Gandhi's work and extended moral support.

Conclusion

Gandhi's endeavour to emancipate the untouchables can be considered as the greatest non-violent social reform movement of the twentieth century. He effectively used the weapons of love, non-violence, compassion and social consciousness to bring about a great social transformation. The entire movement offered a testimony to Gandhi's intense knowledge of the Indian mind, his accurate understanding of the sociopolitical milieu, his unfeigned evaluation of the imperialistic interests of the colonial master, his nonchalant assessment of the efficacy of the weapons in his arsenal and his meticulous political know-how about 'when, where and how to strike'.

Gandhi's works created an unprecedented awareness among both the untouchables as well as the upper castes and made the latter compunctious. At the very same time, it didn't make the former insolent. Such a setting is a desideratum for non-violent social revolution. Only a person with a lesser knowledge of the political culture of the Indian people would have opted the violent path. Comparing to many political systems which brought about radical social change in a violent manner, post-independence social tensions are less in India, thanks to the Gandhian non-violent social transformation. To Gandhi, political and social emancipation were interrelated. So, his crusade against untouchability should be seen as a part of his crusade against colonial subjugation. In both, he shattered the aspirations of the empire.

References

1. A.L. Basham, 1982, *The Wonder That Was India*, p. 35-36, New Delhi : Rupa & Co.
2. *Ibid.*, p. 139.
3. *Ibid.*, p. 146.
4. A.R.Wadia, 1972, 'Gandhi and Untouchability', Gandhi Centenary Papers, K.S. Saxena (ed.), 'Gandhi Centenary Papers', Vol. IV, p. 27. Council of Oriental Research, Bhopal.
5. Arun Shourie, 1997, *Worshipping False Gods : Ambedkar and the Facts Which have been Erased*. p. 221. New Delhi, ASA Publications.
6. D.G. Tendulkar, 1969 'Mahatma : Life of Mohandas Karamchand Gandhi', p. 220. Vol. 3, New Delhi : Publications Division, Government of India.
7. M.K. Gandhi, 1994, *Constructive Programme : Its Meaning and Place*, p. 3, Ahmedabad, Navajivan Mudranalaya.
8. *Ibid.*, p. 5.
9. D.G. Tendulkar, *op. cit.* (n. 6), Vol. 2, p. 36.
10. *Ibid.*, Vol. 3, p. 128.
11. *Ibid.*, p. 167.
12. Har Bilas Sarda, 1946, *Life of Dayananda Saraswati*, Ajmer. (1946).

13. D.G. Tendulkar, *op. cit.* (n. 10), p. 220.
14. *Ibid.,* Vol.1, p. 167.
15. For details, see : *Ibid.,* Vol. 2, p. 35.
16. *Ibid.,* p. 209.
17. The chapter titled 'Dalitisation Not Hinduisation' in Kencha Ilaiah, 'Why I am not a Hindu'.
18. D.G. Tendulkar, *op. cit.,* (n. 9), p. 177.
19. *Ibid.,* p. 180-81.
20. *Ibid.,* Vol. 3, p. 174.
21. *Ibid.,* p. 188-89.
22. *Ibid.,* p. 188.
23. *Ibid.,* p. 191.
24. *Ibid.,* p. 199.
25. For details, see : Babasaheb Ambedkar, 'What Congress and Gandhi Have Done to the Untouchables' and 'Mr. Gandhi and the Emancipation of the Untouchables', reproduced in B.R. Ambedkar, *Dr. Babasaheb Ambedkar, Writings and Speeches*, Vol. IX, Education Department, Government of Maharashtra, Mumbai, (1995).
26. *Ibid.,* p. 142.
27. 'Mitra's Annual Register (1937)', Vol. 1, p. 168 a-p quoted in Arun Shourie, *op. cit.* (n. 5), p. 6.
28. Rajendra Prasad, 1942, *Constructive Programme : Some Suggestions*, Ahmedabad : Navajivan Publishing House.

24

Revolution, Change of People's Mind, not of System

V.K. Muthu
N. Arumugam

Casteism and communalism are the two major social problems which cause frequent civil, political and even military disturbances all over the world even today.

There were and still are people who feel that as long as these social institutions exist, there will be such problems. But another school of thought opines that it is the fanaticism of caste and religion that is dangerous and not the institutions themselves. Whichever thought is correct the fact remains that these institutions have been found to be responsible for the frequent turmoils that we see among the societies. In addition to casteism and communalism, class consciousness is another social phenomenon that causes serious unrest the world over.

While caste and religion thrive in societies since time immemorial, the fact that these institutions rely mostly on arbitrary, irrational and unscientific concepts for their practice, cannot be denied. Since many of the social norms and practices are based on such irrational casteist and religious teachings, it results in injustice to some sections of people with the resultant social disharmony. The unstable and fluid situation due to casteism, communalism and class consciousness in a major part of the world has stirred the conscience of intellectual thinkers the world over and they have also responded to the situation by advocating some strategies to bring about peace and harmony among different nations and societies. This led to the development of two major political philosophies, namely the liberal democratic system and the communist ideology. Even though both these systems trod different means to find solutions to the problems their objective remained the same. What was in the form of 'two different worlds' some years ago has become again a single world after the fall of Soviet-led Eastern bloc under Communist rule. But, still the problems that plagued the world have not abated to any significant extent and continue to persist.

Genuine peace and progress can be established only when the constituent members of different societies are free from wrong beliefs and customs that exist among societies causing unnecessary social problems. Therefore, it appears that the social change that is essential for an orderly, trouble-free world needs to be kindled by the intellectuals at least continually if not continuously. What is needed is recasting of the social order and not a mere change of government or constitution or the use of violence. History has taught us that people's mind can not be changed by force. Therefore, the basic philosophy should be to change the ideas and ideologies of the people to bring about a social revolution. What happened in America, France, Russia and China are only revolts and confiscation of property or bloodshed or only rebellion and upheaval and not revolution. So, it can be easily inferred that when there is violence there is no revolution. Therefore, we can say that real revolution can take place only when people change and their values change. Real revolution always means a fundamental change in people's ideas, ideologies, ethos and values of life.

Mahatma Gandhi was a social reformer par excellence. His approach to the world problems was unique and has no parallel in the entire history of mankind. We also find that he was the only practising theoretician known to the world. He understood the futility of violence and realized the importance of a basic change in the attitude of people. This is very well expressed in his actions during the turbulent days of discontent among Muslims and Hindus in India. The British invaders, as traders, were whipping up the social disharmony that existed between the Hindus and Muslims to perpetuate their rule here. But Gandhi, as a social scientist worked for the unity of Muslims and Hindus. He tried to use the strength of unity of the two communities and truth to defeat the forces of evil.

As a protagonist of peace, Gandhi could realize that the mental barrier that existed between different castes in India was responsible for the problems which impeded India's progress. So, he wanted to create an egalitarian society in India. He took up the cause of the oppressed by relentlessly fighting for the restoration of rights denied to the unfortunate sections of the society. He exhorted the non-Scheduled Castes to shun untouchability and to accept the so-called untouchables into their Hindu fold. While Dr B. R. Ambedkar wanted to annihilate the castes, Gandhi simply wanted the casteism to go. The dual electorate constituency concept proposed by Dr Ambedkar and initially accepted by the British Government was later shelved due to Gandhi's fast unto death. There are many people who believe, specially among the Scheduled Castes, that this was Gandhi's greatest mistake which worked against the interest of the untouchables and thereby seriously delayed the process of social change in India. But, his genuine interest in the welfare of the whole society including the Scheduled Castes can not be suspected if we look at what he had preached and practised in his life for the welfare of the Scheduled Castes.

Mahatma Gandhi's weapons were Truth and Non-violence to bring about social revolution in contrast to the Marxian philosophy of inevitability of violence in revolution. While Gandhian philosophy placed much stress on the change of the heart of people without any force or coercion for renaissance and revolution, Marxian theory laid great emphasis on meeting the immediate and the urgent essential needs of the common man. The failure of communism in the Eastern bloc countries can be due to the fact that they neglected the importance of human values of truth and humanism. Communism was simply content with providing the basic necessities to the people. Human values were not part of their indoctrination campaign. Therefore, that system failed to bring about a fundamental change in the human minds necessary to usher in a lasting revolution. As it only promoted materialistic culture, it failed in the long run to provide peace and stability. Once the strict discipline enforced by law was removed it resulted in the collapse of the system. At the same time we also have to accept that the Gandhian approach too has not succeeded in bringing about a desirable change in the minds of people in our country. It may be because of the fact that, Gandhian philosophy, while stressing upon the importance of human values and virtues, has mostly ignored the immediate basic needs of man, in respect of food, shelter and clothing. As a result, Gandhian philosophy of human values became unattractive to the millions of ill-clad, shelterless and hungry people. It could not also touch the rampant exploitation of the poor by the rich in the name of caste, religion, etc. The materialistic culture brought about and promoted by scientific advancement also enveloped the conscience of people, leading to the neglect of human values.

So, peace and progress needs social revolution. A fundamental change in the values of people is a prerequisite for social revolution. The present political philosophies have largely failed to bring peace and harmony. We find that the caste, religion and class consciousness have hijacked the systems to wrong destinations. Therefore, the only option available to recast the social order is to create a philosophy that will lay stress on human values and also emphasize on obliteration of mental barriers and on integration of mankind. Gandhian philosophy of Truth and Non-violence based on humanism can go a long way in bringing about the long-needed social change.

Part IV

25

Gandhian Secularism

P. Gopinathan Nair

Secularism has increasingly become a subject of topical interest ever since the Khalistan movement and the Ayodhya tangle began to agitate the minds of our people. These movements have challenged the basic assumptions of secularism as provided in our Constitution. This is because we have not honoured the ideals like democracy, socialism, secularism, etc., as enshrined in the Constitution. There is a continuous attempt, overtly and covertly to violate such basic principles and that is where, as a nation we have failed. There is a threat to national integration in the shape of 'linguism', regionalism, casteism and communalism. This threat has engulfed secularism as well.

Gandhian View on the Role of Religion in Social Life : Material and Spiritual

The contribution of Gandhi to the thinking on religion is something unique. He was not a religious man in the conventional sense. He did not belong to any particular religion but, at the same time, he accepted the scriptures of all religions. His religion was that religion which formed the core of all religions.

According to him, every religion is after the quest of one truth of life, the one truth that pervades everything. Gandhi's life was an experiment to realize that one truth.

To Gandhi, life was not divided or compartmentalized into two- the spiritual and the material. Gandhi pulled down the barriers that separated the individual and social aspects of life and also the wall that divided the spiritual and the material. Life for him was one unlimited extensive whole. While, for us, life is compartmentalized into two— the spiritual and the material.

Gandhi experienced that, there was a universal law which governed and animated all existence. He found that this law and the lawmaker are one. Hence, a greater understanding and acceptance of that law was the basis of Gandhi's religion.

This Law is found reflected in the indwelling spirit of every living creature and it governs all creation. All guidance to our life will come from within. The kingdom of God is within us and also around us.

Hence, when we claim that we are followers of this or that religion, we live only in the primary stage of religious understanding. Let us go beyond these narrow religious boundaries, deep into the inner core of each religion. Then, we will discover that there is a common string of universality in each religion. Gandhi was trying to take us towards that universal religion of man.

The universal consciousness extends beyond man to all creation, both animate and inanimate. As Gandhi remarked :

"Not a blade of grass moves without His will".

Realization of this truth is made possible only through a life of love and service. This *sadhana* of love and service is given the name Ahimsa by Gandhi. Ahimsa is the law of life of our species. When we quarrel, hate or kill in the name of religion, we are really violating the basic principles of all religions.

Since the understanding of the ordinary man about this basic principle of religion is limited, fundamentalists find it easy to exploit the common man in the name of religion. Only by educating him and creating the right awareness in him shall we succeed in defeating fundamentalist forces.

Gandhian Approach : Religion and Politics

Gandhi is rightly or wrongly accused for mixing religion with politics. Gandhi himself has answered this question several times. Many have defended Gandhi and many have pointed an accusing finger on him.

Gandhi said that life was one whole and hence in the creation of a new society, we have to take all aspects of life and work for a total change. A new man and a new society was his aim and hence politics and economics which are very vital aspects of life could not be ignored. He worked for a moral, spiritual and cultural awakening together with the battle for political and economic freedom of the people. Gandhi saw life in its totality. The differences between other saints and sages of history and Gandhi was that he was a man of spirituality, engaged in social action and social change. Gandhi had faith in an integrated development which alone could ensure the total evolution of man.

Gandhi and the Hindu-Muslim Question

The advent of Gandhi in India saw an awakening of the masses. Gandhi brought with him his charisma as the hero from South Africa. After his arrival in India, he supported the Khilafat movement through which he roused the Muslim masses. On the other hand, through a programme of non-cooperation, both the Hindus and Muslims were organized against the British raj.

The British then intensified their effort to divide the Hindus and Muslims. Muslim emperors had been ruling over India for seven hundred years before the Britishers came. A section of top Muslims did not want a contingency to arise where they would be ruled by a Hindu majority. This psychology and the divide and rule policy of the foreigners were forces to be contended with.

The ignorance of the masses and their suppression, both among the Muslims and Hindus, proved another stumbling block in bringing about unity among the people. When provincial autonomy came, Hindu-Muslim rivalry again came to the forefront. Gandhi tried his best just before the dawn of independence to thwart the move for partition of India.

Some of his historic battles for Hindu-Muslim unity were fought after the direct action, launched by the Muslim League in 1946.

Gandhi's peace offensive in Naokhali is now a legend and his fast in Calcutta was more than a miracle. Governor General Mountbatten called Gandhi, 'the one man boundary force', when he walked in Bihar to establish communal harmony. His last few months in Delhi and his superhuman efforts for communal harmony while he was there, have now become part of an enchanted period of history.

The question whether all these great efforts were a failure or not is not easy to be answered. Right efforts will bear fruit at the right time and that time is yet to come.

But, was Gandhi wrong in taking certain steps in solving the communal tangle? There are many accusations against him on that score. It is true that the Khilafat movement roused the Muslim masses as never before. This is acclaimed as a great asset to the freedom movement. But some critics accuse Gandhi for keeping Khilafat movement outside the Congress. It is said that the awareness created by Gandhi was used later by communal leaders for the division of the country.

In the early stages, Gandhi negotiated with the leaders but later on he went to the people directly to solve problems. During the British Raj, he was able to cut across communal divisions. The Salt Satyagraha and Quit India movement were able to attract Muslims as participants. But, when the British offered to quit— as was destined— the struggle for power became intense, ending in the partition of India.

After independence, the communal question took new dimensions. But, it is not difficult to find through the fire and smoke of communal agitation, that a vast majority of both Hindus and Muslims have understood the need for a better relationship between them. This is the aftermath of the immense work done by Gandhi, culminating into the sacrifice of his life for this cause.

Communal wrangles after independence, have been directed to capture power at the Centre and in the States. A centralized power structure will always prompt politicians to create communal vote-banks. A decentralized system, as Gandhi wanted, is the surest method of effectively defusing the communal forces in the country.

A Living Model of Secularism

Gandhi was a religious man who accepted the secular way of life. His daily prayers in the morning and evening included prayers from all religions. Wherever possible, his post-prayer speeches were highly enlightening about God, about the brotherhood of man, truth, etc.

Secularism as we have today, is not a comprehensive and positive concept. People at the lowest level are ignorant and superstitious and they suffer from poverty and squalor. Fundamentalist forces in their effort for material gains exploit the masses to fulfil their ambitions. By remaining secular alone, a government will not be able to solve the problems of ignorance, superstition and poverty and give proper protection to the masses from exploitation.

Gandhi surely wanted the State to be secular. But he took the whole question of the abuse of religion as such in a diverse way throughout history and wanted to tackle the question in a basic way. His solution was to take the next step forward and hence in place of secularism his. solution was "Sarva Dharma Sama Bhava" or an acceptance of the equality of all religions. In secularism, the State desists from interfering with the faith of the citizen and protects all faiths. This role of the State is acceptable and necessary.

But, what about individuals? Each individual has a faith in one religion or the other. May be, there are some persons who have no faith in any religion. But ordinarily man is wedded to some religion. If men belong to different religions, then they should learn to study, understand and live with the religion in which they are born. Better understanding of one's religion and learning to live according to the precepts of that religion, is a part of Sarva Dharma Sama Bhava. Only if we know our religion well and live with it, it will be possible for us to understand our religion and then in a consequence, the quality and goodness of other religions also. This is to be done at the individual level.

As members of a society we have to study and understand the religion of our neighbours. This only will enable us to know the real goodness of other religions. We, as social beings, should cultivate the habit of respecting the religions of others and looking at them in a balanced and objective manner.

This was what Gandhi wanted to convey to us by his vow of Sarva Dharma Sama Bhava. This is an explanation of secularism or an extension of its principle to the life of the individual and society.

Gandhi held his prayers under the open sky. This temple under the open sky without any wall and roof is the real temple, where men of all faiths can sit and worship the one God who is visible and invisible as well. This was the best type of secular worship which all can emulate.

26

Gandhi and Secularism

K. Raman Pillai

The concept of secularism has been widely interpreted by eminent scholars from the West as well as from the East. George Jacob Holyoake, who along with his collaborators coined the word 'Secularism' to denote a social ethics based on natural morality, but independent of revealed religion and supernaturalism.

The political antecedents of secular concept are essentially a part of the history of the struggle between the Church and the State. At the height of its ascendancy, the Papacy advanced the idea of the kingdom of God on earth (*Civitas Dei*) according to which the Church must be the kingdom of God and the Pope its head on earth. All authority therefore, belonged to the Pope and not to the Emperor. This was decidedly against the earlier idea according to which, the Emperor had been regarded as the representative of God and the empire was the kingdom of God. The entire history of medieval Europe was replete with this bitter struggle between the Church and the State.

Eventually, the conflict between the Church and the State was resolved, the former confining strictly to spiritual matters and the latter resuming its independence to deal with temporal affairs. This policy of perfect non-interference in each other's affairs has been incorporated in many modern Constitutions including the Constitution of the United States of America. It is known by the name of 'doctrine of wall of separation'.

The long drawn out struggle between the Church and the State and its final outcome clearly show that the concept of secularism in the political arena means in effect State's freedom unsullied by interference from the Church or religious authorities, to deal with the affairs of the State. In the social sphere, secularism symbolized a revolt against the stringent hold and influence of religion on the individual's life. Religion in the early days controlled almost every aspect of man's life.

This great hold of religion on society gave rise to certain movements advocating liberal concept and outlook. In the 19th century the great cooperative thinkers like Robert Owen, Robert Buchanan and others started a cooperative movement to ameliorate the conditions of the working class created by the industrial revolution. Then they realized the adverse influence of religion among the labourers and the opposition from religious authorities. The only way out of the impasse was to remove the influence of religion from the social sphere. The result was the birth of a social movement which was named in 1880 by George Jacob Holyoake as Secular Movement to bring home to the labourers the errors of religion and the benefits of collective society. This organisation prescribed a code of conduct and called it secularism. In short, the concept means a way of life which is essentially outside the religious arena but not necessarily antagonistic to religion or religious beliefs of the people.

A State has been characterized as secular where there is no established religion. This character of the secular State has been almost accepted by all. The state as a secular institution has nothing to do with religion; it neither accepts nor rejects religion but has left it to the individual conscience. This type of secular state can be found in the USA. The object of this state is not negative but a positive one. It remains non-religious because in a multi-religious society, its objective is to give equal freedom to its citizens in religious, political, economic and other spheres. It is not to promote one religion at the cost of other religions. Its position with regard to religion is one of strict neutrality. The USA has accepted the principle of the separation of the Church from the State, as the necessary rod of their concept of the secular state.

Secularism in India

When India became independent, secularism was adopted as one of the basic principles of the Indian state for obvious reasons. The secular idea was incorporated even in the objective resolution placed before the Constituent Assembly. Para-5 of the objective resolution reads:

> Wherein shall be guaranteed and secured to all the people of India justice— social, economic and political, equality of status of opportunity..... freedom of thought, expression, belief, faith, worship, vocations, association, etc.

Para-6 states:

> "Wherein adequate safeguards shall be provided for minorities, backward and tribal areas and depressed classes".

These objectives were included in the Constitution of India and by the Constitution (42nd amendment) Act of 1976, the concept of secularism was included in the Preamble to the Constitution.

Secularism, different from the notion of a secular state is a key, variable to understand the Indian political system. It is directly related to its problems of modernization and development. Secularism has been found as the only practical solution to various problems of the multi-religious state. Indian secularism apparently can be regarded as a bridge to cross over from tradition to modernity.

There is no consensus among scholars and lawyers in their interpretation of secularism in the Indian context. To Justice P. B. Gajendragadkar,

> Freedom of religion is the foundation of Indian secularism". But mere granting of freedom of religion and religious toleration does not make a state secular. Again, multi-religiousness is not secularism.

Apart from religious considerations, there were many other compulsions, expectations and motivations behind the inclusion of secularism in the Constitution of a multi-religious country like India. Jawaharlal Nehru deemed to establish a liberal democratic state. For this, it was necessary to seek willing cooperation from all sections and communities. Therefore, secularism became a matter of policy and ideology, leading to the road to modernization, nation-building and socioeconomic emancipation and reconstruction. Minorities wanted to have secularism for enjoying freedom of conscience, worship and propagation of their religions, individually and through institutional means. In this way, the consensus model of secularism was evolved, developed and improvised in the Constitution of India.

Nehru's Concept of Secularism

Jawaharlal Nehru was the chief architect of this model and as the first Prime Minister, he operated it well to the satisfaction of the minorities. In one of his speeches on Gandhi Jayanti, he expressed his idea that a secular state was nothing but the opposite of communalism and India would be heading towards the secular state. He had said:

> We have said repeatedly that we will not tolerate any communalism in this country and that we are building a free secular state where every religion and belief has full freedom and equal honour ... we have laid down in our Constitution that India is a secular state. It means equal respect for all faiths and equal opportunities for those who profess any faith.

Nehru's concept of secular state did not definitely fall in line with either the types of the secular state of USA or erstwhile USSR. Since the glory of religion lies in giving relief from the dusty and noisy secular life of man, it can not be taken away from the individuals life. Therefore, when it was said earlier that Nehru's secularism was not directed against the internal content of religion, it was meant that this positive and beneficial function of religion was clearly recognized by him. This shows that his secularism does not embark on a meaningless attack on religion as such, but on the other hand, it criticizes the purposelessness and outmoded external manifestations of religion.

Nehru's concept of secularism has mainly four aspects. The granting of equal status to all religions in India constitutes the most important aspect. In a foreword to a book on secularism in 1961, Nehru wrote:

> We talk of a secular state in India... some people think that it means something opposed to religion. That obviously is not correct. What it means is that it is a state which honours all faiths equally and giving them equal opportunities; that as a state it does not allow itself to be attached to one faith or religion, which then becomes the state religion.

The second aspect of Nehru's concept of secularism is that the state should follow a policy of neutrality in religious matters. The resolution of Fundamental Rights, drafted by Nehru and adopted by the Karachi Congress in 1931 stated: 'The state shall observe neutrality in regard to all religions'.

The third aspect of Nehru's secularism is a certain mental attitude on the part of various communities. To Nehru, it was clear that the realization of the secular ideal depended largely upon the attitude adopted by the Hindus towards the minority communities. He emphasized:

> "The Hindus must always remember that the interest and wellbeing of the minorities are their sacred trust. If they fail in their trust, then they injure not only the country but themselves".

Above all, Nehru wanted secularization of all areas of social life. The existence of separate sets of laws governing different religious communities was inconsistent with the ideal of a secular society. In fact, a non-religious approach to politics may very well be described as one of the legacies of Nehru. The whole concept of Nehru's secular state is based on the elementary truth that the individual is the centre of social organisation or group— religious or otherwise and that equal rights should be secured to the citizens through democratic devices, irrespective of caste or religion.

In the Nehruvian model of secularism, religion is deemphasised though not negated as in the western model. Talking to students of Oxford University, Nehru had said that in England, the state had a religion but society was secular and hence its politics tended to be secular. While in India, the state was secular but society was religious and hence the state had to ensure equal protection to all religions.

Secularism is more than laws, concessions and special considerations. It is a state of mind, almost an instinctive feeling which has existed by and large for many centuries in India, when Hindus, Muslims, Christians, Parsis and followers of other faiths lived together in general harmony— irrespective of the religions of their rulers— adhering to their own practices but influencing each other in architecture, dress, music, food and even in their religious evolution. A secular state can be strongly grounded in a secular society and this implies that the people are led out of social backwardness and into forward looking egalitarianism.

Gandhi and Secularism

Gandhi's concept of secularism can be properly understood only in the context of his total philosophy and his idea of the unity of religion. He never looked on social, political, economic and religious issues as if they were in watertight compartments.

Gandhi was the heir to the great Indian spiritual tradition. The teachings of the Vedas the Upanishads and the *Bhagavat Gita* were woven into the very texture of his life. He held truth, to be the highest principle of life. As a corollary of truth, Gandhi upheld non-violence as his loadstar. Love meant for him, not merely the matrix of non-violence, but service to the sick and the suffering, the poor and the downtrodden and the lowly and the lost.

Gandhi rejected the utilitarian doctrine of 'the greatest good of the greatest number' as the end of life. Sarvodaya as propounded by him helps to bring harmony between the conflict of the individual and the state, between the greed of material gain and the spiritual life of man, between organized selfishness and the higher ideals of humanity. Sarvodaya is not a slogan of a political party but a concept, which would dissolve all party factions. It is a battle for order against disorder, it is a battle for planned action and national economic supremacy rather than the nation being the victim of accidental economic development. The ideals of Sarvodaya have their roots in ancient Indian society. It is one step ahead of real democracy. Gandhi gave us a vision of India living in largely self-sufficient villages, purged of the scourge of untouchability in which people of all religions did not merely tolerate but respected each other's customs.

In Rajkot, Gandhi got an early grounding in toleration for all branches of Hinduism and sister religions. Jain monks frequently visited Karamchand (Gandhi's father) and even went out of their way to accept food from the family. Karamachand had, Muslim and Parsi friends too, who used to talk to him about their own faiths and Gandhi listened to them always with respect and often with interest. Being his father's nurse, Gandhi had a chance to be present at those talks. These many things combined to inculcate in Gandhi a toleration for all faiths as he himself admits in his Autobiography.

During his student days in England, Gandhi read Sir Edwin Arnold's translation *The Song Celestial* (*Gita*) and *The Light of Asia* and Madam Blavatsky's *Key to Theosophy*. These books did influence Gandhi tremendously.

"The book, *Song Celestial* struck me as one of priceless worth. The impression has ever since been growing on me with the result that I regard it today as the book par excellence for the knowledge of truth. It was only after some years that it became a book of daily reading", observed Gandhi.

Gandhi read *The Light of Asia* with even greater interest than he did in case of *Bhagavat Gita*. The book, *Key to Theosophy* stimulated in him the desire to read books on Hinduism and disabused him of the notion fostered by the missionaries that Hinduism was rife with superstition. Gandhi read the *New Testament* and it profoundly influenced him. To quote his own words:

> "But the New Testament produced a different impression, especially the 'Sermon on the Mount' which went straight into my mind. I compared it with the Gita. The verses, 'But I say unto you, ye thee resist not evil: but whoever shall smite thee on thy right cheek, turn to him the other also. And if any man takes away thy coat let him have thy cloak too', delighted me beyond measure. My young mind tried to unify the teaching of the *Gita, The Light of Asia* and the *Sermon on the Mount* that renunciation was the highest form of religion appeared to me greatly".

Gandhi read Mrs Besant's book *How I became a Theosophist*. He purchased Sale's translation of the Holy Qura'n and read it. Edward Maitland sent him *The Perfect way*, a book he had written in collaboration with Anna Kingsford. He also sent him another book, *The New Interpretation of the Bible*. Gandhi liked both the books immensely.

Max Mueller's book, *India-What Can it Teach us* and the translation of the Upanishads, published by the Theosophical Society opened up Gandhi's mind further. All this enhanced his regard for Hinduism but it did not however prejudice him against other religions. The essay on 'The Hero as a Prophet' in Carlyle's *Hero Worship* had first introduced him to Islam. Having read the translation of the Holy Qura'n, he read about the life of Prophet Mohammed (PBH) by Washington Irwing and was struck by the poverty and humility of the Prophet and by the courage with which he and his first followers had faced the humiliations and hardships heaped upon them . Gandhi also read a book called, *The Sayings of Zaratushtra*. Thus Gandhi gained immense knowledge of different religions.

After a detailed study of the books relating to different religions of the world, Gandhi arrived at the following conclusions:

(i) All religions are true.

(ii) All religions have some errors in them.

(iii) All religions are dear to him as his own religion, and as much as all human beings should be as dear to him as his close relatives.

(iv) Religion is a personal matter and does not depend on collective efforts and rituals, etc.

(v) Divine knowledge consists of the realization of one's self.

This attitude of respect for all religions was his basic policy. All these are evident from the fact that the prayer at his Ashram at phoenix in South Africa contained selections from all religions and so also in later years. His Ashram was a world in miniature. He pleaded for equality of all religions 'He was non dogmatic, eatholie and secular in thought, word and deed'.

Gandhi stood for the principle of a basic and fundamental unity of all religions. In *Hind Swaraj*, he put it succinctly:

> "Religions are different roads converging to the same point. What does it matter that we take different roads so long as we reach the same goal? In reality there are as many religions as there are individuals".

Gandhi's greatest contribution consists essentially of his interpretation of religion as an outlook, rather than a body of doctrine. As early as in 1920, he wrote in *Young India*.

> Let me explain what I mean by religion. It is not the Hindu religion which I certainly prize above all other religions, but the religion which transcends Hinduism which changed our very nature, which binds one indissolubly to the truth within and which even purifies.

Later he wrote in *Harijan*:

> I can clearly see the time coming when people belonging to different faiths will have the same regard for other faiths that they have for their own.

While Gandhi made religion all important, he dissociated it from its two possible dysfunctions, disunity and stagnation. He looked upon each religion as universal and therefore tried to ensure religious harmony. He viewed religion as a constantly developing force, constantly acquiring better dimensions and giving up the unhealthy elements. Thus he could find in religion alone the basis for the creation of a just society. He worked out the social implications of his religious concepts and made them the basis of his thought and action. The concept of birth and love pervaded all levels of Gandhi's thinking.

While exalting the role of religion, Gandhi also realized that religion had been responsible for some of the most terrible crimes in history, caused by fanaticism and failure to show tolerance and respect for other religions. In the world of Gandhian thought, religion and culture were not strangers but closely related to each other.

Before 1947, Gandhi categorically asserted the inseparability of religion and politics. He wrote:

> I cannot conceive politics as divorced from religion. Indeed religion should pervade every one of our actions. Here religion does not mean sectarianism. It means a belief in the ordered moral government of the universe. This religion transcends Hinduism, Islam, Christianity, etc. It does not supersede them. It harmonizes them and gives them reality.

During the year of independence, Gandhi changed his position and said that a state has nothing to do with religion as it is purely a personal matter. He said:

> Religion is a personal matter and if we succeed in confirming it to the personal plane, all would be well in our political life.
>
> He went a step ahead and declared:
>
> "If I were a dictator, religion and state would be separate. I swear by my religion. It is my personal affair. The state has nothing to do with it. The state will look after your social welfare, health, communications, foreign relations, currency and so on but not your or my religion. That is everybody's personal concern".

No greater proof is needed than this to underline Gandhi's commitment to secularism.

The nature of religious policies of Gandhi is basically ethical and spiritual but not sectional or sectarian. Gandhi was aware of the difference of opinion regarding the meaning of the term 'spiritualising the political life'. He made it clear that to him, 'spiritualising polities' meant inducting all the purities of individual moral life into political life also. He said:

> "I think political life must be an echo of private life and that there can not be any divorce between the two".

Gandhi did not accept every Hindu tenet or practice. He applied the 'acid test of reason' to every formula of every religion. When a scriptural sanction was cited for inhuman or unjust practices, his reaction was one of frank disbelief. In the words of Stanley Jones:

> "Gandhi was a Hindu who was deeply Christian...He was a Hindu by allegiance and a Christian by affinity. He was a Hindu who was deeply Christianised, more Christianised than most Christians".

Gandhi's religion was a rational and ethical one. He would not accept any belief which did not appeal to his reason or any injunction which did not command itself to his conscience. This rational approach towards religion did not prevent Gandhi from paying utmost reverence to the scriptures of Hinduism.

Gandhi told Shriman Narayan on 10th January 1948:

> "I am not a prophet. You should not accept a thing simply because I say it. You should use your own eyes and intelligence. Even if a thousand Mahatmas like me tell you a thing which your brain does not accept, you should reject it at once. You will be able to retain freedom and be worthy of it only if you behave in this manner".

The study of comparative religion, the browsing on theological works, the conversations and correspondence with the learned brought Gandhi to the conclusion that true religion was more a matter of heart than of the intellect and the genuine beliefs were those which were literally lived. This was something beyond the grasp of those who had acquired, (in the words of Swift) enough religion to hate one another but not enough to love one another. In his life time Gandhi was variously labelled a 'Sanatanist', 'Orthodox Hindu', a 'renegade Hindu', a 'Buddhist', a 'Theosophist', a 'Christian' and a 'Christian Mohammedan'. He was all these and more, he saw an underlying unity in the clash of doctrines and forms.

The programme pursued by Gandhi included the uniting of people belonging to all casts and religions in general and Hindu-Muslim unity in particular. How can one say that Gandhi was a revivalist? The characteristics of the movement organised by Gandhi was for fraternization of the ordinary people both Hindu and Muslim. He undertook fasts unto death to ensure justice and equal treatment to Muslims. In September 1947, when riots broke out in Calcutta, Gandhi embarked upon a fast unto death to be broken only if the communal killing stopped in Calcutta. Immediately, there was revulsion against rioting and the people of Calcutta gave their pledge. The Muslim League newspaper, *Morning News* paying tribute to him on behalf of the Calcutta Muslims, forming 23 per cent of the city's population said:

"He was ready to die so that they might live peacefully".

And the correspondent of the *London Times* gently summed up the situation by the remark that : Gandhi had achieved more than could have been effected by several divisions of troops. Gandhi began another fast unto death on 13th January 1948 in protest against communal violence. This lasted up to 18th January 1948, when news reached him that a peace committee, representative of all communities in Delhi had signed a pact, pledging brotherly amity and the protection of the life, property and faith of the Muslim minority. India and the world rejoiced that Gandhi was not to die as a result of his fast.

Gandhi's concept of secularism was evolved over a period of time. His early grounding in toleration for all branches of Hinduism and sister religions began at Rajkot and developed later during his student days in England, when he came across outstanding books on world religions, the inspiration he drew from Tolstoy, Ruskin, Thoreau and Emerson, the experiences at Phoenix Settlement and Tolstoy Farm in South Africa. All these moulded his ideas on religion and philosophy. Although, he was a religious man, he was a religious man with a difference. His religion was neither sectarian nor dogmatic. He applied the acid test of reasoning to everything and was never prepared to accept anything which did not appeal to his reason. He adopted a rationalist approach to all problems including religion. Universal love, he considered was the be-all and end-all of all religions. Although, in early days he believed that religion and politics were inseparable, at a later stage, he changed his ideas and maintained that religion was a matter of personal faith and as such the state should have nothing to do with it.

Gandhi and Nehru stand on almost equal footing as far as their commitment to secularism in the Indian context is concerned. While Nehru's perception of secularism was modern and non-religious, Gandhi's perception was practical and related to religion but not religion in the traditional sense. In essence there was no difference in content but only slight variation in form. Indian secularism is certainly different from the western concept of secularism, where religion and politics are kept in watertight compartments. In a multi-religious and highly pluralistic society such as India, it is not possible to keep religion and politics in watertight compartments and hence an Indian model of secularism was evolved. In the evolution of this model both Gandhi and Nehru played their role and thereby strengthened the fabric of secularism in India.

If secularism in the Indian context means equal respect to all religions, Gandhi was a secularist. If secularism means protection of the legitimate rights of the minorities, no political leader in India was more concerned about it as Gandhi was. Again if secularism implies a rational approach to all political problems, Gandhi could be considered as one who always adopted a rational approach to problems. Judging by any standard, Gandhi was secular and his commitment to secularism is unassailable. According to N. K. Bose, Gandhi was a completely secular thinker in so far as politics was concerned.

The cause of freedom, justice and peace that Gandhi upheld was not only the cause of India's freedom or justice or peace for Indians but, of nations and people all over the world. The best reflection of this aspect of Gandhi is a celebrated sentence from Anatole France:

"He was a movement in the conscience of mankind".

References

1. Jawaharlal Nehru, *Speeches: Volume-II*, 1949-53 (Delhi 1963).
2. M. K. Gandhi, *An Autobiography or The Story of My Experiment with Truth*, Ahmedabad, p. 28 (1983).
3. *Ibid.* p. 57.
4. *Ibid.* p. 58.
5. *Ibid.* p. 114.

6. Dr. M. Kirti Singh, *Philosophical Impact of Gandhism*, Delhi, p. 89 (1994).
7. *Ibid.* p. 83.
8. *Young India*, 12 May, 1920.
9. *Harijan*, 2 February, 1934, p. 8.
10. *Young India*, 10 February, 1940.
11. *Young India*, 31 August, 1947.
12. *Young India*, 22 September, 1947.
13. Margaret Chatterjee, *Gandhi's Religious Thought*, London, p. 58 (1983).
14. B. R. Nanda, *Mahatma Gandhi : A Biography*, London, p. 55 (1965).
15. Stanley Jones, *Mahatma Gandhi : An Interpretation*', New York (1948).
16. Shriman Narayan, *Mahatma Gandhi : The Atomic Man*, Mumbai (1971).
17. Polak, Brailsford and Pathick Lawrence, *Mahatma Gandhi*, Mumbai, p.350-52 (1962).
18. Nirmal Kumar Bose, *Gandhi in Indian Politics*, Mumbai (1967).

27

Gandhi and Communalism

Padma Ramakrishnan

In a country where the influence of religion is so pervasive as in India, it has been found convenient to use religious links for political mobilization. During the freedom struggle in India , the nationalists forged tactical alliances with religio-communal groups and institutions, in order to secure their adherence to the movement. It is argued that the nationalist movement could not develop a healthy, secular and non-religious outlook, because many of its leaders used a language which was enmeshed in religious obscurantism and revivalism. This helped to strengthen communal identities. Tilak blended Hinduism with nationalism and invoked the spirit of resurgent Hinduism to arouse the masses. Unwittingly, this lent a Hindu strain to the nationalist movement, which in turn sparked off an anti-Congress crusade by the Muslims, especially in UP and particularly at Aligarh. Muslim separatism and the two-nation theory espoused by Jinnah became the natural concomitants of such divisive trends. (Gandhi had extended his support to Khilafat Movement, but it was out of Congress fold. So it could not help in bringing Muslims to the Congress camp). However, it must be made clear that neither Tilak nor Gandhi was responsible for the rise and growth of Muslim separatism.

It is not to be wondered that in a plural, multi-religious society like India, communalism would grow as a virus and become a cancerous growth in the body politic. A resume of the events leading to the partition of the country would convincingly attest to the fact that religion was and still is a major force in Indian politics. By the middle of the 1940s, strong identities based on religion emerged in India. The period from 1885 to 1947 saw both the strengthening of consciousness on religious lines and the simultaneous interplay of such forces in politics. In this essay, an attempt has been made to study the phenomenon of communalism, especially in the pre-independence period and its denial and rejection by Gandhi, one of the greatest foes of communalism in India. Gandhi's views on communalism and his approach to the problem, his attitude to the Hindu-Muslim question, his herculean efforts to bring the two communities together under the banner of Khilafat Committee and his opposition to the partition of the country— all these issues have been analysed here, though in a brief and a very selective manner.

Any fair understanding of these views must be preceded by a careful understanding of what communalism precisely means, especially in the Indian context. It is interesting to note that in almost all writings on the subject communalism, the words 'communal', 'communalism' and 'communalist' have not been properly defined or explained. In the absence of an accepted definition, communalism has become a convenient and comprehensive term of abuse. Broadly speaking, communalism has three basic components— firstly it is a process, secondly, it is a method and thirdly and finally it is an ideology. Communalism = process + method + ideology. As a process, it is initiated by interested leaders and parties by which objectively similar groups are transformed into subjectively conscious communities. As a method, it is the making of political demands by such groups on the system which may lead to clash with other groups or with the central authority. As an ideology, it refers to identity and consciousness among certain groups within the same political system, based on ethnic, linguistic or religious identities. Generally speaking, communalism is considered to have a detrimental effect on the interests of the nation as a whole. Communal forces are therefore viewed as divisive, unreal and a sign of political underdevelopment.

Communal politics in India has been criticized because it led to the partition of the subcontinent, which neither resolved the Hindu-Muslim tension in India, nor the regional problems of Pakistan. In addition, it led to armed hostility between the two countries, to two bloody wars and the transfer of population on an unprecedented scale. It may also be noted that the partition of the country did not lead to a homogeneous population in terms of religion in India and that communal riots and communal antagonism still persist. There is a strong attack in the media today on communalism which is ranked as anti-progressive and anti-secular and it is equated with obscurantism and opportunism. Also the recurring clashes between the two communities make it difficult for scholars, to examine the phenomenon of communalism from a less value loaded perspective.

Gandhi's approach to the communal problem in India was unique and a typical communal unity between Hindus and Muslims was a matter very dear to his heart and for which he was prepared to go to any lengths. It is here in his role as an anti-communalist that he has been severely criticised. In spite of his keen desire to achieve communal harmony, Hindu-Muslim unity evaded Gandhi throughout his active life except for a brief spell during the Khilafat agitation. Even though a devout Hindu, Gandhi approached the problem as a well-meaning, persuasive, nonsectarian nationalist. He worked on the assumption that if Hindus and Muslims could be brought together in a joint constructive endeavour, they would see that unity was in their common interest and would learn to live together in peace and harmony.

He devoted his entire life to the cause of Hindu-Muslim amity and in the end, sacrificed his life at the altar of communal harmony.

The roots of communal rivalry can be traced to the Minto-Morley reforms which by creating communal electorates, exacerbated Hindu-Muslim divisions and fostered the spirit of political exclusivism.

Their impact was particularly marked on Muslims who saw the advantage of pressing for special safeguards and concessions. The reforms were therefore a cornerstone in the British imperial policy of divide and rule, a clever ploy to keep estranged one community (Muslims) from the other. The Muslim elite comprised of leaders like Sir Sayyed Ahmed Khan who openly applauded the scheme of communal electorates which had in it the seeds of separatism. There would appear to be a tendency among Muslims to organize in politics on the basis of their faith. Where Muslims form a minority, there frequently springs up a demand that Muslims should be organized as a separate political community, either as a separate nation state or a state within a state. Muslim separatism, like Hindu insularity is *sui generis* and in its contemporary form, it dates back to the sixties of the last century. While each fed the other, neither originated as a reaction to the other. As early as in 1880, the effective leadership of the Muslim community in India rested with separatist elements. There was no Hindu Mahasabha nor an allegedly Hindu oriented Congress in 1885 or 1900. In retrospect, it can be seen that the history of Hindu-Muslim tension in British India can best be explained in terms of attempt made by the Muslim elite to get rid of the minority complex. The Aligarh Movement, the Khilafat Movement and the

Pakistan Movements were manifestations of this fear psychosis. In this attempt, they were aided and abetted by the British, especially the English intellectuals in the Aligarh circle. Leaders like Sir, Sayyed Ahmed Khan worked for close collaboration with the government, as this alone could secure for their community more share than otherwise due, according to the principle of numbers or merit. Alliance with the British was conceived as a powerful force which could counter balance the weight of the Hindu majority especially when the Hindus started 'swamping the Muslims in higher education and bureaucratic positions'[3]. Pakistan was thus born out of the minority complex of Muslims in provinces like UP.

Congress attitude to the Hindu-Muslim problem and its association with Hindu bodies, aggravated the underlying strain and tension between the two communities. In spite of Congress' affirmation of secularism, it was often drawn into activities or associations, pioneered by Hindu revivalists, as for example, in the matter of cow protection in Punjab, many of the leading protectionists were Congressmen. This led Jinnah and other leaders to dub the Congress as a Hindu organization. Thus, except for opposition to British rule, the Muslims, even the nationalist Muslims had nothing in common with the essentially secular leadership of the national movement. Those who remained in the Congress assailed some of its leaders for patronizing Shuddhi and Sangathan movements. Thus, the gulf between the two communities widened further.

By the time Gandhi assumed the leadership of the national movement, Muslim separatism was already a recognized force in Indian politics. However, the Muslim argument in justification of the demand for special treatment had shifted its emphasis from considerations of 'political importance' to those of fear and insecurity in a predominantly Hindu society. Therefore, it is a futile exercise to blame Gandhi for the religious overtones of his approach which many students of Indian politics, consider to be the main cause of the Muslim alienation from the Congress. This seems to me a gross exaggeration, since, Gandhi was not the creator of Hindu-Muslim discord and neither was he responsible for its aggravation. It is true that Gandhi talked in the language of religion, more precisely, which Morris Jones has called 'the saintly idiom'. But Gandhi's conception of religion was nonconformist and non-doctrinaire. It was never a coercive tool to compel others for obedience.

It was Gandhi who made the most impressive attempt to achieve Hindu-Muslim unity. He did so by espousing the Khilafat cause, with the zeal of a Pan-Islamist. It is true that many of his beliefs and practices were rooted in religion and some of the words like Rama Rajya, to which he gave currency, aroused suspicion in the minds of the Muslims. But the Mahatma was an ardent champion of Hindu-Muslim unity and above all, he recognised the importance of drawing Muslims into the Congress fold. No leader before Gandhi had made such an attempt, which may perhaps explain why no other Hindu leader before Gandhi commanded so much respect and influence among the Muslims. From 1919 to 1922, during the Khilafat and Noncooperation days, he was the idol of the Muslim masses and there was hardly a prominent Muslim, with the exception of Jinnah, who did not accept his leadership. This was a vibrant chapter in Hindu-Muslim unity. Gandhi was convinced that without Hindu-Muslim unity, independence from foreign rule was an impossibility. The struggle between the two communities with its undertones of religious, social and economic factors, was also a struggle for political power. Gandhi realizing this, felt sure that there could be no solution to the problem, so long as the British remained in India. As a politician, he realized that without Hindu-Muslim unity, Swarajya could not be achieved. He took the first opportunity to bring a blending between the two communities during the Khilafat and Noncooperation days.

The Khilafat movement with its call for noncooperation against the British is regarded as the high watermark of Hindu Muslim unity, so far unmatched in the history of this country. The Hindu-Muslim *entente* witnessed during this period was one of the greatest achievements of Gandhi, who endeavoured to turn this agitation into an anti-imperialist struggle, with the help of Ali brothers and other nationalist Muslim leaders like Maulana Azad, Dr Ansari, Asaf Ali, Rafi Ahmed Kidwai and the Khan brothers who came to the Congress, by way of the Khilafat Movement. The Khilafat Movement succeeded in bringing an eclipse of the communal forces. Gandhi supported the cause because he was convinced of its justness. By extending his active support to the Khilafat cause, Gandhi hoped to strengthen the bond of Hindu-Muslim unity— "a thousand times more valuable than our connection with the British" —and in helping Muslims in their hour of peril, he hoped to end communal animosities, secure the friendship of Muslims with Hindus and gain their adherence and loyalty to the national movement.

> "If I kept aloof from the Khilafat question," he wrote in May, 1920, "I would consider myself as having lost all my worth---it is through the Khilafat that I am doing the triple duty of showing to the world, what ahimsa really means, of uniting Hindus and Muslims and of coming in contact of one and all".

Gandhi thus made the Khilafat into a national issue thereby hoping to win over the Muslims for the nationalist cause.

In his crusade, initially Gandhi was very successful. His support for the Khilafat agitation did bring the Muslims closer to the Congress as never before. He was able to cement these ties at least for the time being. Also he succeeded in drawing into the Congress fold, a large number of influential Muslims like Ali brothers, Abdul Bari, Dr Ansari and the Khan brothers, This was a notable achievement, unique in the history of Hindu-Muslim relations. This fraternity strengthened the national movement, as Hindus and Muslims fought shoulder to shoulder against the British. It proved to be the heyday of Hindu-Muslim cordiality and a distinct triumph of Mahatma Gandhi.

In the aftermath of the Khilafat agitation, the cordiality between the two communities noticeably waned and there came the parting of the ways between Gandhi and the Khilafat leaders. This was followed by a spate of communal rioting in both rural and urban areas. The Moplah rising of 1921 started the process of misunderstanding between Gandhi and the Muslim leadership and by 1924, Gandhi began to lose the confidence of the Muslims. The unity of the Khilafat days turned out to be skin deep and ephemeral. The outbreak of communal riots, exacerbated the situation. The leaders of the two communities could not maintain impartiality in the event of conflict. As for Gandhi, he was torn between two loyalties and found it impossible to appease the two communities. He was misunderstood by both parties. Muslims resented his so-called partiality to the Hindus while the latter charged him of appeasement of the Muslims. Deeply affected by this sudden turn of events, Gandhi lost confidence in the possibility of Hindu-Muslim unity. It receded as a distant dream. Gandhi lamented:

> "The Hindu-Muslim problem has passed out of human hands into God's hands".

In the midst of growing communal rancour and bitterness and deteriorating Hindu-Muslim relations, Gandhi and the Congress remained as helpless spectators. Thus, closed a vibrant chapter in Hindu-

Muslim accord. Henceforward the *crescendo* of communal frenzy accelerated till it culminated into partition of the country. Gandhi had entered Indian politics through his strong support to the Khilafat agitation and his initial capture of the Congress was due to Muslim support. However, from 1940 to 1947, Gandhi had to watch helplessly the demand for Pakistan and the final achievement of this demand at the immense cost of Hindu, Muslim and Sikh lives. Instead of the emergence of a federal India, he had to live to see the emergence of two antagonistic states— India and Pakistan. Gandhi sacrificed his life in a bid to stop the communal conflagration, arising out of these events. Gandhi was opposed to the partition of the country. He was saddened by the partition and its aftermath. Till the very end, he never got reconciled to the scheme of partition. He told the Viceroy that the British had no right to divide India before quitting. He thought that if partition had to take place, it should have come as a result of understanding between the two parties. But Gandhi was now alone in his desire to avert partition. Congress, which was now made up of tired men, who were unwilling to put up a fight at that late date, accepted the scheme of partition. The utter helplessness of the interim Government owing to sabotage from within by the League members, made Congress skeptical about the possibility of any harmonious government in a united India. They found the situation intolerable and were anxious to escape from it, even by paying the price of partition.

The two great leaders of the Congress, Pt. Nehru and Sardar Patel who were opposed to each other on many issues, joined hands in support of the partition. They were convinced that the only way out was to get rid of the obstructionism of the Anglo-Muslim League combine within the administration which threatened to wreck the country. Therefore, the Congress leaders believed that partition was the only solution to the near chaos in the country. But Gandhi felt differently. Here was the parting of the ways between Gandhi and the Congress. Gandhi was of the opinion that he would rather let the whole country be reduced to ashes than yield an inch to violence.

Gandhi finally agreed to the partition because he felt that the communal problem had warped the judgement of the Congress and he per force agreed to the AICC resolution. He took great pains to stave off the disaster which appeared inevitable to Jinnah, the British and Congress. Gandhi put up a fierce one-man, rearguard action against all those pro-partition forces. Partition thus became a reality but the people had to pay a heavy price since it let loose a virtual blood-bath in many parts of Bengal, Bihar, Punjab and Delhi. The killings and counter-killings continued unabated.

Gandhi's role now became to be pronounced as a mediator, as a saviour of the victims of communal frenzy. Gandhi was no longer the astute politician, bargaining with the British. Gandhi had become the great healer, mending and patching up the wounds, inflicted on Hindus by Muslims and vice-versa. He raised his voice to decry communal atrocities. In the midst of the frenzied killings and counter-killings he poured a soothing balm; he toured riot-torn areas like Noakhali and his frail physical presence infused warmth and solace to millions of shattered homes.

References

1. Mushirul Hasan, *Nationalism and Communal Politics in India*, 1916-1928, Delhi, p. 253 (1979). *Movement in India*, Vol. II, Delhi, p. 377. (1967) Also see Tarachand, *History of the Freedom*.
2. *Young India*, 25 February, 1920.
3. Seal, 'The Emergence of Indian Nationalism', f. n. 6, p. 305.
4. Mahadev Desai, *Day to Day with Gandhi*, Varanasi, (1968).
5. *Ibid*, p. 154-55.
6. B.R. Nanda, *Mahatma Gandhi*, London (1959).
7. Pyarelal, *Mahatma Gandhi: The Last Phase*, Vol. II, Ahmedabad, p. 253-54 (1958).
8. Nirmal Kumar Bose, *Studies in Gandhism*, Calcutta, p. 274-75 (1962).

28

Gandhi : A Living Model of Secularism

A.S. Narayan Pillai

> "Religion is the search after Truth through nonviolent means".
>
> (Gandhi)

> "India is the land of religions... In religion lies the vitality of India".
>
> (Swami Vivekananda)

Gandhi has shown in his life and teachings that to be religious is to be a fundamentalist in the proper sense of the term and to be secular is not necessarily to give up being religious.

Religious Fundamentalism

What does religious 'fundamentalism' mean? In every religion there are certain fundamental, central and basic beliefs and along with these, there are certain modes of worship, many a customs, practices and rites, which are not necessarily as much fundamental. It is the duty of the spiritual guides and heads to make the people aware of the distinction between the fundamental and non-fundamental aspects of the religion. The ordinary people, out of their ignorance may mistake the not-so fundamentals to be the fundamentals and also vice-versa. This in turn results in fanatics, leading to misunderstanding, confusion and sometimes even bloodshed. On the other hand, the truly religious man gives primary importance to the fundamental principles of his own religion as well as those of other religions.

Thus, what is needed is the real understanding and guidance about the fundamental and primary doctrines as the secondary aspects of religion. For this, in our tradition we can look upon the contributions of humanist leaders of India like Sri Ramakrishna Paramahansa, Swami Vivekananda, Rabindranath Tagore and Mahatma Gandhi. They all emphasise upon the principle of unity of all living and the necessity of selfless love of all creatures as the essence of religion. These emphasize the basic unity of the teachings of all religions and reiterate that it is the duty of everyone to cultivate the required proper attitude.

Now, let us examine the contribution of Gandhi in this field. Is he a religious fanatic or a fundamentalist? Does his view of religion help to promote the secular attitude? These questions lead us to a consideration of Gandhi's views and a proper understanding of his conception of religion. Gandhi defines religion thus:

> "By religion, I do not mean any particular creed or Hindu religion but that which underlines and harmonises all religions, that which changes one's nature, which binds one to Truth within and which ever purifies. It is the permanent element in human nature which counts no cost too great in order to find full expression and which leaves the soul utterly restless unless it has found itself, known its nature and appreciates the true correspondence between the Maker and itself."

From this definition it is clear that Gandhi does not speak of any conventional religion. He was born a Hindu Vaishnava but his view of religion transcends all narrow conceptions and harmonizes the essential truths in the religions. In fact, he has a synthetic outlook on religion. He points out that his religion is the religion of Truth. Truth, for Gandhi, is God. Gandhi's maxim, 'Truth is God.' is well-known. What does this maxim signify? It really signifies that God is the supreme principle of the universe. Gandhi asserts:

> "It is that which alone is, which constitutes the stuff of which we are made, which subsists by virtue of its own power, which is not supported by anything but supports everything that exists."

In short, Truth or God is the One Spiritual Principle, the Basic Foundation, the Ultimate Reality and the Absolute Principle of the Universe. To use the Upanishadic term, Truth or God is the "Satyasya Satya", (Truth of all Truth). Gandhi uses the term, Rama as a synonym for Truth or the Absolute Reality or God. For Gandhi, religion is the pathway to Truth-realization.

It may also be noted that Gandhi also calls his religion the religion of Ahimsa. Ahimsa, for him is the means to the realization of Truth or God. The terms, 'Truth' and 'Ahimsa' are therefore inseparable in Gandhi's thought. Truth signifies the Spiritual Realty and Ahimsa signifies the Moral Path to this Truth-realization. Ahimsa, as Gandhi interprets it, is not just non-killing but the purest, positive Love. Love is the empirical expression of the Spiritual Energy and it is the centripetal force which unites all into one.

Therefore, Ahimsa is the only means to Truth-realization, the realization of the Oneness of All or as the Atman, the True Self, over and above the mind-body complex. Gandhi makes clear the inseparable relation between Truth and Ahimsa thus:

> "Truth exists, it alone exists. It is the only God and there is but one way of realising it. There is but one means and that is Ahimsa.

Gandhi defines the religion as the search after Truth through nonviolent means. Speaking again of Ahimsa, he says:

> "Nonviolence is the term I had to coin in order to bring out the root meaning of Ahimsa. In spite of the negative particle 'non' it is not a negative force. Superficially we are surrounded in life by strife and bloodshed living upon life. But some sages who ages ago penetrated the centre of Truth have said: that it is not through strife but through nonviolence that man can fulfil his destiny and his duty to fellow-creatures. It is a force which is more positive than electricity and more powerful than even Ether."

A Sanatani Hindu

It is a well-known fact that Gandhi called himself a Sanatani Hindu. This preference to be called a Sanatani Hindu is that he believed in the permanent, eternal_nature of religion. He gave the following reasons for his preference. To quote his words:

"I call myself a Sanatani Hindu because,

(i) I believe in the Vedas, the Upanishads and Puranas and all that goes by the name of Hindu Scriptures and therefore, in Avatar and rebirth.

(ii) I believe in Varanasrama Dharma but not in its present, popular or crude sense.

(iii) I believe in the protection of the cow, in its much wider sense than the popular one.

(iv) I do not disbelieve idol-worship".

The above statements reveal that Gandhi adhered to certain principles of Hinduism. At the same time, he has reverence for all other religions and their traditions. He tries to live according to the essential principles of all important religions. We can see in him the spirit of self-sacrifice of Jesus Christ, the spirit of restoration of Dharma of Shri Krishna, the principle of Ahimsa of Lord Mahavira and Gautam Buddha, the steadfastness of Prophet Mohammed (PBH) and the adherence to Truth of Harishchandra.

Gandhi's attitude to religion is equal respect for all religions (Sarva Dharma Sambhava). In one of his letters to Naraindas Gandhi from Yervada Jail (dated September 23, 1930), he expressed his attitude towards other religions. It is to be noted that it was one of the Ashram observances. He disagreed with the use of the word, 'Sahishanta' which is translated into English as 'Tolerance'. Tolerance is not the apt word in this context. Tolerance may imply 'inferiority' of the other faiths to one's own faith. But Gandhi asserts that the principle of Ahimsa teaches us to respect all religions and also to show the humility to accept the imperfections of one's own religion. To quote his words:

> "Tolerance" may imply a gratuitous assumption of the inferiority of other faiths to one's own and even respect suggests a sense of patronising, whereas Ahimsa teaches us to entertain the same respect for the religious faiths of others as we accord to our own, thus admitting the imperfection of the latter. This admission will be readily made by a seeker of Truth who follows the law of Love."

We can see that this liberal attitude is the mark of an enlightened religious man. He alone can see Truth as one and its manifestations can be many. As the Rig Veda puts it, 'Truth is one; the wise call it by many names, (Ekam Satya, Vipra Bahuta Vedanti). Gandhi realized this in his life and wanted every person to cultivate this attitude. Religious practices differ. They show variety. Gandhi warned us:

> "All our mutual quarrels centre round non-essentials."

It may be pointed out that the attitude of equal respect for all religious views, to an extent is due to the influence of the Jain tradition on Gandhi's thought. The Jain metaphysical theory of Anekanta Vad teaches us that Reality is many sided. The Jain epistemology points out that since reality is many sided, there can be many relative truths and these relative truths do not come into conflict with one another. They are all true from different standpoints. This is the significance of the Jain Theory of Syad Vad (Theory of May Be). Gandhi claimed:

> "I am an Advaiti, yet I can support Dualism. It is this doctrine that has taught me to judge a Mussalman from his standpoint. Formerly I used to resent the ignorance of my opponents. Today, I can love them because I am gifted with the eye to see myself as others see me and vice-versa. I want to take the whole world in the embrace of my love. My Anekanta Vad is the result of my twin doctrines of Satya and Ahimsa."

Now we come to Gandhi's spiritualization of politics. Gandhi is deeply religious and does not separate his religion even from politics. In fact his devotion to religion leads him to political life. He asserts that life should not be divided into watertight compartments. If a man is truly religious, it must be expressed in every aspect of life.

> "Gandhi saw life as a whole" says K. Arunachalam, "He did not tolerate compartmentalism. To him, Religion, Politics, Economics, Social life etc., can not be segregated. He viewed all these as an integrated whole. It was all right to think of them, as individual entities for the purpose of understanding. But in life, they flow into each other and they can not be divided with a clear cut borderline."

Political life can not be an exception to this. Moreover Gandhi considered political service as the best means for self-realization or Moksha. He said:

> "To see God face to face, one must be able to serve all human beings. God is best revealed in man. Gandhi therefore considered his political service and the formulations of the weapons of Nonviolence, Satyagraha (the moral equivalent of war) as a God-given mission for the propagation of the eternal law of Nonviolence in the world. But like every field, the political field also is to be purified. That is, political leaders must uphold moral and spiritual values. They should work disinterestedly for the welfare of all (Sarvodaya) Then only can we establish 'Rama Rajya".

In fact, Gandhi asserted that the truly religious men--God-fearing, truthful and morally inspired should actively participate in the political affairs. This, indeed is the greatest need of India. It is this which underlies his statement:

> "Those who say that Religion has nothing to do with politics do not really know what religion means."

We should remember that Gandhi upholds two fundamental principles:

(i) All men are brothers

(ii) Equal respect for all religions. Properly understood, this is the true secular attitude.

Henry Polac, one of Gandhi's earliest co-workers in South Africa, refers to this basic attitude of Gandhi. He says:

> "Gandhi does not know how to distinguish a Hindu from a Muslim, a Christian from an infidel. To him all men are brothers, fragments of the Divine, fellow-spirits struggling for expression.

It is a heartbreaking truth that this great leader who preached that secularism was not giving up religion but equal respect for all the religions was shot dead by a Hindu fanatic. Still, this simple man who Churchill once called 'a half-naked Fakir' lives in the minds of all.

Yes, Gandhi is a living model of real secularism. He refers to the fundamentals of religion. But if one tries to characterize him as a fundamentalist (in the ordinary, current sense) or a revivalist or a fanatic, it is a total misrepresentation. It is due to the failure to understand Gandhi's basic religious ideas or due to wrong interpretation of his ideas.

References

1. *Selections from Swami Vivekananda*, Advaita Ashrama, Dezi Entally Road, Calcutta, p. 465 (1975).
2. *Young India*, (12-5-1926).
3. *Collected Works of Mahatma Gandhi,* L. p. 204 (1972).
4. *Brihad Aranyaka Upanishad, III*, 1.9.

5. *Collected Works of Mahatma Gandhi*, Vol. XLIV, p. 90 (1971).
6. *Young India*, 24-4-1924.
7. *Harijan* 14-3-16-1930.
8. *Young India*, 6-10-1921.
9. *Collected Works of Mahatma Gandhi*, Vol. XLIV, p. 166 (1971).
10. *Ibid.*
11. *The Story of My Experiments with Truth*, Navajivan Publishers, p. 420.
12. *Gandhi's View of Lifes*, Chandrashekhar, Sulekha Bharatiya Bhavan, p. 138.

Part V

29

Mahatma Gandhi's Concept of Non-violence

N. Radhakrishnan

> "We have to make truth and nonviolence, not matters for mere individual practice, but for practice by groups and communities and nations. That at any rate is my dream. I shall live and die in trying to realising it. My faith helps me to discover new truths every day. Ahimsa is the attribute of the soul and therefore, to be practised by everybody in all affairs of life", said Mahatma Gandhi.

Can Ahimsa and Satyagraha be moral equivalents to wars and other conflicts that corrode human survival? It is claimed by both Western and Indian scholars that Ahimsa and Satyagraha can be resorted to in any situation involving injustice, in situations where armed resistance is impossible and hence Satyagraha and Ahimsa are better adapted to the role of ultimate instrument of justice. This assertion is partially ambiguous.

As Horsbough said, the prospects of non-violence in the sphere of international conflict may be brighter than is commonly supposed, in spite of our continued belief in armed force. As Gandhi demonstrated through his work, a conscientious effort to make Ahimsa a way of life and not to keep it as a creed is the need of the hour. "Man either progresses towards Ahimsa or rushes to his doom", Gandhi said. Analysed against the background of all what the great teachers of humanity and votaries of Ahimsa did, Gandhi's contribution to the cause is second to none. An incredible optimist that he was, Gandhi believed in the essential goodness of all. He said, "One step enough for me".

As in Gandhi's own times, his notion of non-violence continues to be diversely interpreted and discussed in different parts of the world. While to some it is an ideal that all men should cherish; to an overwhelming number of others it is a value-guiding thought and action.

Many view it as a policy which is desirable and effective only in certain given circumstances. Quite a good number of people all over the world find in it a practical tool to be used according to the capabilities of the user, while some view it only as a technique suggesting one range of actions which may be supplemented or even substituted by other techniques if the situation so demands. Each one of these different interpretations usually is supported by quotations from Gandhi's works and citing Gandhi's actions.

Hurbert Humbrey, Rev. Jesse Jacksons, Senater Diakno, Johan Galtung, Gene Sharp, Erik Erikson and Prof. Richard Keyes found in Gandhi's concept of non-violence a great opportunity for humanity, which will enable mankind to take a fresh look at the problems, man has created for man, disregarding the laws of nature. Francie Huthchins and several others find Gandhi's approach as non-absolutist. To them Gandhi's view of non-violence explicitly or simply included motive as well as act, so that Ahimsa or non-violence was both psychic and corporal.

Thomas Clark and several others find great scope for the practical application of the non-violent mode. William Robert Miller, James E. Bristor, William Stuart Nelson, A.J. Minto, Ted Duncan , Willock, Michael W. Sonneleitner, Glenn D. Paige and a few other scholars and pacifists find in the Gandhian non-violence a model that can well become the basis for the twenty-first century man to experiment with, while the SGI President and one of the most profound thinkers of our times Dr. Daisaku Ikeda views Gandhian non-violence as a potent force and an instrument to secure justice and peace.

A cursory glance reveals that during the last five decades since the assassination of Gandhi, a very considerable degree of intellectual effort went into the appreciation and understanding of the concept of non-violence than ever before in different parts of the world. This ranged from deep sociological analysis of the dimension of the conflict to the policy implications of the Gandhian mode. Many see in the Gandhian non-violence clues to ways of dealing with national problems of tensions, conflict, arms race and war. Inevitably, what most of the analysts, critics, followers or admirers have seen in Gandhi, is a 'Challenge rather a stereotype'.

It is natural that different levels of perception developed as it spread globally. Since Gandhi represented a model value system, it is quite natural that people viewed Gandhi from different social, political and territorial positions. Berlin's Mayor, Klaus Scuts was categorical in his assertion, "Non-violence does not mean passivity or political vegetarianism".

It is an active attitude, it permits fight for justice, challenges the opponent to declare himself. Gandhian concept of non-violence never visualized surrender to evil or injustice, but 'pitting of one's soul against the will of the tyrant'. The philosophy of soul-force visualizes three kinds of persons. The first category is that of the coward who supinely submits to injustice in order to save his skin. While the second category is that of the brave man who is eager to redeem injustice by brute force-methods willing to kill and ready to be killed. The third is the superior person, the Satyagrahi, the believer in and practitioner of non-violence, who in the fullness of his strength using soul-force method forgives the doer and attempts to convert him to 'right' through non-violence and love.

South Africa was the laboratory of Mahatma Gandhi. The twenty one years, Gandhi spent in South Africa witnessed great changes both in his private and public life and also much of what Gandhi did later in India had been tempered by the South African experiments.

His Ashram life and its beginning in the Phoenix Ashram in South Africa, while non-violent resistance, simple life, Charkha spinning, non-violent struggle and insistence on simple life, all had their origin there. In fact, Gandhi had already become the Mahatma in the making by the time he left South Africa for India. His was a heroic struggle involving several millions of people over a long period. And when Gandhi was doing all this how did the local population of the Blacks react to it? There is no doubt that by and large Gandhi was fighting the inhuman and discriminatory laws enacted by the Pretoria regime. But, he was equally fighting a system that was perpetuating racial discrimination and inhuman treatment to fellow human beings in the name of colour and nationality. The general situation faced by the Blacks in South Africa was not very different from that of the Indian settlers. It would be naive to believe that the black population was insensitive to what was happening in South Africa under the leadership of Gandhi. Though, he was concentrating on the Indian population, the issues he was fighting for had importance far beyond what the

Indians in South Africa were trying to secure. So, it can be said that Gandhi influenced them considerably when the Gandhian struggle was on in Natal, Pretoria and other places. But then as the law of nature teaches us, the seeds sown always take some time to sprout. The Gandhian pattern of non-violent resistance had to wait until Nelson Mandela came to the scene. There again, one cannot deny that the African National Congress (ANC) was considerably influenced by Gandhi. By and large, the ANC movement remained within manageable limits of violence, though quite on a few occasions the movement became very violent too. It was largely due to the influence of Gandhi. Two points arise here : Was it the brute force of minority White regime that kept the Blacks at bay or their incapability to rise in revolt and finish off their opponents? One thing that emerges from their experience is the difference in the manner in which they conceived non-violence as a creed and a strategy. It was conceived in a creative and positive manner and in their own way the black majority wanted to give it a fair trial.

The ANC leadership, including Nelson Mandela seem to be familiar with and appreciative of Gandhi's work and the success of his campaign. Mandela's speech after two days of his release from jail on 11th February, 1990 was significant in the sense that besides referring to his indebtedness to Gandhi, he said, "Another strand in the struggle against oppression began with the formation, right here in Natal, of Indian Congress founded in 1884, begun a tradition of extra-parliamentary protest that continues with the present. The next decade saw the increasing radicalisation of Indian politics under the leadership of Mahatma Gandhi....... In 1906, Bambatha led sections of Africans in a war to destroy the poll tax, against oppression of the British Government". Another passage Mandela had quoted before his arrest was from Jawaharlal Nehru.

> "There is no easy walkover to freedom anywhere and many of us will have to pass through the shadow again and again before we reach the mountain tops of our desires".

It also indicated that Mandela was studying the Gandhian option carefully. Since then, Nelson Mandela and ANC have come a long way, winning their goal. Now, South Africa is an independent nation, free of apartheid and all sorts of discrimination and Dr Nelson Mandela, its President till recently.

Dr Martin Luther King in USA, in the sixties had in his own way added new dimensions to the Gandhian non-violence in order to make it an effective instrument to fight against evil. But then, as is seen both in South Africa and in USA, when the fight derives its strength from moral and spiritual considerations and depends on the quality of suffering, it takes quite a long time to effect what we call the change of heart which is the aim in a non-violent struggle, as opposed to an armed struggle where the result is quicker. Let us remember, even in an armed conflict nowadays victory to either of the party is not assured and it is not as easy as it used to be. The racial violence which Los Angeles and some other parts of the USA witnessed, some time ago, speaks volumes how fragile our civilization is. It is actually an ominous portent and a disturbing reminder to what has been simmering underneath the welter of modernity and progress.

It also shows how skin-deep our pretension of equality of human beings is. And that such racial disturbance should occur in the land of Abraham Lincoln, Thoreau, Emerson, Walt Whitman, John Kennedy and Martin Luther King and that too after several decades of the physical killing of the demon of racial discrimination, is really surprising. It means that the dream of Martin Luther King who dreamt of a day when 'on the red hill of Georgia, sons of former slaves and sons of former slave owners will be able to sit down together at the table of brotherhood, is still far away.

No doubt, the American Blacks have won several rounds with remarkable success, yet, as the Los Angeles violence suggested, the dream of Dr King— "when my four children will one day live in a nation, where they will not be judged by the colour of their skin but by the content of their character"— remains a dream. Gandhi warned humanity as early as in 1909 when he published his first book, *Hind Swaraj* that a civilization bereft of human considerations is 'Satanic'.

Dr King was greatly influenced by the teachings of Mahatma Gandhi, since his school days. So, it was natural that he adopted the Gandhian doctrine of non-violence as the most effective weapon against racial segregation in the US. He once said, explaining his philosophy:

> "I believe in a militant, nonviolent approach in which the individual stands up against an unjust system, using sit-ins, legal action, boycotts, votes and everything else, except violence or hate.

> Acknowledging his indebtedness to Gandhi, he further said :
>
> "From my background I gained my regulating Christian ideals. From Gandhi I learned my operational technique".
>
> Dr King referred to the Montgomery bus boycott programme : "This is a protest of passive resistance depending upon moral and spiritual forces. We will return good for evil. Christ showed us the way and Mahatma Gandhi showed us it could work".

Explaining why the US Negro has not taken to more radical ways to gain civil rights, he said,

> "The basic reason is that the American Negro has faith in that he can get justice within the framework of the American democratic setup".

That Gandhi continues to inspire a considerable section of the American opinion is a fact which cannot be wished away. What E. Stanley Jones, himself a great pacifist, said about Gandhi assumes significance:

> "I bow to Mahatma Gandhi, but I kneel at the feet of Christ and give him my full and final allegiance. And yet a little man, who fought a system in the framework of which I stand, has taught me more of the spirit of Christ than perhaps any other man in East or West".

There are quite a few among the liberal pacifists in the West who found in Gandhi the argument against the inevitability of the deterministic social order dominated by Darwin and Marx. Albert Einstein, Aldus Huxley, Oswald Garrison Villard, Roger Balwin and many others were able to see in Gandhi a reinstatement of the Renaissance— faith of the perfectibility of man. In contrast to this group there was the religious pacifists such as A. J. Maste, John Nevin, Haynes Holmes and Norman Thomas who found in Gandhi 'a moral equivalent of war'. There may not be a Martin Luther King now in the USA but the number of votaries of non-violence both as a political strategy and as a creed has increased and there are several internationally famous pacifists who are champions of nonviolence. Johan Galtung, Homer Jack, Dr Glenn D. Paige and Gene Sharp are some of the ardent supporters of non-violence.

The spilling of blood in both the former Yugoslavia and Czechoslovakia and the uncertainties created by the events following the dismemberment of the USSR should be viewed as the inescapable result of incongruities grown around a philosophy which by and large did not care about the pure means in achieving ends. Here comes the relevance of the Gandhian insistence of purity of means and ends, something which the communist block always scoffed at. The Gandhian concept of non-violence seems to have attracted the attention of the youth of Czechoslovakia. There is an awareness all round that non-violence which is as old as hills and which is based on primordial instinct of man to live and let live happily would be an answer to the seething problems they face. Following the Soviet invasion of 1968, in that country, there was a Gandhian protest mainly organized by the youth. From the youth the message gradually spread to the elders. It may be of interest to note here that the Czechs organised extremely useful programmes during the Gandhi centenary. The Speaker of the National Assembly of Czechoslovakia said in a message, "Gandhi's thought is of special significance".

The hapless victims who were caught up in the cross-fire of dismemberment and vaulting ambition of political leaders of Czechoslovakia looked up to the Gandhian concept of non-violent social transformation more than ever before. In Yugoslavia also the fast emerging political scenario offered very disturbing pointers. The USSR, Czechoslovakia and Yugoslavia, the three main pillars of communism in Europe defused and as reports indicate the Gandhian alternative is very much being examined in these countries which are faced with the threat of political extinction.

There is no doubt that the present century has been a glorious one in terms of man's continued conquest of nature, including the outer space. Materially man has reached the zenith of his achievements.

The rapid technological strides that have changed the life-style of man has also induced in him a new sense of both insecurity and hope. Hope on his ability to rise like the phoenix to reconstruct from the ruins and the indomitable spirit— never to yield. The insecurity stems out of the profound understanding that unless material progress is tempered with the waters of spiritual values and concerns, humanity will land itself on the desert sands of its creation.

Europe overawed the rest of humanity with its superior might through an intelligent harnessing of the fruits of science and technology while other continents particularly Asia and Africa continued to be enveloped in spiritual and philosophical pursuits. The appeal of the Buddha, despite the tidal wave of material progress swept almost the whole of the South East Asia, while the Indian civilization and the Chinese civilization made feverish attempts to come to terms with the new challenges. The Asian continent which was condescendingly described as 'developing' while the African region with its infinite natural resources and tremendous manpower was described to be the 'dark' and 'underdeveloped' continent because it suited the colonial exploiters to keep it so. But it did not escape the notice of the impartial observers that Africa is only a sleeping giant who, when awakes will be a formidable force to reckon with. Though, the hangovers of the centuries-old colonial exploitation still hampers different countries, there is no doubt that a rejuvenated African continent which would be self-confident of its inherent strength will play a crucial role in the 21st century. Brushing aside these seething problems, Asia and Africa which have several common features would challenge the West and as and when this happens it would mark a new phase in human history.

Johan Galtung points out that Gandhi has become a part of the world political culture and Gandhi is bound to influence the course of the Twenty-first century. This is made amply clear from the manner in which the fast-spreading Soka Gakai movement under the presidentship of an unbelievably energetic and creative person Dr Daisaku Ikeda has been emphasizing the Gandhian method for world peace. The SGI leadership has shown remarkable awareness of this factor as is evident from the thrust, SGI President Dr Ikeda gives in recent times to the propagation of Ahimsa as enunciated by Shakyamuni Buddha.

The growing awareness of a world without war which is one of the cherished goals of humanity could not be a distant dream. A spiritual awakening supported by cultural, educational and social movements is on the cards as we move close to the threshold of the Twenty-first century. Then what kind of changes are we expecting? It cannot be anything other than a non-exploitative and just society where no man will die of hunger, where everyone's self-respect will get prime place and where none will be segregated in the name of the colour of his skin. Well, if we are dreaming like the king of an Utopia, even then to dream is a pleasant experience. The tragedy of the fellow men is still denied of opportunities for growth and luckily the winds of change that have set in, hold out promise thanks to the remarkable work in this field by several motivated groups. As Keats sang, "If winter comes, can spring be far behind"?

It may look refreshing and inspiring to the votaries of peace and non-violence all over the world to realize that the epoch-making changes in South Africa, resulting in the death of apartheid owe their inspiration to Mahatma Gandhi's heroic work in South Africa at the beginning of this century as Nelson Mandela acknowledges. It was precisely a hundred years ago that Gandhi set his foot on the soil of South Africa. Gandhi who was invited to South Africa as a lawyer to fight a court case, found on his arrival, the situation highly mortifying and humiliating for any human being to tolerate. He was aware of the inhuman segregation, a section of Indians were facing back in his home country in the name of untouchability. But, what was faced by Gandhi in South Africa was beyond his imagination. The fact that a man could be segregated in the name of colour of his skin and could be denied of his basic rights, came to him as a rude shock. Millions of the local black population and the Indian settlers (most of them indentured labourers) were languishing in inhuman conditions. Gandhi too became a victim of this dehumanizing practice not once or twice but on several occasions. On June 7th in 1893 a few months after his arrival in South Africa, while travelling by train in a first class compartment, he was thrown out of the bogey at the Petermauritzburg station. His only crime was that he was black and the blacks were not permitted to travel in first class. On another occasion, he was denied travel by a coach along with white passengers. He was denied hotel accommodation once and taking pity on him a kindly soul offered him accommodation on condition that he would not come down to the dining room and instead would remain in his room and take his food also there. On another occasion, he was pushed down by the guards for having dared walk along a road in the vicinity of the residence of some important white government official. Later, Gandhi came to know that the blacks and 'coolies' were not allowed to walk along that road. Gandhi could also see that the children of the blacks were also not allowed to study in the schools along with the white children. These were only some of the visible symptoms of the dreaded apartheid practised and there were many more humiliating aspects, which made Gandhi think and eventually transformed him into what he became later— Mahatma Gandhi, a great leader, reformer and thinker of modern times.

30

Rediscovering Mahatma Gandhi

T.N. Jayachandran

Fortunately, I have had the benefit of living during the last twelve years of the Mahatma's life. When the tidings of his death shocked and numbed Indians and rocked the entire world, I could only gaze into nothingness with indescribable reverence.

Pandit Jawaharlal Nehru, who was the most affected person by the death of Bapu personally went to the All India Radio station in Delhi and broadcast to the nation a message which by itself was (and still is) a classic-crisp in form, clear in convictions, resolute in ideas and firm in forecasts. He said in a voice choked with sorrow but clear :

> "The light has gone out of our lives and there is darkness everywhere and I do not quite know what to tell you and how to say it. Our beloved leader Bapu as we call him, the father of the nation, is no more............ The light has gone out, I said and yet I was wrong. For the light that shone in this country was no ordinary light. The light that has illuminated this country for many years will illuminate this country for many more years and a thousand years later that light will still be seen in this country and the world will see it and it will give solace to innumerable hearts. For that light represented the living truth and the external man was with us with his eternal truth, reminding us of the right path, drawing us from error taking this ancient country to freedom .... All this has happened. There is so much to do. We could never think that he was unnecessary or that he had done his task. But now, particularly, when we are faced with so many difficulties, his not being with us is a blow most terrible to bear". Pandit Nehru concluded his message in words which were equally forthright and stunning: "A mad man has put an end to his life".

I quoted Nehru's message at length not only because of its historic relevance but also of its contemporary significance. It is a sorry and sharp reminder of how India and Indians have been rude and crude in not only not paying homage to Gandhi properly but also casting aside his ideas and way of life. Year after year, since his death in 1948, Gandhi was slowly cast into oblivion, his ideas given the go-by as impractical, his advice discarded as the idealistic and his programmes abandoned as visionary. It is strange that it required a Britisher in the form of Sir Richard Attenborough to discover Gandhi and give him back to the world through his film *Gandhi* in 1986. In a way, it is not yet time for his rediscovery as its only a decade and a few years, since he was discovered; but it looks as though we have to discover and rediscover Gandhi every year. Our minds have become corroded by corruption in life, thoughts and deed and our conscience numbed by selflessness and our hearts shattered by violence.

I am not suggesting for a moment that Gandhi's perception of life is the most ideal or his thought system the best. As a matter of fact, it is my humble belief that his model of life was suited only for the ideal man and therein lay the seeds of its failure. He showed to the rest of the world that a leader of the people must live in utter simplicity, notable nobility and vivid transparency. In other words, the model itself was an ideal, hardly possible for anybody even to keep as a model let alone live it. The nearest that most of the Gandhians have come to Gandhi's ideals is in wearing Khadi—very often adulterated and silken. Unfortunately, people have come to identify this spotlessly white apparel with power, its blatant misuse and corruption. Barring the very few true Gandhians who are ignored, insulted, injured and humiliated, most of the people who wear khadi are hardly able to pronounce the Mahatma's name correctly and are totally ignorant of his life and ideals.

Leaving aside the mundane trappings of the Gandhian system of life and thought, it has to be emphasized that its predominance and greatness lay in the fact that its approach to political and economic problems was ethical and humanistic. His religion was non-conventional and non-traditional. He was dead set against religious obscurantism and dogmatism even though he regarded politics and religion as inseparable. Unfortunately, in the current day world, this Gandhian dictum is sought to be revived in the most dreaded form by equating communalism with religion. Gandhi emphasized upon the equality of all religions and laid the foundation of a secular India; whereas what is sought to be emphasized now is the superiority of one religion over the other in the name of our heritage.

As a humble worker in the field of education, I think it is my duty to refer to Gandhi's views on education. He was not an educationist in the conventional sense of the word, but his thoughts, experiments and views mark him out as a born educationist and a great teacher. His outlook on life was integrated and comprehensive and this had given him a true perception of real education. According to Gandhi, education is the building-up of character. Education that helps to build up sound character and promotes self-development is true education. As Gandhi himself pointed out :

> "People have no idea of what education truly is. We assess the value of education in the same manner as we assess the value of land or of shares in the stock exchange market. We only want to provide such education which would enable the student to earn more. We hardly give any thought to the improvement of the character of the educated".

Nothing can be more true or prophetic about the state of education in the country today. Gandhi firmly believed in the dignity of labour and felt that there is a great need in our country for creating a suitable atmosphere for 'productive work' which should form an important part of our education. In his words:

> "True education of the intellect can only come through a proper exercise and training of the bodily organs, e.g. hand, feet, eyes, ears, nose, etc. But unless the development of the mind and body goes hand in hand with a corresponding awakening of the soul, the former alone would prove a lopsided affair."

According to Gandhi, education means an all-round drawing out of the best in child and amenably, mind and spirit. He believed that for the proper and effective implementation of his scheme of education, it is of the utmost importance that the teachers should be all men of character who are inspired by spirit of service. They should look upon education as a duty which they must perform and be content only with a living wage. The latter part of this Gandhian exhortation will hardly be acceptable to the teaching community even though they will swear proudly that they are teaching only as a duty.

There can be no better comment on the contemporary situation than the exhortation in the National Policy on Education: 'All teachers must teach and all students study', where is the Gandhian scheme of education and where are we?

There is a plethora of Gandhian literature; but in a situation in which Gandhi is even fading from memory, who has the inclination and the time to read him ? Gandhi is probably one of the greatest writers of our time—a strange combination of Tolstoy, Bertrand Russell, Einstein and Abraham Lincoln. He had no claim to scholarship or erudition. Life was his greatest teacher and his own unending source of inspiration. During his busy life, he wrote whatever he wanted to write about whatever he was interested in. His first article appeared on 7 February 1891 in the *Vegetarian* magazine of London about vegetarians in India. His last article was written on the day of his death—30 January 1948—an article suggesting that the Congress should be converted into a service organisation. Gandhi's writings have been consolidated and published in a hundred volumes which are more than adequate for a lifetime reading. His greatest contribution is undoubtedly his autobiography, *My Experiments with Truth*, in which he declared that his life is not more than his own experiments with truth.

Probably the true exposition of Gandhi's soul has taken place in his letters. They are thousands in number which could be compiled into a sizeable number of volumes. Most of them are in his own hand. It was partly of his daily routine and there were days when he wrote as many as fifty letters with utmost economy of space and words, a large number of them being in postcards. Most of the letters, the people write are ephemeral, but in Gandhi's letters there is history, philosophy, caution and consolation, advice and suggestions, severe criticism and solid specimens of concentrated love and kindness. To read them is an experience in itself.

There is no point in suggesting, that nobody in India should be allowed to come out of school or college, without studying at least Gandhi's autobiography and a few of his articles and letters because it should have already been done. It would appear that at present the task of educating students and people on Gandhi is left mainly to some research and service organizations. Unless teaching and learning Gandhi becomes part of our daily life, we will not be able to realize the meaning and significance of the cardinal principles of the Gandhian edifice—truth and non-violence.

There is no leader of the world worth his salt, who has not written or spoken about Mahatma Gandhi. But, I would consider that the best tribute has come from the greatest scientists of our time, Dr. Albert Einstein. He said :

> "Gandhi, the greatest political genius of our time, indicated the path to be taken, he gave proof of what sacrifice man is capable of, once he had discovered the right path. His work on behalf of India's liberation is a living testimony of the fact that man's will, sustained by an indomitable conviction is more powerful than material forces that seem insurmountable. Generations to come will scarcely believe that such one as this, ever in flesh and blood, walked upon this earth".

Unfortunately, the prophecy of Einstein has come true; and more unfortunately, the first to prove his prophecy are we Indians. It is in this context that efforts to study more about Mahatma Gandhi become all the more meaningful. Let us rediscover Gandhi, pay homage to his memory in word and more particularly, in deed.

Index

501/60 1RD2